BEYOND

COSMIC

DICE

Moral Life in a Random World

BEYOND COSMIC DICE

Moral Life in a Random World

Jeff Schweitzer

and

Giuseppe Notarbartolo-di-Sciara

JACQUIE JORDAN, INC.

*To Jeff's wife Sally, Giuseppe's wife Flavia
and his children Marco and Bianca, and to our families
and dear friends who not only tolerated but encouraged
our quixotic and uncertain quest that spanned well
more than a decade to bring this book to life.
Such unconditional support, even if misplaced in
our flawed characters, was the inspiration we needed
to continue when the outcome was anything but certain.*

Beyond Cosmic Dice: Moral Life in a Random World

Published by Jacquie Jordan Inc.

Interior book design by Barbara Aronica-Buck
Interior illustrations by Paula Cobian
Book cover designed by Jonathan Fong

ISBN-13 978-0-9819311-0-4

www.tvguestpert.com

www.JeffSchweitzer.com

First Printing April 2009
Printed in the United States of America
10 9 8 7 6 5 4 3 2 1

ACKNOWLEDGMENTS

Life in all forms is nothing
but a roll of the cosmic dice.

In the world of biology, a proximate cause explains *how* a particular bit of anatomy functions, while the ultimate cause explains *why* in terms of a creature's evolutionary history. Those two concepts apply perfectly to the genesis of *Beyond Cosmic Dice*. Both deserve recognition.

The evolution of this book can only be understood in the context of Monique Raphael High and Ben W. Pesta, who together are this book's ultimate cause. Ben took us seriously when nobody else would. That he did so is still a source of amazement to us, for he was somehow able to glean from the manuscript the essence of our idea buried obscurely in dense and dry prose. For his initial confidence in us we will be forever grateful. But his contribution did not end with his early encouragement. He subsequently introduced us to his wife Monique, who as our literary agent rescued the project from a certain death. Under Monique's careful and skilled guidance the book slowly took shape, and eventually assumed a form that could be presented proudly to the public. Whatever success we ultimately have as authors can be attributed directly to Ben and Monique, for without them this initial project, leading to all others, would have never come to life.

Monique's gallant efforts to attract potential publishers led, in this highly connected world, to Jacquie Jordan and Darice Fisher, who are in fact our book's proximate cause. The intense energy of this dynamic duo can only be described as a sustained explosion. The shock wave resulting from their ceaseless efforts blasted away every conceivable barrier to the publication of *Beyond Cosmic Dice*.

With sleight-of-hand that would do a Las Vegas magician proud, Jacquie and Darice created a media presence for us out of thin air. That accomplishment rivals in importance the writing of the book itself, for in today's world without media experience an author has little chance to sell his wares. Yet to get on television or radio, an author must demonstrate previous experience on those media, creating an obvious, frustrating and seemingly unsolvable dilemma for the uninitiated. That is but one of the many mysterious obstacles that Jacquie and Darice knocked down with practiced ease.

Beyond Cosmic Dice exists because of the initial efforts of Ben and Monique to create a solid structure, an anatomy that would stand the test of time; you have the book in hand because Jacquie and Darice were able to introduce this new creature to the world. We are eternally and deeply indebted to this amazing team of professionals.

CONTENTS

Foreword by Darren Campo   ix

Prologue: Nevertheless, It Moves   1

Introduction: The Age of Little Bugs   7

PART I: HUMANKIND IN PERSPECTIVE   19

Chapter 1 / Wanted Dead or Alive: A Definition of Life   21

Chapter 2 / Primordial Soup to Nuts: A Brief Tour of Evolution   49

Chapter 3 / Getting a Head: The Human Branch of the Evolutionary Bush   67

PART II: RELIGION AND MORALITY   99

Chapter 4 / Myths and Mysteries: The Origin of Religion   100

Chapter 5 / Why Ask Why? The Meaning of Religion   115

Chapter 6 / Commandments from Above: Exploring Religious Morality   133

PART III: A NEW NATURAL ETHIC   143

Chapter 7 / Off the Beaten Path: Secular Moral Theory   144

Chapter 8 / God, Greed and Glory: Motivations for Moral Behavior   166

Chapter 9 / Reflections in the Pond: Redefining Who We Are   178

Chapter 10 / Getting Our Act Together: A New Morality   197

Chronology of Major Ethical Theories   225

References   231

FOREWORD

by Darren Campo
   author of *Alex Detail's Revolution*

Wow!

Beyond Cosmic Dice is actually a thrilling suspense novel. With every turn of the page I was pulled along trying to find some shred of evidence that humans really are the ultimate pinnacle of evolution. I was constantly saying, "but wait a minute, what about."

I was trying to outwit each argument, but I was no match for the authors, Schweitzer and Notarbartolo-di-Sciara.

What is truly remarkable, is that Schweitzer and Notarbartolo-di-Sciara are not merely taking us on a Bill Bryson-esque journey to show us our true place in the universe, they're up to something. They use this great knowledge to take a stand on everything relevant in our lives today. Bravely so in many instances.

These facts are clearly written by authors who a have a deep respect for life, deeper still because they hold all forms sacred and always have a sense of humor about it, as they pull the veil off our conventional wisdom. And as I read, I finally had a great realization that in seeing beyond traditional definitions of life, every single thing in the universe is alive or somehow closely connected to the living.

You gotta love two guys who preach moderation in moderation – never let the rules keep you from testing your limits. My hat is off to them!

PROLOGUE
Nevertheless, It Moves

*The root of all superstition is that men observe when a thing hits,
but not when it misses.*

— Sir Francis Bacon

In 1612, Galileo encountered powerful opposition to his view that the
sun was the center of the solar system. Based on his observations, Galileo
claimed that the Earth revolved around the sun, a conclusion that was in
direct contradiction to teachings of the Church. His idea also contradicted the widely accepted world system proposed by Aristotle in the
fourth century BCE, and later refined by Ptolemy. Galileo was simulta-
neously challenging the orthodoxy of the Church and the revered Greeks.
Not only was Galileo attacking the concept that the Earth was the center
of the universe, he was at the same time dethroning the idea that humankind was sitting at a special place in the cosmos. Both his intended
idea and the logical consequences of his conceptual framework were a
threat to established authority, and were a direct challenge to a central
tenet of the Catholic Church.

The iron-fisted resistance that Galileo encountered when confronting
entrenched religious authority is relevant to our efforts today to articulate
a new foundation for moral behavior divorced from any religion or god.
A small detour describing Galileo's fate will help put in historic context
our current efforts to challenge long-established dogma.

The link between morality and religion has been established so firmly
over the past 2000 years that any shift to a strictly secular model will strike

many as heretical even today, on a par with Galileo's transgression; that is so in spite of the long history of secular moral theories challenging religion over the past few hundred years. None of those challenges has been too successful. Life in the 21st century offers no refuge: religious authority is not to be questioned. Just the act of publishing some cartoons critical of a prophet caused riots worldwide and dozens of deaths. In the United States, the religious right has hijacked the Republican Party, creating what is close to a theocracy, one that seeks to impose on the general population a narrow, intolerant religious moral code.

Galileo's observations were a significant threat to the world order because he verified by direct observation the heretical ideas put forth by Copernicus seventy years earlier in *The Revolution of the Heavenly Bodies* (*De revolutionibus orbium coelestium*), published shortly after Copernicus died in 1543. The Church was not amused by Galileo's advances in astronomy, or by his support of Copernicus. In 1614, Father Tommaso Caccini denounced the opinions of Galileo in the church of Santa Maria Novella, claiming Galileo's ideas about the movement of the Earth to be false. Galileo went to Rome to defend himself against Caccini's charges, but to no avail. In 1616, Galileo was formally admonished by Cardinal Bellarmini and told that he could not defend Copernican astronomy because such teachings went against the doctrine of the Church.

The Church's opposition to Galileo was no surprise given earlier and predictable reactions to Copernicus. Upon hearing the views proposed by Copernicus, Luther remarked at a dinner in 1539 that "this fool [sometimes translated as 'that fellow'] wishes to reverse the entire science of astronomy; but sacred Scripture tells us that Joshua commanded the sun to stand still, and not the Earth." Rarely has an epithet been so far off the mark, for Copernicus possessed one of the greatest minds of his times. Such is the blinding power of religious fervor.

In spite of a growing body of religious opposition, Galileo obtained permission to publish his ideas when his friend and supporter, Maffeo Barberini, became Pope Urban VIII. The Pope insisted only that Galileo would, in addition to presenting his heliocentr all the evidence to support prevailing dogma center of the solar system. As promised, in hi *ing the Two Chief World-systems* (*Dialogo sop mondo*), published in 1632, Galileo presented the religious position, but he carefully and convincingly demonstrated with science and mathematics that the Church's view was not supportable by any evidence.

The character Galileo used in the dialogue to support the Church's view was named Simplicio, a not-too-subtle slight, and Urban VIII suspected that this imperial and slightly ridiculous character was loosely based on none other than himself. For good reason, too, for Galileo used Simplicio to argue the point about God's omnipotence made by Barberini himself in previous discussions with Galileo. Adding further insult to the Church, the book was written in Italian, not Latin, in order to increase readership. Galileo was subsequently arrested for this work in October that same year, under the all-encompassing charge of heresy. The Pope became one of Galileo's harshest and most unforgiving critics. His pride was wounded.

The wording of the document condemning Galileo is powerful testament to the dangers of dogma.

> We say, pronounce, sentence and declare that you, Galileo, by reason of these things which have been detailed in the trial and which you have confessed already, have rendered yourself according to this Holy Office vehemently suspect of heresy, namely of having held and believed a doctrine that is false and contrary to the divine and Holy Scripture: namely that Sun is the center of the world and does not move from east to west, and that one may hold and defend as probable an opinion after it has been declared and defined contrary to Holy Scripture.

Under threats of torture and death, an unpleasant fate to consider, the Inquisition forced Galileo to renounce his views and to make a public statement that the Earth stands still and the sun revolves around the Earth. He complied in order to avoid burning at the stake, and wrote the requisite abjuration. The boilerplate language in his retraction is revealing in light of Galileo's clear understanding that the Earth moves around the sun:

> I abjure with a sincere heart and unfeigned faith these errors and heresies, and I curse and detest them as well as any other error, heresy or sect contrary to the Holy Catholic Church. And I swear that for the future I shall neither say nor assert orally or in writing such things as may bring upon me similar suspicions; and if I know any heretic, or one suspected of heresy, I will denounce him to this Holy Office, or to the Inquisitor or Ordinary of the place in which I may be.

So Galileo not only submitted to the Church, he basically agreed with this language to become a snitch.

Yet, when submitting this strongly worded retraction, in which he affirms the Church's view that the Earth remains motionless at the center of the universe, he is said to have muttered, "Eppur si muove . . . " (Nevertheless, It Moves . . . .) Historians of Galileo doubt seriously he actually uttered this phrase, but the story, whether factual or not, has taken on significance as a metaphor for the struggle between the search for truth and religious dogma.

Considering the powerful forces arrayed against him and the horrific consequences of being condemned, Galileo's mumbled and perhaps apocryphal insistence that data must be evaluated objectively provides inspiration even today. By rejecting prevailing views, and by relying instead on careful collection and analysis of data, Galileo helped revolutionize scientific inquiry to a profound degree still felt four centuries later.

Galileo, however, was not infallible, nor are the methods he introduced without flaws. His extreme confidence in his power of observation led him to mischaracterize Saturn's rings, with great authority. He later revised his views based on observations made more than two years later, but never did properly describe the rings. Rings were simply not in his world view, and his mind was constrained to interpret what he saw in context of what he thought was possible. Galileo's failure to recognize the Saturnian ring system teaches each of us that even our most deeply embedded assumptions must be questioned as we examine the foundations of morality.

In spite of his fallibility, Galileo's example illustrates the great potential of the human mind and the greatness of the human spirit when freed from the tyranny of dogma. His understandable capitulation to the forces of the Inquisition also serves to remind us of ever-present and often intense pressures to accept prevailing views simply because such views are widely held.

INTRODUCTION
The Age of Little Bugs

D'ou venons nous? Que sommes-nous? Ou allons-nous?
(From where do we come? What are we? Where are we going?).
— *Paul Gauguin 1897*

As a minor branch on a vast evolutionary bush, modern humans have been roaming the Earth for no more than a few hundred thousand years of the Earth's 4.5 billion-year history. Ours has been a brief presence, with too little time to demonstrate whether the evolution of large brains is a successful strategy for long-term survival of the species.

Human beings are not inevitable, and our brief existence is not preordained to be extended into the distant future. If *Homo sapiens* is to have a continued presence on Earth, humankind will reevaluate its sense of place in the world and modify its strong species-centric stewardship of the planet. Our collective concepts of morality and ethics have a direct impact on our species' ultimate fate.

As are all creatures, humans are a genetic experiment resulting from selective pressure, random mutations, and pure chance that our ancestors avoided extinction from catastrophic events such as meteorite impacts. Our ancestors made it far enough to yield us, but the prospects for our future survival are not particularly bright. In *Extinct Humans*, authors Ian Tattersall and Jeffrey H. Schwartz note that extinction is the biological norm; so far, at least, the pattern of evolution for humans is no different from the rest of the Earth's fauna.

Humans are certainly unique, with our combined abilities to reason, to communicate with complex language, and to modify our environment on a global scale. But cheetahs are unique, too, in their ability to run over

100 km per hour (60 mph). Sperm whales alone can dive to 2000 meters (nearly 6100 feet) on a single breath, and hummingbirds are the only aviators that can hover in mid-air, shift sideways and fly backward by flapping their wings up to 200 times per second while precisely controlling the wing's angle of attack. Specialized bugs live in deep-sea volcanic thermal springs in temperatures up to 113 °C (235 °F), where no other creatures on Earth could survive.

Each species, including humans, occupies a special place on the evolutionary bush according to its unique characteristics. Humans happen to possess a well-developed central nervous system as one of our defining traits, and this evolutionary development has provided us with the ability to contemplate ourselves and our future. But large, complex brains are simply another extreme in the development of animal traits, just as speed and strength are found in extremes in other animals. Our large brains do not confer upon us any special status among our living cousins, and it is the height of folly to claim that evolution was driven toward humans as the pinnacle of achievement. One could claim with equal validity that evolution advances toward a pinnacle of speed, or that bacteria are the perfect creation because only they can occupy extreme conditions of temperature, salinity, pressure and acidity. The evolution of large brains confers no exalted status on the human race.

But unlike cheetahs or bacteria, our particularly notable evolutionary achievement enables us to reason and communicate, and we therefore have a monopoly on making any claims about our status in the world. This monopoly has led to the self-serving and comforting conclusion that humans are somehow separate from, and superior to, the rest of the animal kingdom. The long-term survival of our species may require that we change this perspective.

In an often-told story, a group of ministers asked the famous scientist J.B.S. Haldane to characterize God based on Haldane's knowledge of the natural world. He replied that God apparently has an "inordinate fondness for beetles."[1] He had this opinion because about twenty percent of

---

[1] *Multiple versions of this quote have proliferated over the years. The original quote is probably closer to the following: "The Creator, if He exists, has a special preference for beetles . . . .*

all known species of animals in the world are beetles. But even in his great wisdom, Haldane was wrong. God apparently has a greater propensity for prokaryotes, organisms comprised of just one cell, so small they can be seen only in powerful microscopes.

While our sensitivities may be offended, we are living not in the Age of Man but in the Age of Bacteria and Archea, or "bugs" as they are generically known. These single-celled germs are the most successful of all life forms, and have been dividing away for more than three billion years. Bacteria have been found to live in virtually every conceivable environment at extremes of pressure, temperature, salinity, radiation, alkalinity and acidity. A spoonful of good quality soil may contain *ten trillion* bacteria representing more than *ten thousand different species*. More than one million bacteria are found in one milliliter of seawater, and these constitute most of the ocean's biomass. The ocean holds many drops. Even more abundant by number in the ocean's waters are viruses, packing in roughly ten million per milliliter. That means that viruses lock up as much as 270 million tons of carbon, more than twenty times the estimate for the amount stored in the Earth's supply of whales.

Unwittingly referring to bacteria, Mathew 5:5 says that "Blessed are the meek, for they will inherit the Earth," and indeed they shall. For regardless of the fate of humanity, bacteria will likely survive. The urgent question becomes: for how long can we delay or prevent that fateful day when humans, and perhaps all mammals, are just another extinct evolutionary experiment, while bacteria continue their unparalleled dominance?

Even acknowledging the obvious success of bacteria, changing our perspective toward a more humble understanding of the status of humans in the living world will be difficult. For millennia, peoples of nearly all cultures have been taught that humans are special in the eyes of their god or gods, and that the world is made for their benefit and use. This is made clear in Genesis 1:1, which states:

> God said, "Let us make man in our image, in our like-ness, and let them rule over the fish of the sea and the birds of the air, over the livestock, over all the Earth, over all the creatures that move along the ground."
>
> So God created man in his own image, in the image of god he created him; male and female he created them.
>
> God blessed them and said to them, "Be fruitful and increase in number; fill the Earth and subdue it. Rule over the fish of the sea and the birds of the air and over every living creature that moves on the ground."

We should pause here to raise three important points. *First*, citing passages from Genesis does not mean to imply that all religions every-where support a species-centric viewpoint, or to suppose that humankind occupies an exalted status. However, the focus is on the Judeo-Christian worldview because of its pervasive and widespread practice in the west-ern world. *Second*, the goal of this Introduction is not to attack or to den-igrate religion. The point is to illustrate beyond any doubt the *fallibility* of religious doctrine, and from that, demonstrate the fallibility of reli-gious morality. By necessity, the foundation of morality as practiced today must be questioned if we are challenging the validity of that moral code, with the goal of demonstrating that morality must ultimately be divorced from religion and god. *Third*, as we explore further the impact of reli-gious morality on society, we will focus much of the discussion on the Catholic Church, but only as a representative of religion, not as the only problem. With over one billion followers baptized globally, the Church's version of religious morality remains a powerful force in societies around the world. But by no means is the Church alone in promoting a false and dangerous moral code.

Evangelical Protestants in the United States pursue a moral agenda that attacks gays, women, and minorities. Now firmly established in all branches of government Evangelicals work hard to limit a woman's right to choose her own reproductive destiny. They support the death penalty even when DNA evidence has, since 1989, exonerated 172 prisoners condemned on death row. Apparently the sanctity of life has its limits. Evangelical Protestants deny the reality of climate change and allow industry to dump more poisons into the air and water, perhaps in hopes of accelerating the arrival of the Apocalypse. They relentlessly insert their particular brand of religion into public life, fighting for school prayer and the teaching of Intelligent Design in public schools. The religious right wing willingly erodes the separation of church and state, supporting the display of the Ten Commandments on government property, and promoting government-funded faith-based initiatives. The inmates have taken over the asylum.

Radical Islam is certainly no better, relegating women to nothing but chattel while spreading terror globally. The consequences of religious fervor were seen clearly on September 11, 2001. Those 3000 people died a horrible death in the name of religious morality imposed by extremists. The hijackers objected to western moral decadence, and the infiltration of horrible ideas like equality for women into their medieval societies. Exhibit A on the list of Islamic countries that institutionalize the degradation of women is Pakistan, our stalwart ally in the fight on terror. Citing Islamic Law, General Zia ul Haq mandated in 1979 that the responsibility for proving rape rests with the victim, who will otherwise be punished by death for adultery. To prove rape, the victim must produce four male or eight female witnesses to the crime. In 2002, in Chorlaki, Pakistan, Zaafran Bibi was repeatedly raped by her brother-in-law, and from that bore his child. For her crime, she was sentenced to death by stoning. For being raped.

Any disagreement with Islamic doctrine can mean death. In Afghanistan, Abdul Rahman was sentenced to die for the crime of converting to Christianity. This example of extreme intolerance is mainstream thought in the Islamic world: the Shari'a (Islamic Law) states that a Muslim who abandons his faith can receive the death penalty. The Afghan constitution, based on Islamic law, embraces that concept. International pressure forced the Afghan government to exile rather than execute Rahman.

We are not picking on the Catholic Church; the ideas we discuss next using the Church as an example apply broadly across all monotheistic religions.

Now, let's return to Genesis. The Biblical passage, found a couple of pages earlier, gives humans the special status of being made in God's image, unlike any other creature on Earth, and clearly implies human dominance over all other living things. Humans are told to "subdue" the Earth and "rule over" the air, land and sea. These religious teachings not only condone but actively encourage humans to view the environment as separate from them, put here for their pleasure. In this worldview, no deep moral obligation exists to preserve resources for future generations.

The explicit religious mandate to exploit natural resources remains clear and unambiguous, in spite of recent efforts to harmonize religion and environmental sciences by numerous academic and international organizations, including The Forum on Religion and Ecology, the largest international multireligious project of its kind, and the Pontifical Academy of Sciences, founded in 1936 by the Vatican to promote scientific progress compatible with the Church's teachings.

The argument used by those seeking reconciliation between religion and environmental protection point to the integrity of all creation, or reverence for all things created by God, insisting that religion and concern for the environment are not only compatible, but have been so all along. Those are welcomed sentiments. In fact, as is frequently the case, the Bible contains contradictory passages about the natural world, reasonably allowing for such an interpretation. Old passages can also simply be reinterpreted to fit the facts or to be compatible with newly adopted ideas. Pope John XXIII said in 1961:

> Genesis relates how God gave two Commandments to
> our first parents: to transmit human life – 'Increase and
> multiply' – and to bring nature into their service – 'Fill
> the Earth, and subdue it.' These two commandments are
> complementary. Nothing is said in the second of these
> commandments about destroying nature. On the con-
> trary, it must be brought into the services of human life.

But the harsh facts of human history belie this benign revisionist interpretation of the meaning of "subdue." The preponderance of unambiguous passages in the Bible giving mankind dominion over nature's
bounty argues against any idea that religion is environmentalism in dis-
guise. As Renaissance scholar Lynn White famously wrote in 1967, "We
shall continue to have a worsening ecologic crisis until we reject the Christian axiom that nature has no reason for existence save to serve man."
His words remain true forty years later, when religious conservatives in
the United States view resource extraction as an inalienable right. Our
natural resources are under growing threat from a world view that
encourages mining on federal land, weakens protection for species,
habitat and wetlands, accelerates deforestation, and promotes drilling for
oil in the Arctic National Wildlife Refuge, one of Earth's few remaining
pristine areas.

Then there is the Biblical admonition to increase in number to fill the
Earth. When written, in times when death rates were high, the population
small and resources abundant, this mandate was easily justified. With over
six billion people now calling Earth home, the divine mandate to multi-
ply might now be viewed in a different light from when promulgated millennia ago. Yet the Church remains unyielding. The official Church
position was reaffirmed in 1995 by Pope John Paul II, who condemned
all artificial contraception as a "conspiracy against life." To their credit,
80% of Catholic couples in their reproductive years ignore the Pope on
this issue; sex provides a powerful incentive to discount the ramblings of

a celibate old man. But the Church's position has real and tragic consequences, even if the laity rebel.

In Latin America and Africa, bishops officially object to the use of condoms, recommending instead abstinence to prevent AIDS. The bishops steadfastly hold this view even in Sub-Saharan Africa, where 26 million people are infected with AIDS and more than 3 million more new infections occur each year. In Zambia, nearly 20% of the adult population is infected. Still, the bishops loyally follow the Pope's mandate.

But a rapidly spreading AIDS epidemic is certainly not the only consequence of religious morality imposed on the question of family planning. Unwanted pregnancies in poor countries condemn women to an unrelenting cycle of poverty. Only when women gain control over their reproductive destiny and have access to education can the cycle be broken. But the Church, with a concerted campaign against condom distribution, actively seeks to prevent women from gaining such control. This policy contributes directly to the suffering of millions of people relegated to hunger, disease and illiteracy. The war against contraception, without concern for short-term suffering and the long-term consequences for human survival, is another sign that religious morality is deeply and tragically flawed.

Beyond "policy" errors such as obsolete ideas of family planning, scientific discoveries over the past 2000 years have proven many Biblical assertions to be factually in error. Let us come back to the Church's insistence that the Earth was the center of the universe as another example of how the supposedly infallible and eternal teachings of the Holy Scriptures are not. Three hundred and fifty-nine years after Galileo's conviction, the Pope issued in 1992 a statement acknowledging that the Church's prosecutors did not "interpret with great circumspection the Biblical passages that declare the Earth immobile." This linguistic contortion attempts to show that the Bible was not wrong, but simply that the Bible was not interpreted with appropriate clarity during the Inquisition.

But the Bible was and is utterly clear in stating that the Earth is immobile, and that the sun revolves around the Earth. Referring to the sun, Psalm 19:6 says, "His going forth is from the end of the heaven, and his circuit unto the ends of it; and there is nothing hidden from the heat thereof." Psalms also say (104:5) that "He established the Earth upon its foundations, so that it will not totter, forever and ever." Solomon, speaking from divine inspiration in Ecclesiastes 1: 5, 6 claims, "The sun riseth and goeth down, and hasteth to his place: and there rising again, maketh his round by the south, and turneth again to the north." Joshua 10:13 states the following:

> And the sun stood still, and the moon stayed, until the people had avenged themselves upon their enemies. Is not this written in the book of Jasher? So the sun stood still in the midst of heaven, and hasted not to go down about a whole day.

If any doubt remains, the Church claimed the following in Galileo's abjuration: " . . . a doctrine that is false and contrary to the divine and Holy Scripture: namely that Sun is the center of the world and does not move from east to west . . ."

For more than 1600 years, the Church denied any ambiguity in this view, vigorously defending as *indisputable, divine fact* the notion that the Earth was the immobile center of the universe. Galileo was to burn at the stake for questioning this divine fact. The Church held onto geocentrism tenaciously until contrary evidence became irrefutable. The solution to this glaring discrepancy between fact and Scripture was to suddenly declare that nothing in Scripture requires the Earth to be the center of the universe, thereby sweeping 1600 years of violently enforced dogma under the rug. That is quite a broom and a mighty big rug!

Even today in the 21st century, the Church claims that Galileo shares blame because he made unproven assertions. The best the Pope could muster was that he regretted the "tragic mutual incomprehension" that had caused Galileo to suffer. As the new millennium settles in, the Church still claims that Galileo was wrong! The dissonance between Scripture and fact is not a problem relegated to earlier centuries, but remains relevant today.

The Bible's clear statement about the age of the Earth, off by more than four billion years, is another example of an important factual error. This error, of course, has implications for creation. Also related to the Church's view on creation, the Pope in 1996 was able to admit only that evolution is "more than just a theory." With each new discovery proving a Biblical assertion wrong, the Church retreats to the safety of errors in interpretation or dismisses the discrepancy as unimportant. Yet these accumulating factual mistakes must call into question the certainty with which the Church claims the Bible is infallible, since their previous insistence has proven unsubstantiated. *These doubts about infallibility apply, too, to the Church's teachings on morality.*

That religious morality has failed is made clear by humanity's current fate, and the sad state of the planet. Religion has had 2000 years to prove itself worthy as a guiding moral force. Yet the result of that 2000-year experiment is war, poverty, hunger and suffering across the globe as humanity consumes itself; in addition, after two millennia, we see overpopulation, depletion of nonrenewable resources, and accelerated degradation of the environment because our current moral foundation is not suited to guide us away from that destruction.

Long-term survival of humankind may depend on our ability to define a new moral code that adapts the human species to the demands of the future, completely independent of God and religion. (A distinction must be made here that is explored in greater detail later: long-term survival of the species is not a *motivation* for adopting a new code, but a possible *consequence* of doing so.) If humankind's welcome on Earth is to prove sustainable, and if large brains are indeed adaptive, we will reexamine our responsibilities toward each other and understand better our dependencies on the physical world around us and the resources that support our existence. Just like all other beings, humans follow the rules of nature. Now, if we are to take another path, one unique to our species, we must decide for ourselves on the basis of a deliberately chosen model, within the constraints of nature.

What is that other path? All species exploit the environment to the maximum extent possible, until competition, predation, resource depletion, disease or other constraints limit growth and expansion. Social animals, from insects to mammals, find equilibrium between cooperation and competition among conspecifics and potential enemies. Human survival strategies are little different from those pursued by other species except that we have a huge technological advantage. In struggling to survive, humans have successfully co-opted a significant percentage of the planet's available resources, and alternately waged war and pursued peace within and between societies. Our reliance on technology to exploit resources, and each other, has had global affects over a short time period, unlike other species similarly striving to survive. As a result, our efforts to survive and prosper may have the paradoxical effects of causing our extinction, either directly through the use of weapons of mass destruction or through the degradation of the resources on which we depend.

Fortunately, the large brains that gave us technology and war also give us the ability to choose, personally and collectively, to behave for the greater good and to be concerned with the fate of distant generations. Humans have a unique capability, even if not always fully realized, to worry about the fate of the planet.

With our large brains, we find ourselves contemplating an important crossroad in our evolutionary history. Do we continue plodding along like all other species, exploiting resources and each other to the maximum extent possible, blindly marching toward our own extinction? Or do we rise to the occasion, and grab the opportunity unique to our species? Humans are special, not because we are made in God's image, and told to rule over the Earth, but because we have the amazing potential to choose a future in which we thrive and develop in a just society while coexisting with a healthy natural world. If we fail to seize our opportunity to create such a future, we will be no more than bacteria with library cards. The choice is in our hands, not God's. We are special if we choose to be, if we ourselves decide to use our big brains to manage wisely our relationships with one another and with our environment. That is the essence of a new natural ethic, and that is the new path. We can choose to rise above the common destiny and course of other species, and realize the full potential of being human.

This book sets out to define a natural ethic based on a fundamental shift in our perception of place in the world, and to contrast this new philosophy to extant beliefs and practices. A natural ethic is pursued without ulterior motive for personal gain in this life or in the hereafter. This new natural ethic is sought not in fear of punishment nor in search of reward, but is sought for no reason other than it is what makes us human.

The first important step is to demonstrate that a natural ethic *must* be divorced from God and religion. The notion that morality and ethics do not derive from religion is not new. Over 200 years ago, the English philosopher David Hume dedicated himself to showing that moral life can be lived and fully explained without the resources of religion and free of any reliance on divine authority. This view is uplifting, positive and above all, human. It may also be essential to the survival of our species. But separating ethics from religion is just the first step, albeit an extremely important one, in pursuit of a natural ethic. We must go further and remove any motive for self-reward in moral behavior, and we must reevaluate the place of humanity in our physical world as a moral imperative.

All of these elements, and their interrelationships, will be explored in depth in the following chapters. We begin with a digression in the first chapter. The journey to appreciate human life must begin all the way back at the definition of life itself as a first principle. Placing human life in the context of a new definition of living and non-living creates a foundation for understanding all that ensues, including how humans relate to each other, other forms of life, and to the supporting physical environment.

PART I

HUMANKIND IN PERSPECTIVE

CHAPTER 1

Wanted Dead or Alive:
A Definition of Life

*The most difficult thing in life is to
know yourself.*

– Thales of Miletus

There is nothing special about the substances from which living things are made. Living things are collections of molecules, like everything else. What lies at the heart of every living thing is not a fire, not warm breath, not a 'spark of life.' It is information, words, instructions.

— *Richard Dawkins*

God is one of the
Leading causes of
death — George Carlin

... ...ng, all of us have a bias toward life. We are not to blame, for our first reference point is our own existence. We view life as special, something unique, divine, sacred. We naturally consider life as inherently superior to inanimate objects that do not enjoy our vital fluids. Being dead is less interesting than being alive.

But our fealty to the living, while understandable, obscures some uncomfortable truths. As comedian George Carlin observed with his typically offbeat take on the sanctity of life: "If everything that ever lived is dead, and everything that's alive is gonna die, where does the sacred part come in? I mean, life is sacred? Who said so? God? Hey, if you read history, you realize that God is one of the leading causes of death."

Our preconceptions, our biases, and our self-serving tendency to view life as sacred derive in part from the fact that life is mysterious and notoriously difficult to define with precision. The difficulty arises because every characteristic that was supposed to be unique to life has ultimately been found in nonliving systems. Each new description of life seems to be stymied by excluding some form of existence that can reasonably be deemed alive, or including something clearly not animate. Aibo the robotic dog keeps nipping at our heels.

We could just ignore Aibo's troubling bark, accept that we will never have a perfect definition of life, and move on to other pursuits. But that would eliminate the need for this chapter, an unpleasant consideration, and perhaps bring on other dire consequences. One must first have a re-fined understanding of the essence of life in general in order to compre-hend *human* life in particular or, more to the point, human existence in relation to other forms of life and our supporting physical environment. Wrestling with the difficult task of defining life is necessary if we are to understand humanity's humble place on Earth, the first step toward cre-ating the foundation for a new natural ethic. Plus, we just like a good challenge.

Historically, the effort to distinguish life from nonlife has proven so difficult partly because the quest has been based on an erroneous as-sumption. Dating back to the early Greeks and across millennia to mod-ern times, great minds have recoiled from the notion that life might be a matter of degree, because our intuition so strongly demands that some-thing be alive or not. But our intuition serves us poorly here.

Most people would logically reject the conclusions from quantum mechanics that an electron will exhibit the properties of either a particle or wave depending on how we measure its activity. But that duality has been proven experimentally to incredible degrees of precision. Just as in the quantum world, the more rigorously we attempt to define life, the more we encounter ambiguous cases that test our assumptions, stretch the limits of our definitions, and demonstrate where intuition and com-mon sense falter. With even modest scrutiny, the essence of what makes something alive quickly becomes nonintuitive when we are presented by forms that defy easy categorization such as crystallized virus capsules or bacterial spores. Then we have prions, nothing but raw protein, contain-ing no genetic code at all. Yet these proteins self-replicate, and cause hor-rible brain-wasting maladies such as mad cow disease, scrapie, and Creutzfeldt-Jakob disease.

While philosophers and biologists have failed to meet the challenge of defining life, in their labors lie clues to how this impasse can be over-come. The fact that scientists have discovered no simple quality that de-fines life, after endless years of effort, is an important clue that life is not something materially different from nonlife but instead represents a natural place along a continuum from simple to complex.

History has failed to give us a good definition precisely because life was viewed not as this continuum from inanimate to animate but as a huge leap from one to the other. To be alive meant having a special essence, something beyond the normal mechanisms that governed inorganic chemistry and physics. Invoking "vital forces" to explain life endures today in much of the general public. But vitalism, this endowing the living with a life force, is tautological and explains nothing. If something is alive, it must have a life force; if it is dead, a life force must be absent. That is not helpful.

We now know that no life force exists. The laws of physics and chemistry are indifferent to our struggle to define life and operate identically on the same principles whether we deem something to be living or dead. The carbon, nitrogen, phosphorous, iron and other atoms that come together to form our bodies are just that: the same elements that are found in the iron skillet in our kitchens and the nitrogen in the soil fertilizing our gardens. The atoms in our bodies are not special or endowed with any properties different from the atoms in every object around us. Iron is iron is iron, whether attached to hemoglobin in our blood or flaking off the hull of a rusting ship.

In defining life, we will appeal to philosophy and logic in addition to natural history and basic biology. But before going any further, let's pause to clarify two concepts critical to the definition of life that have already been introduced. The first is the notion of a continuum, and the second is the idea of atoms. Both are fundamental to any understanding of life, so we will wander off our direct path toward a definition to explore these in brief.

A continuum describes a whole, no part of which can be distinguished from neighboring parts except by arbitrary division. The best example is the electromagnetic spectrum in the region of visible light. You know without hesitation when something is green (Astroturf) or blue (the new M&M candy), but cannot say exactly when one color yields to the next. Any attempt to define where one color ends and the other begins becomes arbitrary because green turns to blue across a smooth gradient of frequencies with no inherent boundaries. A pristine lake might be green-blue or blue-green or turquoise, but not clearly green or blue. This nature of the electromagnetic spectrum applies to the idea of living and nonliving as well. If we call green "inanimate" and blue "animate" we see that no boundary exists between the two because they transition one to the other with no intervening gap.

Atoms deserve special attention since everything we know, both alive and not, is an aggregation of atoms. A quick story about these basic building blocks of nature and their astronomical origin will help demystify the stuff of which we are made and help make the concept of life's ambiguity more accessible.

The simplest and lightest atoms such as hydrogen, helium, and some lithium formed just moments after the Big Bang. A star derives energy from the combining of these lighter elements into heavier elements through nuclear fusion. Our own sun is currently fusing hydrogen to helium, a process that will occupy most of its lifetime. After the hydrogen supply is depleted, the star will burn helium to form progressively heavier elements such as carbon, oxygen, silicon, sulfur, and iron. Up to a point, fusion releases energy and is therefore self-sustaining, which is why we see the sun shining every morning, unless you live in Seattle.

But the creation of elements heavier than iron requires the input of energy and is not self-sustaining. Some other source of energy is needed, and that comes from the explosion of a supernova. A massive star will eventually deplete its energy source of lighter elements. The star will collapse into itself when no longer supported by the release of nuclear energy through fusion. If the original star was sufficiently massive, the collapse will release a huge amount of energy in a spectacular explosion. The resulting supernova supplies the energy necessary to support fusion of nuclei heavier than those of iron. The explosion also causes a blast wave that ejects the elements into interstellar space. Some of this dust is eventually gathered up in planets, like Earth, as new solar systems form. Every single carbon atom in your body and every carbon atom in the charcoal at the bottom of your barbecue comes from such interstellar dust.

Derived from stardust, the elements in your body exhibit no special properties. Carbon is carbon. Nitrogen is nitrogen. As far back as 1828, Friedrich Wöhler proved the point when he synthesized urea during his attempts to make ammonium cyanate, demonstrating that compounds once considered the provenance of life (like urea) could be made from ordinary inorganic materials, all derived from the detritus of spent stars.

Atoms are just atoms, so the premise of vitalism, which gives the stuff of life some special property, is demonstrably false. Any definitions of life deriving from vitalism are doomed. But more modern efforts to describe life fall short, too. The most recent edition of the Encyclopaedia Britannica offers a typical definition of life as a "state characterized by the ability to metabolize nutrients (process materials for energy and tissue building), grow, reproduce, and respond and adapt to environmental stimuli." At first, that sounds perfectly reasonable, but the Britannica definition is in fact completely inadequate.

Fortunately, much can be learned from this encyclopedic attempt, as well as from earlier efforts to define life. One way to approach the issue is to examine, one by one, the characteristics that have been included in previous definitions of life, and determine why each is wanting. Good advice. That is what we will do.

The fatal flaws in each characteristic called upon to define life all fall into just three simple categories: the trait is present in some nonliving systems (growth, for example), the trait is absent in some living systems (movement), or the trait can be determined or defined only across generations (evolution, reproduction), depriving us of the ability to determine if the beast before us is alive or not. Every single character or trait that has been used to define life suffers from one or more of these three deficiencies. Now, if you accept that statement at face value and do not need to be convinced, you can skip to the last paragraph of this chapter, then move right on to Chapter Two. Otherwise, allow us to persuade you that life, while wonderful, amazing and awe-inspiring in its complexity, is not special.

AUTONOMY

Some scholars have evoked autonomy or self-determination as a key characteristic of the living. The idea is attractive intuitively because we all know that a rock just "sits there" while a dog will search for a toy to initiate a vigorous game of tug-of-war with his owner. Some inner drive seems to give living organisms volition. The trajectory of a thrown ball is fairly predictable; but a bird thrown in the air will take a path over which the pitcher has no control. That is why we have baseball instead of bird-ball. The ball has no volition but the bird does. Even bacteria actively swim away from noxious stimuli.

But two major difficulties arise when trying to use autonomy to define life, even if we recognize the clear difference between birds and balls. First, autonomy implies a system that is organizationally closed, with internal regulation of its components, with a clear distinction between self and nonself. The idea works well in many cases, like dogs, but fails in many life forms less photogenic than golden retrievers. Parasites are a good example. Parasites tend to evolve toward greater simplicity. Generations accumulate genes resulting in characteristics that allow them to use more and more of their host's biological machinery. In other words, they become less and less autonomous to the point of being anything but.

A strange case of this is found in the deep sea anglerfish. Finding a mate in the dark ocean depths is a serious challenge, even more difficult than in the dark corners of the local bar. But the male anglerfish only has to find a partner one time because he lives permanently as a parasite on the body of the much larger female, deriving nourishment from her blood. This presents a case where the male has evolved from a fully formed fish to nothing more than parasitic genitalia, a state of being that surely reminds some female humans of their male counterparts. The male is not autonomous, yet remains alive.

The second problem is that "we are what we eat." No organism is independent of its environment. Place an organism in a sterile environment absent any nutrition or oxygen, and death soon follows. Thirdly, autonomy implies at some deep level that an organism is a closed system, which if true would violate the Second Law of Thermodynamics (see "Resistance to Entropy" below). Ultimately, the basic idea of autonomy is fatally flawed since we are fully dependent on the environment from which we are supposed to be autonomous.

REPRODUCTION

Reproduction is the most obvious and robust characteristic of living beings. Except when it is not. No discussion of defining life can go long before bringing out the venerable mule. Most mules would be offended if anybody suggested they were not alive, yet all mules are sterile, and therefore unable to reproduce. While mules serve as a poster child for the fact that not all living things can reproduce, they are not alone. We also must consider a human male born with immobile sperm or a woman with non-functioning fallopian tubes. Clearly such individuals are alive, but can bear no children. We should also not exclude from the living any children who have not yet reached puberty; they are alive and kicking but unable to reproduce. Many social insects have entire castes of workers that are sterile, but their sting and bite will prove them very much alive. Viruses, whom we will meet repeatedly in these discussions, cannot replicate on their own; they must commandeer the machinery of the infected host.

The notion of invoking reproduction to define life brings along another critical problem. Standing in a group of friends, you could not possibly know if any of them were alive. You would have to wait until each had kids, that is, if reproduction is necessary to define life. Including reproduction in the definition of life leads to the ridiculous conclusion that we cannot evaluate whether something right in front of us is alive or not until the thing replicates.

Reproduction as a defining trait of life brings with it a further embarrassment: nonliving things can reproduce. Fires can self-propagate, consuming nutrients to do so, and some crystals can reproduce in an appropriate medium. If beings that are clearly alive are unable to reproduce, and nonliving systems can, the concept of reproduction loses some appeal as a defining characteristic of life.

STABILITY, CHANGE AND EVOLUTION

Evolution and mutation are commonly called on to assist in defining life. I.S. Shikloviskii and Carl Sagan proposed, among many possibilities, that "a living system is any self-reproducing and mutating system which reproduces its mutations, and which exercises some degree of environmental control." These authors come to this conclusion in part because life has the odd property of promoting stability through variability.

Reproduction in biology is imperfect, so that copies are not identical to the parents (or parent in the case of asexual reproduction). Changes from parent to offspring provide the target against which natural selection can act to yield potentially hardier varieties of the original. Variation allows for adaptations to a changing environment across generations.

Variation arises because of the enormous complexity of the reproductive machinery. Think of the information contained in John Smith's chromosomes as equivalent to all of the books in the Library of Congress. Every single letter of every single book on every shelf has to be copied when John wants to mate. The same is true for Jane Doe, whom John just met in a bar. After a few drinks, John and Jane go home and consummate their new relationship. During that act, half of John's books are shuffled together with a randomly selected half from Jane's library to produce

Jill nine months later. Jill is the product of a brand-new and unique combination of the books bequeathed by John and Jane. Errors can be introduced in this process in many places, from the original job of copying more than a billion letters to combining the wrong books together during the shuffle. The errors are random and usually are either neutral or detrimental to survival. But every now and then an error introduces a small survival advantage, which can be passed on to future generations.

Stability and change are clearly important features of life. None of this is particularly useful, though, in helping us to define life. One huge problem immediately presents itself. Mutations become evident only across generations, so we have the same conundrum encountered earlier with reproduction and variability. That means if mutation is required to define life, we would not know if anybody or anything standing before us were alive or not. We could not know if our dog were alive until we saw her litter and detected mutations in the pups. Any definition of life that requires us to wait across generations for the final answer is inadequate.

Software creates another problem for evolution as a defining characteristic of life. Even modestly simple programs can be written to mutate and evolve, and more complex programs can mimic behaviors with downstream impacts on further mutations. We resort to semantics by calling such programs "artificial life" but regardless of the label, abiotic systems clearly can exhibit stability, change and evolution.

RESISTANCE TO ENTROPY

Entropy is a sophisticated concept that when stripped to its core means that things tend to fall apart. Over time, things decay and disorder increases. That is why you spend so much time doing repairs around the house: you are fighting entropy, the natural tendency for nature to seek the greatest amount of disorder. Entropy is an increase in disorder in your everyday world, like that rusted heap of an old car sitting on cinder blocks in your neighbor's yard. But at a deeper and more interesting level, entropy is really something else. Entropy is nature's relentless drive toward equilibrium. If you put a glass of cold water in a warm room, soon the temperature of the room and water will be exactly the same. The room lost a little energy and the glass of water gained a little energy, until there was no difference between them. The room and the glass of water have reached equilibrium. A new car becomes the heap on cinder blocks as the car seeks equilibrium with the disordered state of materials making up the car before General Motors put them all together. That is an increase in entropy, an increase in disorder, over time.

Erwin Schrödinger defined life as matter that *avoids decay into equilibrium*, squarely placing his money on the idea of entropy. According to Schrödinger, life postpones the natural tendency for energy to flow toward a state of uniformity (equilibrium) by assimilating nutrients, otherwise known as food, from the environment. Nutrients are chemically processed, or metabolized, to yield the energy necessary to fight entropy.

Think of eating a cashew. Prior to succumbing to your appetite, the nut is highly ordered and structured. But once you are through extracting minerals, vitamins and salts from the poor thing, not much remains of its original order. Sitting in the Planters can, the nut is like the shiny new car, perfectly ordered and whole. After passing through your gut, the nut quickly becomes like the rusted chassis blighting the front lawn. For its vital contribution, remnants of the nut are awarded passage from your body as waste. The nut has gained entropy so that you can fight off disorder.

At first glance it would appear that life, avoiding decay, would violate nature's law that entropy always increases. But the Second Law of Thermodynamics stipulates that entropy *in a closed system* always increases. No law of physics is violated by life because as the organism loses entropy with increased order and structure, the environment gains an equal amount of disorder. The "system" in question encompasses both the organism and its environment.

Unfortunately, Schrödinger's definition fails to exclude clearly abiotic matter. We recently discussed one example. The sun fusing hydrogen to helium is self-sustaining, increasing order and structure. The Second Law is not violated because the region near the sun gains equal amounts of disorder through heat and other energy losses. Nothing about Schrödinger's definition excludes the idea that hydrogen is a nutrient, and fusion is metabolism. The sun resists entropy through the metabolism of nutrients. Yet the sun is clearly not alive by any commonsense definition. Nonliving systems can resist entropy; the talent is not exclusively in the domain of the living.

CONVERSION OF MATTER AND ENERGY

Living things have the ability to take matter and energy from their environment and change it from one form to another. Plants convert sunlight and carbon dioxide to cellulose and sugars. Herbivores convert plants and their sugars to meat and movement through the process of digestion. Carnivores do the same favor to herbivores. That is a good story, with a happy ending if you are the carnivore, but relying on the flow of matter and energy to define life leads to immediate trouble. As Paul Davies points out, the Great Red Spot of Jupiter is sustained by a flow of matter and energy and has been for millennia, yet the spot is a meteorological phenomenon, not life. A Nestle factory converts raw materials of sugar and starch, with a dose of electricity, into chocolate chip cookies. Systems that convert matter and energy from one form to the other are found routinely in the world of the nonliving.

METABOLISM

For us to make it through a day, we must chemically convert energy stored in food into useful energy we can tap for vital functions like moving, mating and watching reality T.V. One might easily conclude that this process of metabolism is an essential characteristic of life and therefore must be included in any definition of life. But that conclusion would be wrong. Our best friend the virus can be crystallized and put on a shelf in a jar, sitting inert for ages with no metabolism at all. Some bacteria when encountering adverse conditions can encapsulate into spores, and remain in a state of complete dormancy for hundreds of years with no metabolic activity. But the virus and bacteria can be quickly revived into rapidly reproducing organisms under the proper conditions.

Perhaps only "simple" forms of life like bacteria and viruses suspend metabolism, so that we can dismiss these cases as minor aberrations. But no, even complex animals, such as rotifers, can enter into a state of dormancy and remain there for years. Rotifers are microscopic but multicellular animals with a head, a mouth with a jaw, a body with internal organs, a nervous system, a digestive tract and a posterior foot with two or three toes, depending on the species. While they do not present much of a photo op on the Serengeti, rotifers are real, live animals, vastly more complex than viruses and bacteria. Rather than roaming the savannah, they live most commonly in freshwater and marine habitats but can also be found in soil, in mosses, and associated with lichens on rocks and trees. When their environment dries out, rotifers can desiccate to an encysted form that is completely dormant. The cysts are nothing but particles of dust that blow in the wind. But in the presence of moisture, even after long bouts of dormancy, the animal becomes fully active again.

Some things that are clearly alive, therefore, do not metabolize, at least for extended periods of time that in some cases can encompass hundreds of years. The absence of metabolism cannot be used to exclude the possibility of life.

The presence of metabolism is equally inadequate to define life. Our previous example of fire consuming oxygen is but one nonliving system in which environmental chemicals are converted to energy for the purposes of reproduction and movement. We could try to avoid this fire trap by noting that fire releases all of the oxidative energy of its fuel as heat, trapping none for useful work as is usually seen in the living. But fire moves uphill, a form of work, moving against gravity, with what could seem like volition and purpose. Plus, we have the unassailable example of stars burning fuel to create matter as a reminder that metabolism is not a unique marker of life.

EXCRETION

The process of metabolism creates waste that must be eliminated from the body or machine creating the waste. If metabolism fails to define life, perhaps its byproduct might help. But what really is excretion but a release of entropy? Waste itself is the disordered residue of things once more highly ordered. The cashew is not recognizable when what remains comes out the other end. Waste and heat are the currencies used to balance the entropy books, keeping tabs on the decrease in entropy (increased order) in your body and the concomitant entropy increase (loss of order) in the environment, discarding that not used for useful work in the business of life. Excretion is a critical link between metabolism and resistance to entropy. But just as neither of those was found to be helpful in defining life, the connection between the two is of no greater assistance.

Excretion fails to help us define life also because examples are found abundantly in the abiotic world. An automobile consumes food in the form of gasoline, metabolizes the hydrocarbons to produce useful work to get us to work, and excretes waste through the tailpipe in the form of carbon dioxide and other pollutants. Most industrial processes function similarly. Every smokestack on the horizon is the equivalent of an animal's rear end, the place where waste is excreted into the external environment after consuming raw materials to extract energy for work to produce essential goods like Cheetos®.

MOVEMENT

Many living things move under their own power, toward food and mates, away from predators and in a search for shelter. But consider the misunderstood sponge, often confused for a plant. A sponge is an animal, which just happens to be sessile. Coral is another immobile animal. Most plants do not move. The fact that these organisms cannot move makes them no less alive, whether plant or animal. The absence of movement, then, is not an indicator of nonlife. Many things that do not move are alive.

While movement through space, from point A to point B, is the type of motion typically invoked when discussing motion as a characteristic of life, it is not the only game in town. Even the sponge, stuck in place, has *internal* movement, using collar cells with tiny little hairs that, on an average specimen, move about 2000 liters of sea water across its pores every day. Plants have internal flow of materials from roots to leaves. So maybe movement, if we include the internal kind, can after all define life: if it moves, it is alive; if it does not move, it might be alive. But no, even that is not possible.

Whether internal motion or the more obvious kind, the presence of movement is definitely not an indicator of life. Machines move. A team at Stanford University won a $2 million prize from the Defense Advanced Research Projects Agency (DARPA) by building an "autonomous robotic vehicle" that successfully negotiated a course in the Mojave Desert, driving with no human intervention over 131 miles of unpaved roads and obstacles including tunnels, narrow cliffs, power lines, barbed wire fences, cattle guards, rocks and boulders.

Robots in automobile factories move in ways that would make the most agile gymnast envious. Karcher makes an autonomous vacuum cleaner, the RC 3000 RoboCleaner, which moves throughout the house with no human guidance. The RC 3000 returns to its base station for cleaning and charging before setting out again for another round of cleaning. The base station automatically empties the dirt from the robot; since the owner does not need to empty the dirt bin, the vacuum can clean all day with no human intervention. Motion or absence thereof is a poor characteristic to distinguish life from the nonliving. That little machine scurrying across your kitchen floor is the reason why.

AUTOPOIESIS

Autopoiesis describes a process, first articulated by two Chilean biologists, Humberto Maturana and Francisco J. Varela, by which an organism self-maintains its unity or identity through self-production of its components. Only an autonomous system that is closed structurally and operationally can exhibit this property. Two problems immediately present themselves when trying to apply this concept to the definition of life. The first is that autopoiesis requires autonomy. If we remember the diminished male anglerfish, reduced to nothing but a pair of testes parasitizing the female, we will recall that autonomy is problematic as a defining trait of life. Autonomy is further discredited by acknowledging that no organism is independent of its environment. Autopoiesis therefore rests on a concept, autonomy, which we have already shown to be questionable in the realm of life.

HOMEOSTASIS

While autopoiesis and autonomy require a closed system, homeostasis describes a complex open system that protects its structure and functions in the face of external changes by regulating its internal environment to maintain a stable condition. The most obvious example of this type of dynamic equilibrium is thermoregulation, your body's ability to maintain a nearly constant internal temperature in the face of widely varying air temperatures. You also maintain innumerable other physiological parameters within tight specifications, including glucose levels, oxygen, carbon dioxide, salts, pH and water content. The body accomplishes this task of maintaining stability in a changing environment through negative feedback mechanisms, responding in a way that counteracts any direction of change. Blood sugar levels offer a good example: when sugar levels become elevated, the pancreas secretes insulin, which accelerates the storage of glucose in liver cells in the form of glycogen, removing glucose from the blood. When sugar levels fall, the pancreas secretes glucagons, which help break glycogen back into glucose, increasing blood glucose levels.

Protein production is controlled in a similar way. When protein A becomes too abundant, it triggers the creation of protein B, which destroys protein A. But protein B degrades quickly on its own, so when there is not enough protein A to trigger production of protein B, protein B fades away, which allows concentrations of protein A to build up again, until once again it hits a level that starts anew the production of protein B.

Finally, we have a process, homeostasis, which seems to be unique to life. But no, we do not. Plenty of physical systems exhibit true homeostasis. The thermostat control in a friend's house turns on the heat when the temperature falls to 69 degrees Fahrenheit, and turns on the air conditioner when the temperature reaches 73 degrees. His house is thermoregulating to maintain a narrow range of temperatures through negative feedback.

Electrical systems commonly maintain constant voltage in very tight specification through negative feedback. Even the common toilet uses the same mechanism to fill up to a predetermined level after being flushed.

Homeostasis can also be found in much larger systems. We need not rely on the toilet to make our case. Population balance in an ecosystem is also the result of homeostasis. This can be seen readily in the relationships between predator and prey. If a predator such as a fox becomes too abundant, rabbits, a fox delicacy, will diminish in number as they are overharvested. Eventually, the rabbit population will decline precipitously enough that the fox population can no longer be supported. In the absence of enough food the fox population crashes. With vastly fewer foxes around, surviving rabbits do what they do best and soon the population is back to strong numbers. With so many rabbits jumping around, the few remaining foxes, with plenty to eat, start reproducing and increasing in number, continuing the cycle. The population of both predator and prey is kept in check within relatively narrow values. This is an example of how the ecosystem itself maintains balance through homeostasis. An ecosystem is comprised of living things, of course, but in itself is not alive.

The climate system of Earth is stabilized through complex systems of negative feedback loops that have maintained the global average temperature to a few tenths of a degree over millennia in a perfect example of homeostasis. These feedback loops are why Earth is balmy and habitable, compared to Venus, where a runaway greenhouse has scorched the surface with temperatures of about 900 degrees Fahrenheit. Of course, dumping billions of tons of greenhouse gases into the atmosphere might change the equation on Earth in the next few centuries. In any case, living and nonliving systems, both large and small, exhibit homeostasis, which makes the property useless as a defining trait of life.

COMPLEXITY

Even the simplest of living things is extraordinarily complex, which might imply that complexity itself is a sign of life. To explore that possibility, the idea of complexity has to be further refined into two distinct categories. *Structural complexity* refers to how many parts a machine or organism has, and how elaborately those parts are connected. *Functional complexity* describes the behavior that results from the underlying structure. The two ideas are distinct: a highly complex structure could behave simply, and a simple structure could exhibit complex behavior. Perhaps one or both types of complexity are the key to defining life.

What is commonly meant by life's functional complexity is that living things tend to exhibit nonlinear behavior, in which a simple input can yield a wide range of unpredictable outcomes. Your sedate eighteen-year-old daughter getting a tattoo of a dragon on her right breast after seeing a picture of one on her favorite rock star would be an example of unpredictable behavior in response to a simple stimulus.

Unfortunately for those of us trying to define life, however, simple physical nonliving systems can also exhibit complex nonlinear behavior. A novice amateur can build an electric circuit in which the output strength does not vary in any way proportionally to the strength of the input. This type of behavior is also commonly seen in the field of optics. On a grander level, global weather is a classic example of nonlinearity where the eventual outcome is extremely sensitive to initial conditions. This is known as the butterfly effect, the idea in meteorology that a butterfly flapping her wings in France can create a disturbance that in the chaotic motion of the atmosphere will amplify large-scale upper-level motion in the Pacific to create a monsoon in Japan. Living and nonliving systems exhibit nonlinear behavior.

If functional complexity fails to define life, we might look to structural complexity to save the day. The idea would be that the structure of life is inherently more complex than abiotic systems. The idea is attractive and holds true for the majority of cases. But some physical systems are more structurally complex than the simplest biological organisms. Imagine FedEx as a unitary system, with multiple airport hubs, warehouses, thousands of employees, fleets of trucks and airplanes, conveyor belts, sorting equipment, scheduling software, fuel deliveries, and hierarchies of management. One could argue that the structure of this organism of overnight delivery is more complex than a simple virus with RNA residing inside a protein capsule. Nor do viruses offer the only example of extreme simplicity. Mycoplasmas are bacteria so small they were long categorized incorrectly as viruses themselves. A researcher may well have an easier time learning the secrets of mycoplasma structure than penetrating the inner workings of FedEx.

Even so, mycoplasmas are impressively complex. While the FedEx argument presented above serves to make a point, the idea is a bit of a stretch really. One might reasonably say that biological complexity *on average* is greater than that found in the nonliving world. Complexity does seem to be an inherent characteristic of life at some level, while the same cannot be said for physical systems. All life is complex. All physical systems are not complex. The problem is that not all complex things are alive. We are further burdened by the fact that quantifying complexity in biological and abiotic systems is fraught with assumptions, inaccuracies and unknowns, so that the effort to define complexity becomes as difficult as the underlying struggle to define life. We swap one intractable problem for another. Determining the point at which complexity reaches a level that defines life appears to be impossible.

ORGANIZATION

The concept of organization, when used as a defining characteristic of life, is simply functional and structural complexity under another guise. The idea is that living things are comprised of numerous systems and subsystems such as molecules, cells and organs, that all must work together in an intricate balance of rates, gradients, volumes and concentrations in order to function as a self-contained organism, supposedly in a way not found in nonliving systems. All of the systems must cooperate and coordinate. Your heart beating furiously in a fight-or-flight response would not do much good if you are trying to get to sleep. All of your organs must constantly adjust to the output of the others to maintain equilibrium.

One possible implication is that since the organization of a chimpanzee is more elaborate than that of a bacterium, the primate is more alive than the germ. In any attempt to define life, introducing a gradient of more and less alive is unhelpful, and in fact counter to the goals of the exercise. Or if both chimpanzee and bacterium are considered alive to the same degree because both are organized in some complex way, the implication is that life is defined by some threshold of organization. In that case, the same arguments relating to complexity would hold true here, making organization a useless concept. Or consider an airplane factory, with its hundreds of robots and humans, material inputs and outputs, corporate and government bureaucracies, the conversion of energy and matter, and waste. The organization of the myriad systems and subsystems must all work together harmoniously to produce an aircraft. In the end, organization is a concept too amorphous to be helpful in our quest to define life.

GROWTH AND DEVELOPMENT

Growth can be defined simply and intuitively as a physical increase in size. Since scientists have a propensity for precision, they view growth more formally as an increase in volume or area in a structure resulting from the conversion of materials from the environment into components of the structure. Immediately we can see that by itself growth is clearly not an indication of life. Observe the surface of a metal chair sitting outside, and rust will be seen to grow in all dimensions. Crystals grow. A rock rolling downhill will tend to grow in size if moving over an appropriate substrate by adding deposits to its surface. A pond of water grows in volume during a rainstorm. Buildings grow during construction. A campus can grow by adding land and buildings to the site. Not all things that grow are alive.

But perhaps all things that are alive grow. With the exception of viruses, which assemble rather than grow, that is true. Even bacteria reproducing through binary fission double in size before splitting in two to make a better half.

All forms of life that reproduce sexually grow from a fertilized egg into something bigger. Furthermore, in most biological systems this growth is more than just an increase in size; growth is a product of development, during which the organism changes not only size but shape and organization during the transformation from egg to adult. Not simple growth, but growth seen as a result of development might be the stuff of life. But no, even the concept of development does not help us. Cars, refrigerators, and computers all grow and develop during production, changing shape, growing, increasing in complexity. Growth and development are important characteristics of life, but not defining ones since many nonliving systems grow and develop.

We see yet another problem unrelated to the fact that nonliving things also grow and develop. The concern is similar to what we encountered with evolution and reproduction. If we come upon the adult form of an animal never seen before, and we rely on growth to define life, we would have to admit we could not determine if the thing was alive or not.

The common flaw with growth, development, evolution and reproduction is that we are attempting to define life as a process of transformation unfolding over time rather than as the result standing before us. In all cases the approach is inadequate.

RESPIRATION

We usually think of respiration as breathing in and out. But biologists have a different definition, perhaps the result of spending too much time in the lab. Respiration is the process of converting food energy into a form of energy that your cells can use. Respiration gets its fuel from digestion. Digestion breaks down food into molecules such as glucose and carbohydrates. Respiration takes these products of digestion and converts them into a specific type of chemical energy that your cells can use to function properly. You eat to make fuel for respiration. You breathe to give your cells the oxygen they need to burn this fuel to power the essential functions of life.

Inside our cells, aerobic respiration involves combining glucose with oxygen, which yields energy plus carbon dioxide and water as waste. For those who enjoy symmetry, this is the exact reverse of the reaction that takes place with photosynthesis, a process in which plants use the energy of sunlight to combine carbon dioxide and water into sugar and oxygen.

With that yin and yang of life energy, we can safely say that all things that respire are alive. But alas not all things that are alive respire. We have our venerable examples of viruses and prions, which do not. Prions you will recall are those self-replicating proteins, containing no genetic material, that cause mad cow disease and scrapie. But respiration has another big problem in the form of dormant life, the same stumbling block we encountered with metabolism. Bacterial spores and encysted rotifers do not respire until reanimated. Rotifers are the most important exception here because they provide an example of a complex animal that can endure long periods with no respiration at all. We cannot use respiration to define life.

RESPONSIVENESS

Animals react favorably at the sight of a mate, pull away from extreme heat, cold or pain, and migrate toward the smell of food. Unicellular organisms move away from noxious chemicals, toward or away from light, or up a gradient of desirable molecules. Plants respond to light, and some to touch, such as the Venus flytrap and other meat-eating plants.

But responsiveness is clearly not confined to the living. The RC 3000, that little robotic vacuum that could, responds to touch, moving away from walls and other barriers in a relentless assault on dirt. Thermotropic liquid crystals, the basis for mood rings popular in the 1970's, change color in response to slight changes in temperature. Modern sewing machines respond to software programs that guide stitching patterns. Nonliving things are responsive, and not all living things respond, as we have seen with dormant life. Responsiveness is no help to us in defining life.

INFORMATION

The quote from Richard Dawkins at the beginning of the chapter, from *The Blind Watchmaker*, moves the debate from the substance of life to the information that guides how molecules are put together. Living things carry within themselves a set of instructions on how to develop into a specific type of living thing. That information is fully contained within each organism's genetic material in the form of DNA. Every cell in your body has a complete set of DNA, which acts like the blueprint for an architect building a house. Your DNA contains all the instructions for making you. That is impressive, but somebody needs to read the blueprint to convert the plans into bricks and mortar. That is the role of RNA, which translates the code embedded within DNA, converting the information in the DNA into proteins, the building blocks of all life. If DNA is like an architect with a complete set of blueprints, then RNA is like the general contractor, who reads and translates the architect's plans to build the new structure. In this analogy, the new structure is a set of proteins, which in fact is what you are.

The one exception to this tidy rule of biology, going from DNA to RNA to proteins, is one class of virus that contains only RNA. They have cut out the boss, DNA, and decided to use RNA as the way to encode everything necessary to make a virus. But even in this case, the boss has the final word. Once such a virus infects a host, the virus reverse engineers its RNA back into DNA! In any case, think of DNA and RNA as *information* that each organism uses to build itself.

Dawkins's appeal to information to help us define life solves some immediate problems. A spec of dust that is a rotifer contains its genetic code whether animated or dormant. A bacterial spore retains its full complement of DNA. We even partially solve the problem posed by viruses, which contain enough genetic material to direct the genetic machinery of *the infected host* to make more viruses. We can safely say that any live thing contains a genetic code that describes how to make that thing,

Life i DNA, RNA
Genetic code
Prion - exception
Ability to use it.

indirectly in the case of vi[ruses] ... es this conclusion, but as a free-standin[g] ... for now.

So perhaps we have fi[nally] ... [de]finition of life. We might conclude simp[ly that the pre]... RNA) defines life. How elegant! We are so close, but no, once again we have been foiled, because not every thing that contains a genetic code is alive. An animal that has recently died retains a full complement of DNA, but is still dead, just as dead as Monty Python's parrot. We might salvage the situation by saying that life is defined by the presence of DNA or RNA *and the ability to use the information* to create new copies of the genetic material. That solves the dead animal problem. But then we revisit the dormant life issue, because bacterial spores, crystallized viruses and encysted rotifers are not capable of using their genetic material to make copies during their periods of dormancy.

Using information content to define life runs up against another problem. The genetic code is digital. Instead of being a binary system of 1s and 0s as in the computer world, the genetic system is quaternary, having four distinct states rather than two. Either way, we have an immediate and obvious case of a nonliving example of information stored digitally. Computer code can contain enough information to replicate itself, and the computer has the ability to use the information to do so. The existence of digitally stored, self-replicating information cannot define life because examples are found in nonliving systems. Also, as storage media become denser and smaller, the discrepancy between the enormous amount of information contained in an incredibly small space in a cell and the information content on a computer chip becomes slightly less dramatic every year. Although the gap in information storage in biotic and abiotic systems remains gargantuan, one can imagine that the discrepancy will disappear one day. And that leads us to artificial life.

ARTIFICIAL LIFE

Artificial life is the simulation of biological functions through the use of computer models, robotics, or biochemistry. Many businesses and books are devoted to the topic. However fascinating, though, we can find no assistance here in our journey to define life. Whatever clever creation arises out of this field of study, nobody could define the result as alive or not in the absence of a good definition of life. The field of artificial life would benefit from a clean, distinct, unambiguous definition of life, because experts in the field would then know if they had succeeded in making something lifelike. But, inversely, progress in the field of artificial intelligence does nothing to advance a definition of life. Even if Aibo the robot dog advanced to the stage of speaking English, making your breakfast, and driving you to work, we still could not say if Aibo was alive or not in the absence of a good definition of life.

FINAL AMBIGUITY

As we have noted, nobody would deny the existence of green or blue, yet nobody can define when one color becomes the other. That inability to draw a clear line between them does not diminish the reality of the two colors. We accept the existence of clearly identified colors even when the transition between frequencies in the electromagnetic spectrum is absent of any clearly delineated boundary. Life is no different. We know at the extremes when something is alive or not, with no ambiguity, just as we know something is green or blue. Other cases are ambiguous, just as we do not know when green becomes blue. A virus could be alive or not, simply depending on your perspective. In some cases, such as viruses, bacterial spores, and prions, defining matter as alive or not becomes arbitrary, an exercise in semantics, rather than a window into the deeper workings of nature. We might be obsessed with attaching a label of "living" to something, but that something simply sits somewhere along a continuum of complexity regardless of the label finally affixed, aloof to our discomfort. Think of a virus as blue-green and prions as turquoise.

The region along the spectrum where abiotic transitions to biotic is a zone of ambiguity that exists because life is not an all-or-none phenomenon, and because the stuff of life is the same stuff as nonlife. Previous definitions of life have fallen short because of a common commitment to find a spark that simply does not exist. Definitions struggled to capture something essential about life that was not found in the abiotic world, rather than accept that no such distinction can be found. Definitions of life were meant to reflect somethin   ther than serve as a useful tool for cate   *Life — table*   y all have failed.

There is no single unambiguous   es of life are complex; most metabolize, g   time. But not all do, and not all have all o   hys-ical systems also share these same   trou-bling; it reflects the reality of nature. "Life" is an *arbitrary label* we apply to distinguish extremes of complexity along a continuum. We know that a block of pure quartz is not alive and that a screeching kid in the restaurant is; whatever label we paste on all those cases in between is a convenient convention but in no way reflects any fundamental break or division between the living and nonliving.

We are not the first scientists to reach this conclusion about life. Josephine Marquand suggested in 1968 that we "avoid the use of the word 'life' or 'organism' in any discussion of borderline systems." Norman Horowitz in 1955 and John Keosian in 1964 concluded much the same as we do here. Even the 1968 Encyclopaedia Britannica stated, "There is no point along the continuum of existence from the simplest atom to the most complex animal, at which a line can be drawn separating life from nonlife." Notice, however that Marquand, Horowitz and Keosian are not household names, nor is the Britannica observation widely cited. The idea of a continuum of complexity, with simple inorganic systems at one end and the highest life forms at the other, is a bit difficult to digest and does not satisfy the human need for easy answers. The idea also moves against the grain of our intuition about something being alive or not. So we put up some resistance. But resistance is futile.

With a new perspective on the phenomenon of life, we are now prepared to explore how humanity fits into the big picture. Being humble about who and what we are is easier when we recognize our kinship not only with our cousins in the animal kingdom, but also with the dirt under our feet and the charcoal in our barbecue.

CHAPTER 2

Primordial Soup to Nuts:
A Brief Tour of Evolution

*The highest possible stage in moral culture is when we
recognize that we ought to control our thoughts.*
– Charles Darwin

*I have been studying the traits and dispositions of the
"lower animals" (so called) and contrasting them with the traits
and dispositions of man. I find the result humiliating to me.*
— *Mark Twain*

When Charles Darwin published *On the Origin of Species* in 1859, he exposed the world to a momentous discovery every bit as significant and disorienting as when Copernicus discovered that the Earth was not the center of the universe. For the first time in history, human beings were seen not as creatures of divine origin, but instead as a product of nature, an animal like every other on the planet. Imagine yourself back in that amazing year. The day before Darwin's book was published, you wake up thinking yourself the image of God; the next morning you realize you have the face of a monkey. Not everybody immediately embraced this rude demotion from god to goat. Resistance to the idea was inevitable. But have absolutely no doubt: evolution is one of the most extraordinary, successful, thoroughly documented scientific discoveries in human history. Evolution through natural selection is an indisputable fact, just as we now know that the Earth orbits the sun.

Sometimes the word "theory" associated with evolution is misunderstood to mean that the concept is not well established. Oddly, that burden is not shared by the Theory of Relativity. Einstein apparently hired a better publicist than Darwin, if not a more skilled barber. In any case, we know now, unambiguously and with certainty, that *Homo sapiens* is a normal and by no means inevitable result of evolution operating under the same principles that yielded the shrew, dung beetle, cholera bacterium and oak tree.

This book is not a treatise on evolution, but we can hardly avoid the subject if we want to place humankind in its proper context to create a new moral foundation. Before we can answer the question of how life evolves, though, we must first address a preceding concern: that is, where and how did life originate? After all, life had to start somewhere in order to evolve. This question of origin is quite distinct from the quest to define life that we explored in the first chapter: even with a perfect definition of life that includes all living things and excludes all things not living, we would still need to ponder that initial spark.

THE ORIGIN OF LIFE

While the questions of life's origin and definition are distinct, one informs the other in a significant way. You may not have realized in reading Chapter 1 that we have solved the age-old problem of what came first, the chicken or the egg. That dilemma derives from the notion that life can derive only from life; if true, we can see the problem immediately. If new life comes only from a previous generation of the living, what started the process when no life was around to propagate the first generation?

We hinted at the answer to this fundamental question in the preceding chapter. As we will soon see, life is not needed to create life, an arbitrary designation along a continuum of complexity. With that conclusion, however, students of science history might eye us suspiciously as relics of the 17th century. Perhaps we endorse spontaneous generation, the idea that some life forms routinely arise all of a sudden from nonliving stuff, particularly decomposing matter? Aristotle noted that mud and river water were important ingredients in the generation of frogs, eels and even mice. Methods changed over the centuries, so that in the 1600's, mice recipes were calling for incubating wheat husks and sweaty underwear in an open container for 21 days, during which time sweat would penetrate the husks, converting them to mice. Maggots were said to arise spontaneously from rotting meat.

To see why we are not resurrecting the dead theory of spontaneous generation, let alone the use of sweaty underwear, we need to revisit the late 1600's. From the time of Aristotle until 1668, spontaneous generation was taken as a given, unquestioned by educated people. But then an Italian physician, Francesco Redi, hypothesized that maggots in meat were the result of flies laying eggs after being attracted to the odor of decaying flesh. In 1668, Redi proved his idea correct when he showed that meat sealed to prevent access by adult flies did not generate maggots, throwing into doubt nearly 2000 years of unchallenged assumptions. Competing experiments supporting and refuting spontaneous generation battled back and forth for the next 150 years, further refining and building on Redi's work. But no experiment convinced the other side to abandon ship.

At the turn of the 19th century, scientists were still engaged in this heated debate, dividing into two warring camps whose views were largely shaped by religion and politics, rather than by science. In the context of modern times, the composition of the two sides is a bit confusing. The Catholic Church fought against spontaneous generation because the idea conflicted with Genesis, which states that all life was created in six days. If life was indeed being created in rotting meat, that would present an embarrassing problem for the Church. In contrast, materialists, those cold-hearted scientists in white lab coats, *supported* spontaneous generation as proof that God played no role in the origin of life. Early advances in science seemed to support the materialists. Introduction of the microscope revealed a fantastic world of microorganisms that truly did seem to develop from nothing. Just put a bit of hay in some water, wait a few days, and see new life in water that previously had held none.

This raging debate was largely resolved by an experiment completed by Louis Pasteur in 1859, the very same time Darwin published his masterpiece. What a year! Pasteur is best known for germ-free milk. But he made an equally important contribution in 1860. He compared two flasks of water, one of which he sterilized by boiling. He then showed that no life subsequently formed in the previously boiled water, debunking any notion of spontaneous creation of life where none existed before. Based on his experiments, all but the most ardent supporters of spontaneous generation had to throw in the towel. But like creationists and "intelligent design" advocates today who cannot accept the fact of evolution, die-hard proponents of spontaneous generation would not let go, proposing ever-more desperate ideas to explain away indisputable experimental results. Over time, though, all but the most fanatic opposition died out, and support for the idea of spontaneous generation eventually fell into the category of flat-Earth science.

But wait just a minute. If life can arise from nonliving sources, are we not indeed resurrecting spontaneous generation? Not even close. Life arose once, and only once, early in Earth's history from a combination of inorganic chemicals. That history has no kinship to the idea that new life springs routinely and spontaneously from some vital force. To grasp the difference, we need to ponder a deep paradox. *The creation of life destroyed the very environment in which life was created.* Once life was established, the favorable initial conditions would no longer be present; any chemicals that might come together to create new life would be eaten by existing critters! The presence of life created com ~~rials, so the chemicals needed for a second genes~~ available. (That is true at least as a general condi ~~treme and isolated conditions could occur in whi~~ environment is recreated.)

On early Earth, the atmosphere contained no that precious gas is the byproduct of photosynthesis in plants, which convert carbon dioxide and sunlight into sugars, with oxygen as a waste product. We breathe plant waste. Life first formed under these anaerobic (no oxygen) conditions, in an environment that would kill us instantly. Life destroyed the crucible from which it came, making life's creation a one-time event.

Let's think about this paradox for a minute longer. Plants evolved in an atmosphere with no oxygen, along with all other early life forms. But then plants started polluting this pristine environment with dirty and

[handwritten marginal note:] Early earth - NO O_2. Byproduct of plants. We breathe plant waste.

deadly oxygen as a waste product. Plants themselves are indifferent to the presence of this pollutant, because oxygen is not toxic to plants. As long as they have access to carbon dioxide and sunlight, life for plants is good. But the other early life forms were not so lucky. Oxygen is extremely deadly to them. As plants became more and more numerous, more and more oxygen got pumped into the atmosphere. Eventually, after millions of years, oxygen became abundant, creating the environment in which subsequent life evolved. Aerobic, oxygen-loving critters, like us, got to come out and play, while anaerobic bugs, which die in the presence of oxygen, had to hide away in the few remaining dark places that were protected from the deadly gas.

So to beat a dead horse, let us reiterate that life could develop only one time from abiotic sources as a unique event, at least on Earth. The very presence of life, and a changed atmosphere, prevent a new genesis.

If the origin of life can be explained in general terms by the laws of physics and chemistry, we still face the burden of providing a few details about the actual mechanism of creation. Modern theories make the point that the mechanisms by which nonliving materials yielded life can eventually be fully understood without invoking any unknown or mysterious forces. Future developments will almost certainly lead to a complete synthesis of life in the lab, which will prove beyond any doubt, if nothing else, that life can come from nonlife under the right conditions. Until we are fortunate enough to witness the creation of a microscopic Frankenstein in a Petri dish, how do we support the hypothesis that life began with a boiling bath of mud?

Any newly gathered group of golfers will be unable to refrain from mentioning the mighty Tiger Woods for more than just a few minutes after convening. The very subject of golf and Tiger have become synonymous; thinking of one leads to thoughts of the other. In the quest to understand the origin of life, Tiger's equivalent is Stanley Lloyd Miller. While Dr. Miller does not enjoy the wealth or acclaim of golf's most famous son, his impact will be felt long after the next great athlete comes onto the scene. To understand his contribution, we must again to go back in time to revisit the year 1953, when Miller published his findings in *Science* as a young graduate student under the guidance of Harold Urey at the University of Chicago. Miller was not the first to propose that life originated in a prebiotic soup in which chemical selection took place. He was the first, however, to create such a soup experimentally.

Recreating what was then thought to be the composition of the Earth's nascent oxygen-free atmosphere of methane, ammonia and hydrogen, Miller boiled some water to represent evaporation from the ocean, and then energized the system with an electric charge representing lightning. What he created were amino acids, which are the building blocks of proteins, the foundation of biology. The importance of this experiment is difficult to exaggerate. He formed complex biological molecules from a few simple gases. Eventually, after many refinements and later advances in analytical chemistry, Miller detected the formation of thirty-three amino acids, including nearly half of those found in all living beings on Earth. Other scientists subsequently showed similar results, with smaller yields, using ultraviolet light as the energy source.

Miller may well have gotten the composition of the early-Earth atmosphere wrong, and may have used the wrong source of energy. Those parameters are still debated. Even if so, none of that diminishes the incredible accomplishments of Miller or his colleagues. What these scientists did was create an experimental link between the world of the nonliving and living.

In spite of the enormous importance of Miller's experiments, a bowl full of amino acids is not life. Miller built humankind's first indisputable bridge across the chasm that was thought to separate the living from the nonliving, but the land on the other side was and remains vast and largely unexplored. How do we actually get to life from the biological building blocks in a prebiotic soup?

We noted earlier that we solved the age-old problem of what came first, the chicken or the egg, by demonstrating that life has a nonliving origin. But the story is not yet complete. In claiming that life developed from a brew of chemicals on the early Earth, we have created a brand new "what came first" problem. All forms of modern life contain either RNA or DNA as genetic material. The problem we face is that both RNA and DNA require elaborate proteins to assist in the replication process. So if genes are needed to make proteins, and proteins are needed to make (replicate) genes, what came first, genes or proteins? All we have done is shrink the chicken-egg problem down to molecular size, but the problem remains.

We would avoid this new dilemma if only we could find some form of genetic material that could replicate itself without the assistance of any proteins. In fact, the Holy Grail in understanding the origin of life is to find a completely independent self-replicating molecule that extracts energy from the environment to fuel its own replication. We need to find a "molecular chicken!"

Discovering a truly self-replicating molecule would bring us a long way toward a potential explanation for the origin of life. That is precisely why Thomas Cech and Sidney Altman won the Nobel Prize in Chemistry in 1989 for their work earlier in that decade. What these scientists found, working independently, is that RNA molecules, real genetic material, can catalyze certain chemical reactions with no help from other molecules or proteins. Cech called the new molecules *ribozymes* ("molecular chickens" did not sound sufficiently official) because they not only carried genetic information in the form of *ribo*nucleic acid (our friend RNA) but also acted as catalysts, the normal role of proteins in the form of en*zymes*. This work validated an idea presciently put forth by Carl Woese way back in 1967 before ribozymes were even discovered. Cech and others went on to evolve ribozymes that took on ever-more complex catalytic functions, to the point that some of the modified ribozymes can copy short stretches of themselves with no assistance.

The power of duplication is such that even if one such self-replicating molecule arose just once in one place, in just two days there could be trillions of copies if replication times were short. Those huge numbers generated in a short period are important, because survival would be ensured even if the first self-replicating molecule were unstable, or stable only under the right conditions, but easily degraded otherwise.

So are we done? Can we go home now? No, because this is almost certainly not how life got started. This "RNA World" is full of significant problems and gaps. This and every other theory on the origin of life suffer from the fact that the condit[ions]   [pr]obably never be known with certainty. E[a]   [n]o fossil record, and would be obliterated [   ]   [1]s. Scientists also continue to debate w[   ]   Origin Event most likely took place. Diff[   ]   [th]e sites such as deep-sea hydrothermal v[   ]   [sh]allow lagoons or hot sulfur springs. The[   ] details, but not in the solid conclusion that *at some point a mix of chemicals came together in a way that eventually self-organized into something we call life.* That requires neither a miracle nor the invocation of any divine intervention. The discovery of small segments of self-replicating genetic material is an important proof of concept, even if a more plausible means of creating life is eventually found.

[handwritten note: Life / Carbon based / – iron, sulfur needed / Genetic code – same]

While large gaps in our knowledge remain, we can nevertheless conclude with confidence that we are all descendents of a chemical stock brewing in some nasty primordial soup. That common ancestry is seen all around us. You are that rhododendron in your garden, and the aphid gnawing its leaf. All forms of life are carbon-based. All use the same energy package to power life's functions. All rely on the elements of iron and sulfur to support normal operations. But here is the clincher: every form of life known on Earth uses the same genetic code, using the exact-same alphabet and language to make the stuff of life. That fact is perhaps one of the most fascinating, important and monumental discoveries ever made since the dawn of time. Even more important than knowing from which rehab treatment a tabloid star recently escaped. When we see that an elephant, a yeast cell and a rose share the same internal machinery, right down to the most basic biochemical pathways, we can easily understand that we are all drawn from the same broth, whether bacterium, fungus, plant or animal.

Those who wish not to believe that we are the spawns of soup might object that a common machinery of life does not prove common ancestry. Perhaps the machinery we see is all that is possible if life is to exist, so of course all forms of life would share the same biochemical pathways and genetic codes. Common pathways and functions prove nothing other than the fact that such pathways are necessary for life. Well, that idea can easily and conclusively be proven wrong.

Molecules come in two forms, just as your hands do. Your hands are mirror images of each other, and all molecules have the equivalent of a left and right hand. Like your hands, they differ in spatial orientation but function the same. Amino acids, those building blocks of life, are no exception and all come in left-hand and right-hand varieties. Both kinds are found in equal amounts in Miller's primordial soup. Amazingly, though, every single amino acid in every single animal is the left-handed kind. No right-handed amino acids are found in any form of life on Earth. But left-hand amino acids are not necessary for life. Scientists have shown in the laboratory that everything functions just fine if all right-handed amino acids are used instead. Life need not be based on left-hand amino acids, yet every form of life indeed is. The fact that all forms of life share the same biochemistry, combined with the fact that other pathways are possible but never found, indicates strongly that all life is derived from a common ancestor. Or perhaps God is left-handed, and this is His idea of a practical joke.

THE EVOLUTION OF LIFE

Once self-replicating genetic material was found in the soup, Darwin's favorite subject took central stage. Evolution just means change over time, but we should be a tad more rigorous than that. Charles himself defined evolution as "descent with modification . . . caused by the accumulation of innumerable slight variations, each good for the individual possessor." Keep in mind that this insight about the *mechanism* of evolution is amazing, considering that universities had not yet invented courses in genetics. The bottom line is that the great diversity of life that we see around us comes not from some grand design, but from random changes during the imperfect processes of genetic replication that result in mutations accumulating over many generations.

The key idea is that the random genetic mutations just mentioned take place in a large number of individuals in each generation, and that these diverse individuals demonstrate a variety of traits and behaviors, which make some individuals more fit than others to pass on their genes to the next generation. But the copying process is terribly complicated, and in the parlance of modern politics, "mistakes are made" during replication. So the descendants of the most successful moms and dads are not exact replicas of the parent generation. In this way, new characteristics can appear in a population. If enough new characteristics develop in a subset of the original population, a new species can result.

How the environment acts on the new traits and behaviors of each generation is what we call "natural selection," the mechanism by which species evolve over time under environmental pressures. There is no grand design, and no grand designer. Natural selection is undirected, unguided and as cold and uncaring as the wind. Richard Dawkins elegantly frames this as "nothing but blind, pitiless indifference."

Thanks to Chuck Darwin, natural selection allows us to understand the development of nature's diversity and complexity without resorting to divine tampering. Through Darwin's insights, we can understand that life on Earth began as a natural event, and that evolution is a random process with no direction or drive. The male peacock would probably agree that any rational design would [*Complexity is*] of a ridiculously large tail, which leav [*Not progress.*] But because natural selection is uncarin; st big enough to attract painfully picky fer the next time you are pumping iron at t to make the competing male next door dy's lunch.

With that little background, we come to the most important point about evolution. *Evolution does not inevitably lead to greater complexity, and complexity is not a measure of progress.* This critical point must be understood if we are to place humankind in context of other living beings and appreciate our humble position in the biosphere. You think you are more interesting and more important than *E. coli.* You're not. This requires some explanation.

About 3.5 billion years ago, single-celled organisms were alone in the world. Now we have multicelled creatures with fingers and toes, not to mention antibiotics. So does not that mean we obviously went from simple to complex? In fact, no. Evolution drives always in the direction of better adaptation, but better adaptation may or may not be more complex. Stephen J. Gould explained this better than anyone in his "drunken walk" analogy.

Gould starts his story with a drunk leaning against a wall. The inebriated fellow suddenly begins stumbling about without direction, finally falling into a nearby gutter. Now, the drunk reached the gutter not because that was a predetermined destination to which he was methodically moving. He was just staggering randomly to and fro, and at any given time the drunk was just as likely to be moving away from his former resting place against the wall as toward it. But the wall bounds his movements in one direction, and as a consequence, on average he will likely be somewhere away from the wall. Eventually, he'll topple over into the gutter just by chance. Gould points out that an organism can only be so simple and still be alive, and this limit of simplicity corresponds to the wall. If life began "at the wall" in the form of the simplest possible cells and then randomly evolved, average complexity would eventually and inevitably increase, since moving in the other direction of greater simplicity is not possible. So the development of greater complexity does not imply a systematic trend of any kind, just that there is more room away from than at the wall. In fact, the tremendous success of bacteria demonstrates that even as complexity was evolving into multicellularity "away from the wall," much was happening to the evolution of life right at the wall as well.

Other creatures beyond bacteria also show that evolution does not inevitably lead to greater complexity. Often, parasites evolve toward greater simplicity as generations accumulate genes resulting in characteristics that allow them to use more and more of their host's biological machinery. A deep-sea tube worm known only by its scientific name of *Osedax* is a good example. The male has been reduced to nothing but a "sperm package" residing inside the female worm. Female comedians can have a field day with this... Anyway, the male is a tiny sperm factory living his entire life imprisoned within his mate, surviving off a bit of yolk, doomed to perish when the yolk is exhausted. *Osedax* males have reached a pinnacle of simplicity, evolving ever further away from complexity. Evolution has no goal toward which progress can be measured.

Mark Twain saw this clearly in his oft-quoted comment on what was then the world's tallest building, the Eiffel Tower. Since the Earth is about 4.5 billion years old, Twain got the age of the planet wrong, from Lord Kelvin's estimate, but he got the idea right with his usual wit and sarcasm.

Man has been here for 32,000 years. That it took a hundred million years to prepare the world for him is proof that that is what it was done for. I suppose it is. I dunno. If the Eiffel Tower were representing the world's age, the skin of paint on the pinnacle knob at its summit would represent man's share of that age; and anybody would perceive that the skin was what the tower was built for. I reckon they would. I dunno.

There is no ladder of progress or cone of evolution with a base of lower animals and a peak crowned with the human species. Instead the image of life is one of a large bush, with many branches and sub-branches, all leading to a variety of life forms, each a pinnacle in its own right.

Just as evolution drives toward no species, no species is inevitable. Certainly not the scrawny, weak, hair-challenged apes we call humans. Natural selection is inherently inefficient and messy because selection works largely by elimination rather than toward a goal. Natural selection yields traits adapted to a given environment by eliminating those traits that are not. The process is constrained in that selection can only work with structures, materials, and behaviors at hand. We see how the same chunk of clay is molded to different purposes in genes that are preserved across the animal kingdom, serving different functions. Genes that protect gills in fish are present in mice, for example, but they play an obviously different role. Feathers likely evolved first in function as heat insulation, but the very characteristics that made feathers good insulators also by chan[ce ... fo]r flight.

Chance plays a [...] al selection cannot anticipate future cala[...] l to its environment might well perish ir [...] ges, such as those caused by the impa[...] ount of adaptation can prepare for tha[...] o unknown future conditions.

When conditions change abruptly and radically, only randomly will some species have traits, adapted to other circumstances, which happen to be suited to survival in the new environment. Life in all forms is a roll of the cosmic dice. All species roaming the Earth today are a contingent product of ancestors that possessed a set of adaptations that for no reason other than luck allowed for survival when environmental conditions changed rapidly or catastrophically. This history reflects no march of progress toward humans, or any other species.

In times of greater sanity, we could stop here, confident that no further exposition of evolution would be necessary to emphasize that human beings are just another animal with no bragging rights in the history of life. But these are extraordinary times. In spite of evolution's unprecedented success in explaining the living world, in spite of the fact that evolution is one of the greatest triumphs of science, creationism and intelligent design have crept into the mainstream of American thought and into public school curricula in several states. A poll conducted by the People for the American Way Foundation showed that only 37% of the population believes evolution should be taught to the exclusion of creationism. A Gallup poll in 2001 showed that 40% of Catholics in the United States believe that God created human life in the past 10,000 years. These grim statistics would have even surprised Pope John Paul II, who way back in 1996 reaffirmed that the Church accepted evolution, although with some strong caveats, and about 150 years late.

If we fail to change course and overcome this shameful level of collective ignorance about creation, we will soon be forced to teach the "stork theory of reproduction" in schools as an alternative to the "theory of sexual reproduction." But why stop there? We could soon be teaching that the sun orbits around the Earth as the Bible claims, as an alternative to the "theory of orbital mechanics." Only by understanding the fundamentals of evolution can we put an end to the madness of creationism and intelligent design, and regain a rational sense of our place in the universe.

So we need to dive a little deeper into the gene pool. Evolution is a fact, an undeniable, proven fact. Only some of the details of the mechanisms of evolution fall under the category of theory. Cancer is a fact, though not all the mechanisms leading to malignancy are understood, even with all of our tremendous advances in molecular biology. Opponents of evolution attempt to paint the idea as "only a theory," but that misses two important points. A grand idea, such as general relativity, can be well-established but remain under the rubric of a theory because the idea encompasses and explains a broad range of phenomena. Second, in the world of science, fact means "confirmed to such a degree that it would be perverse to withhold provisional consent," as Stephen Gould has so elegantly said. Advances in genetics, microbiology, molecular biology and paleontology have established evolution as a fact every bit as certain as the existence of atoms. To deny evolution is to deny everything known to science, a position that is patently absurd.

You might be asking by now, with some exasperation, how any of this is even remotely related to the topic of this book on ethics. In fact, the notion that evolution has no direction or purpose, and no drive toward complexity, is central to our effort to place humans in proper context relative to all other living beings and to overcome some deeply embedded ideas about other animals and the physical world around us.

We are faced with the need to combat a fierce bias. Humans generally believe that our species is superior to and separate from the animal kingdom, that we are the end point of the evolution of life on Earth. That notion is not only false but extraordinarily dangerous. The idea that humans were created in the image of God has had grave consequences for other animals and for the natural resources that sustain us.

Golda Meir once said to Israeli military leader Moshe Dayan, "Don't be so humble, you are not that great." That admonition can be applied more broadly to the entire human race. We as a species pretend a false humility before our gods, but we are simply not as great as we would like to believe. Since our early ancestors first organized into clans, nearly all cultures have taught that humans are special in the eyes of their god or gods, and that the world is made for their benefit and use. Across cultures and time, most myths concerning the origin of life, and of human life in particular, hold an exalted place in the world for human beings.

Christian origin myth, badly and inconsistently told in Genesis, is by no means unique in placing humankind in an exalted position. With a few notable exceptions, Greek gods came in the form of human beings, apparently all of whom went to the gym regularly. The female gods all appear to have flat tummies and pert breasts, while their male counterparts boast the ultimate hard bodies, even before being displayed in stone.

We want to suggest a different perspective of humanity based on the idea that human beings are no more special than a butterfly, a gazelle or a paramecium. Our species is nothing but a normal consequence of natural selection, and certainly not the pinnacle of evolution. We are nothing special, and bacteria are the proof.

We have focused before on bacteria, but we are not quite done. For regardless of the fate of humanity, bu[...] ily live without us, but we would die qui[...] le to kill every bacterium in our body, w[...] h. Rapid asexual reproduction is one key [...] e ria populations can double every tw[...] e comes two, then two become four in [...] e eight in the first hour. Not too impres[...] ht bacteria would hardly catch your eye. But at that rate, left unabated, a single bacterium would produce in just 24 hours more than one million billion billion (10^{24}) offspring. In forty-eight hours, the progeny of just one bacterium would weigh 400 times the weight of the planet. Of course, food scarcity, waste buildup and other constraints prevent such ridiculous proliferation. One might question this continuing and odd fascination with bacteria, but they indeed teach us a vital lesson. We must be humble in the face of their biological dominance and impressive longevity.

Our ancestors made it far enough to yield us, but the prospects for our future survival are not particularly bright. As are all creatures, we are a genetic experiment resulting from selective pressure, random mutations, and pure chance that our ancestors avoided extinction from catastrophic events. In the history of life, 99.9% of all species that have ever lived are now extinct. (The rate of extinction, currently nearly 1000 times the *rate*

[Handwritten annotation: "Bacteria can Live without us. We cannot Live without Bacteria. 99.9% of all species are now extinct"]

seen historically before humans entered the scene, is what causes present concern with loss of biological diversity, not the fact of extinction itself.) Extinction is the norm; our brief cameo is by no means preordained to become a leading role comparable to that played by single-celled germs.

We keep forgetting that our highly developed cerebral cortex does not confer upon us any special status among our living cousins. People easily embrace the idea that humanity is set apart from all other animals. But nothing could be further from the truth. Humans are nothing but a short-lived biological aberration, with no claim to superiority. If evolution had a pinnacle, bacteria would rest on top. When the human species is a distant memory, bacteria will be dividing merrily away, oblivious to the odd bipedal mammal that once roamed the Earth for such a brief moment in time.

Our self-promotion to the image of God is simply embarrassing in the face of the biological reality on the ground. There is a loss of credibility when you choose yourself for an award.

CHAPTER 3

Getting a Head: The Human Branch of the Evolutionary Bush

The deepest sin of the human mind is to believe things without evidence.
— Thomas Henry Huxley

Man is the only creature that refuses to be what he is.
                                                    – Albert Camus

A Swedish researcher by the name of Carl von Linné became a proud parent in 1758 when he sired a new field of science that we now call taxonomy. He devised a standardized method of classifying plants and animals to bring shape and order to the unruly bush of life. You may know this scientist more famously as Carolus Linnaeus, a translation of his name to Latin, the language in which he published. By either name, his system is still used today. In the Linnaean system, all forms of life are identified, in descending order, as belonging to a Kingdom, Phylum, Class, Order, Family, Genus, and finally, a Species. This hierarchy of taxonomy is memorized by students of introductory biology with the mnemonic King Phillip Can Order Fresh Green Spinach.

In this system, our particular species is categorized first as Animalia, because after all we are not plants; then Chordata because we possess a backbone (supposedly); Mammalia because we have hair and nurse our infants; Primates because we share common characteristics with apes, monkeys, and lemurs; Hominidae because we are separated from other apes by walking on two legs; *Homo* to recognize our ancestry with other human types; and finally *sapiens*, a species name meaning "wise," perhaps a conclusion drawn somewhat prematurely or too optimistically.

We know that these wise Hominid primates are late arrivals in the history of life, a tiny remote twig on a vast bush. Through various fits, starts, and dead ends from *Australopithecus* to *Paranthropus*, through various *Homo* species like *erectus* and *habilis*, to modern *sapiens*, our lineage is short. Our most ancient direct-line ancestors only go back at most a few million years. Modern people, looking like us, have been around for only about 100,000 years. Take a Cro-Magnon from 35,000 years ago, give him a shave and a suit, and he would look just like your banker and lawyer. He would behave better than either. If we go back much further than that in time, the appearance and behavior of our ancestors will start to diverge from what we expect from our professionals today.

In the previous two chapters, we established that these newly-arrived bipedal primates occupy a humble place in Earth's evolutionary history, a perspective necessary if we are to begin redefining our relationship with our planet. The next step is to define in the contemporary world what it means to be human today within the context of our short evolutionary history. What exactly is this experiment we call modern *Homo sapiens?*

The first answer to this question is that we are not as human in the physical sense as we once thought. The vast majority of our cells are not human at all, but instead, are comprised of microorganisms located in our eyes, mouth, nose, ears, skin and gut, representing about 1000 different species and as many as 8000 subspecies. Bacterial life dominates not only the Earth's biosphere but also the ecosystem of our own bodies. Microorganisms outnumber our human cells by ten to one. Your intestine alone is home to one hundred trillion microbes. Most of the genetic information found in our bodies is nonhuman. The organisms that we host are not invaders or parasites, but an integral part of our internal ecosystem, helping us digest food, produce vitamins and fight against disease. They are us and we are them. Jeffrey Gordon at Washington University points out that *we are really a composite of species.*

Even our genome, the DNA found in truly human cells within our bodies, does not do much to define us. The genetic material found in chimps differs from human DNA by only 1.23%. A more familiar figure you may have encountered is 3% or 4%. These different conclusions do not reflect any uncertainty about the genomes, only diverse methods of analysis. Think of comparing two versions of the same book sold and edited by different publishers. One difference can be measured by comparing every letter in every word in both books. But you could also compare the books by word count or number of paragraphs. The percentage difference between the two depends on what comparison is being made. The same holds true when comparing genomes.

But even these small differences of a few percent exaggerate the disparity between the two genomes. Most genes that differ between chimps and humans are considered "neutral" in that they code for proteins that do not confer any obvious difference between the two species. That leaves even fewer genes available that can be responsible for us writing this book and the chimp not.

From the perspective of composition, therefore, we are more bacterial than human and not much different from chimps genetically. That certainly provides a humble base on which to define humanness. Yet even acknowledging these facts, common sense tells us that we are obviously a distinct mammalian species. While we may be no better or worse or higher or lower than a mouse or an elephant, an elephant walking down the sidewalk would catch your attention, whereas another human would be less of a show. Somehow we are different. The nature and meaning of that difference is what needs to explored.

Surely humans are unique, just as the monarch butterfly and slime molds are unique, as we define species. The question is: are humans unique in a way qualitatively different from all other life forms? Are humans "uniquely unique"? Are humans unique in a way beyond a list of traits that define us as a species? If the answer is no, as we believe it to be, then the question of how to define humans, and human interactions with other animals, needs to be rethought. We are either the image of God, or not.

Past attempts to define a human being have failed for the same reason that attempts to define life failed: the basic assumptions underlying the quest are wrong. We desperately want to find a single trait or capability that can be a defining characteristic, anything that can prove we are special. That search is futile because no single trait, behavior or capability can define humanity.

Instead, a unique combination of traits, all found to some degree in other animals, defines who we are. As emphasized before, humans are a species and therefore can be characterized as a unit distinct from others. At some point, throw in enough variables and a human can be defined. What is striking in the attempt to describe humanness is how difficult the task turns out to be.

We humans have always thought of ourselves as particularly intelligent, proudly noting our compassion, humor, altruism and impressive capacity to generate language, mathematics, tools, art, and music. In citing this self-serving list, filtered to our benefit, we assume that humans possess, and other animals lack, these honorable traits or capabilities. We ignore the inconvenient fact that we choose to define and measure intelligence in terms of our greatest strengths. We arbitrarily exclude from the definition of intelligence higher brain functions in other animals. We would be low on the list of smart animals if we included in our basic definition of intelligence the ability to use self-generated sonar to explore the environment and to communicate, as dolphins do so well.

We are using a bizarre circular logic here, working backward from a desired result. We look at all of our capabilities as humans and then declare that those very sets of capabilities are what make us better than other animals, if not the image of God himself. That approach to defining ourselves as superior is a bit outrageous. Imagine playing a game of football, during which your team unilaterally stops the play and declares that the contest will be decided by measuring the total weight of the players. Conveniently, you know beforehand that your team weighs more than the other, ensuring your victory. The other team might well object, noting that the game should be decided instead on which quarterback can bench press the most weight. Funny enough, they know before deciding on that criterion that their quarterback will win that particular competition. As with these teams, in defining superiority we are just arbitrarily choosing characteristics that we know will put us on top.

But even when we give ourselves a big handicap by creating self-serving definitions that we know beforehand will prove advantageous, the categories of "uniquely human" talents are shrinking rapidly as we learn more about other animals and their adaptive behaviors. Characteristics previously considered special to our species have eventually been found, at least to some degree and often with some humor, elsewhere in the animal kingdom. Let's take a look.

BRAIN DEVELOPMENT

Starting right from the top, what could be more human than a big brain? Unfortunately, even our most obviously defining trait turns out to be less unique than previously thought. Our primate cousins give us a serious run for the money. The frontal lobe of the brain was considered the very hallmark of human evolution, the highest evolved component of the most evolved organ. But studies by Katerina Semendeferi, a professor of anthropology at U.C. San Diego, and her colleagues now find absolutely nothing disproportionate about the human frontal lobe in comparison to great apes. That gorilla giving you the evil eye is smarter than you think.

Even so, our brains are still bigger in the absolute sense; we can still say "mine is bigger than yours." Our brains weigh more, even if gorillas share with us a proportionately big cortex. We have bigger brains compared to our body weight as well. That must make the difference. Surely, with heavier brains we are more intelligent, right?

INTELLIGENCE

Without a doubt, human beings possess a level of intelligence, self-consciousness and self-awareness *greater by degree* than is found in any other animal. Evidence suggests that no animal besides the human kind is aware of its own mortality, the ultimate expression of self-awareness. Only humans bury their dead ceremonially. Dogs and cats do not put on elaborate state funerals for their fallen leaders. Chimpanzees do not visit their lawyers to make out a will in anticipation of impending death. For centuries, philosophers have taken this highly developed sense of self in humans to mean that intelligence does not exist at all in other animals. Descartes was convinced that animals completely lacked minds, and his influence is felt even today. Even Stephen Jay Gould, no species-centric chauvinist, concluded that consciousness has been "vouchsafed only to our species in the history of life on Earth."

With all due respect to the late Professor Gould, perhaps one of the greatest evolutionary biologists of our time, and to Descartes, the issue is not so simple or clearly delineated. As with almost all aspects of comparative biology, intelligence, self-consciousness and self-awareness are elements of a continuum rather than phenomena with sharp boundaries between species. Intelligence and self-awareness do not belong exclusively in the domain of humankind. To demonstrate this point, we must first remove any ambiguity about what is meant by "intelligent," "self-conscious," and "self-aware." We should also throw "empathy" into the mix of definitions, as this word is often associated with self-awareness.

A rough hierarchy exits among these concepts. One must be intelligent to be self-conscious, and in turn, one must be self-conscious to be self-aware. Finally, self-awareness must be present to feel empathy. So we begin with intelligence, the first ingredient in the recipe for self-awareness, in order to explore how these "human" capabilities are distributed throughout the animal kingdom.

Intelligence cannot be precisely defined, for reasons we will see shortly, so the best we can do is offer some rough correlations to the underlying idea. Intelligence can be thought of as the ability to learn from experience (acquire and retain new knowledge) and to subsequently apply that new knowledge with flexibility to manipulate or adapt to a changing environment. Or we can view intelligence as the ability to create abstract thought, beyond instinct or responses to sensory input.

Beyond these definitions, becoming more precise is treacherous. The primary difficulty in defining and measuring intelligence precisely is that mental acuity is situationally dependent. A cat under water would not look too intelligent, but a porpoise might. On the other hand, you would be severely challenged to teach a porpoise to climb a tree. You may well be able to solve math problems, but your dog will learn more quickly and more effectively than you ever could to sniff out the drugs in your colleague's suitcase and to notify you of the contraband. An animal's intelligence, or more precisely *its ability to manifest its intelligence*, is tightly correlated with its natural environment, and its evolutionary adaptations.

Dozens of books have been penned and many careers have been devoted to defining and understanding intelligence, so rather than delve any deeper we simply emphasize here the most important point: intelligence, however we define the concept, is not an all-or-nothing phenomenon. No universal measure of intelligence can be meaningful because animals have diverse adaptations that define the context of intelligence, making interspecies comparisons suspect. Intelligence is found by degrees across the animal kingdom, and not in some nice neat linear correlation with some other trait like the development of mammary glands. Being smart seems to be a trait unique to human beings only when we artificially designate our particular suite of characteristics as the definition of intelligence, proving that circular logic is not too intelligent.

SELF-CONSCIOUSNESS

For most of human history, people were convinced that no animal could be self-conscious, with Descartes representing the poster child of this viewpoint. More than any other trait, our ability to be conscious of our own existence was seen to endow humans with something special, making them different and better than other animals. Self-consciousness was considered the ultimate expression of humanness. We will see, though, that some animals indeed exhibit this most human of traits, and that in fact, self-consciousness is probably widespread in the animal kingdom. Breaking down this particular illusory wall dividing humans from all other creatures is a giant step toward developing a more realistic assessment of our place in the world.

The very idea of self-consciousness is not without controversy, and the scientific community is not unified in defining the concept. For example, some scientists use the term "self-conscious" in the sense that we use the term "self-aware" below, that is, an animal's thought about thought, in which an animal has a "second order representation" of its own mental state. That means an animal not only thinks but also thinks about thinking. Some scientists call the ability to "think about thinking" self-consciousness and others call it self-awareness. This academic parsing is why cocktail parties at a professor's house can be so stimulating.

But we believe the two concepts of awareness and consciousness are quite distinct, and should not be confused one with the other. Self-awareness represents a further refinement of self-consciousness. We will get to higher-order self-awareness shortly. For now, for our purposes, a simple definition of self-consciousness can be distilled to: *understanding that you as an individual are distinct from the external environment, and at the same time recognizing that others are similarly aware of you as an individual.* If we accept this formulation, autistic humans in the most extreme cases would not be self-conscious, perhaps an explanation for many of the behaviors manifested in this condition, including social isolation.

The idea deriving from our definition is that I can only recognize Ralph as a unique person if I first understand that I too am an individual. With this meaning then, the ability to recognize other individuals is perhaps the most important indication of an animal's being self-conscious. The notion of self-consciousness is therefore amenable to experimental investigation because we can test for individual recognition. We have a window into the mind!

Where in the animal kingdom should we look first for signs of self-consciousness? Individual recognition and therefore self-conscious-ness would most likely be found, but not exclusively so, in highly social animals where survival depends on recognizing dominant individuals and, in turn, dominating those lower in the social hierarchy. We all learn this in high school. Animals that pair-bond for life, and therefore can recognize a mate among many conspecifics, are also more likely to be self-conscious, at least by our definition.

For sticklers of logic, one implication here is that an animal can be self-conscious without being self-aware. That is, an animal can recognize itself as an individual among other individuals without knowing anything deeper about its own mental state. But at the same time, gregarious animals would also have evolutionary pressures to recognize not only the dominant animal in the group as an individual but also his emotional state and that of others in the hierarchy. You might get more food if you know to approach a kill when the big guy is in a good mood. So while it is possible to be self-conscious without being self-aware, the development of one trait might typically lead to the other.

By itself, though, the concept of self-consciousness is not terribly satisfying; mainly because it is tautological by invoking the concept of somebody else's mental state to define yours (you recognize that others see you as an individual). This type of argument is a hint that the notion of self-consciousness is not fully adequate. In fact, when we ask whether a creature is self-conscious, what we really want to know is something deeper about that animal's knowledge about itself.

SELF-AWARENESS

Self-awareness is a further refinement of the concept of self-consciousness (while others would invert this relationship) in that you not only recognize yourself as an individual relative to others and the physical environment, but you are aware of your own mental state, including your own internal thoughts independent of the external world. Your thoughts are unavailable to anybody but you until you decide to expose them to the external world either through behavior or some type of communication. Self-awareness depends on no other creature but you. You would be self-aware even if you were the last person on Earth, with no other sentient being to recognize your presence. *Self-awareness is your brain acknowledging its own existence.*

Do animals other than humans have this talent of self-awareness, or have we finally found a trait unique to our species? If found elsewhere, to what degree do other animals have a true "theory of mind," that is, an understanding that others also have independent thoughts, with different and separate beliefs, desires, mental states, and intentions? Again, these questions can be answered empirically.

We can experiment directly with the idea that an animal has a self-image and knowledge of the concept of self. G.G. Gallup describes how: place a chimpanzee, let's call him Alessandro, in a room in which he finds a large mirror. After a brief period in which Alessandro has become familiar with the room and the mirror, anesthetize him. While he is asleep, paint a dot of yellow paint on Alessandro's forehead, and gently place him back in the room. After waking up, most animals will not notice or react to the dot, continuing to treat the reflection in the mirror as another animal. But Alessandro, and his fellow chimpanzees and orangutans, will recognize the image in the mirror as themselves, touching their foreheads and examining the dot. That demonstrates that Alessandro knows the forehead in the mirror is his, *and that he normally does not have a dot on his head.*

One could object that this experiment in fact only demonstrates self-consciousness, rather than self-awareness, proving that Alessandro recognizes himself as an individual. This is a gray area. We cannot state with certainty from this particular experiment if Alessandro is aware of his own mental state even if the results hint in that direction. Nevertheless, we have from this and other observations at least an indication that primates like Alessandro might be truly self-aware. We also have evidence that mammals other than primates share this talent with humans. Using a modified version of Gallup's procedure, mirror self-recognition has been demonstrated in bottlenose dolphins, magpies and elephants.

Dolphins and porpoises have also demonstrated, in striking form, originality and creativity, both tangential indicators of self-awareness. An animal can only be creative in context of understanding its own behavior and intent, something that requires a level of self-awareness. Likewise, the act of creating something new, the capacity for originality, usually requires a deep understanding of one's own internal representation of the world as it now exits, also a feature of self-awareness. Animals that clearly demonstrate originality and creativity are likely self-aware, at least to some degree.

At the Makapuu Oceanic Center in Hawaii, trainers working with a female rough-toothed dolphin named Malia praised or fed her fish only for behaviors that had not been previously rewarded. Within a few days, Malia began performing novel aerial flips, corkscrews, new tail flaps, new twisted breaches, and other never-before-seen behaviors. Malia learned early on that the trainers were looking for new acts, not repetitions of previously demonstrated talents. As her repertoire expanded, she needed to create ever more unique combinations of movements to get a reward, which she did with aplomb, performing stunts so unusual that trainers could not have otherwise encouraged the behavior through standard training techniques.

This propensity for originality and creativity was not a fluke unique to one individual. Another female rough-toothed dolphin by the name of Hou soon followed in Malia's flipper steps. This tendency for originality increased in situations outside of training as well. Hou taught herself to leap over tank partitions to join other dolphins in an adjoining tank, something rarely seen before. Malia, not to be outdone, wanted to catch the attention of a trainer over at another tank. She jumped from the water, slid across more than six feet of pavement (wet from splashing), and gently tapped the trainer on the ankle. Originality and creativity, once unleashed, seem to transfer broadly. This is a good demonstration of applying knowledge flexibly in a changing environment, a hallmark of intelligence, self-consciousness and self-awareness.

Malia and Hou seem to be the aquatic equivalent of primates in terms of intelligence and self-awareness. Many species of cetaceans, like the bottlenose dolphin, live embedded in a complex social structure, with apparently content-rich communications and unambiguous individual recognition, important indicators of self-awareness. Dolphins are also one of only a few species besides humans that engage in recreational sex. They have naturally complex and rich play behavior. Anybody who has been to an aquatic amusement park will walk away with the thought that dolphins are sentient beings. We have a deeply intuitive sense that cetaceans are self-aware, driven in large part by our observations of their creativity and originality.

But we must always be on guard against the danger of anthropomorphizing animal behavior. The popularity and cuddly image enjoyed by cetaceans are why we must be particularly cautious in drawing easy conclusions. We have a natural affinity toward fellow mammals, even if aquatic, so we are predisposed to believing they are more like us than not. The alliance with cetaceans, however attractive, is illusory. Dolphins and porpoises live in a vastly different medium than humans, making any attempt to define their mental state or degree of self-awareness as difficult as with any other animal, mammal or not. This is perhaps one of the clearest examples where mental acuity has to be recognized as a trait closely associated with an animal's environment and evolutionary constraints. We do not know what living in a society surviving in the open ocean really means. Nevertheless, with those caveats clearly recognized, dolphin biology, behavior, social structure and communications skills together would seem to indicate a high degree of self-awareness, even if difficult to quantify beyond self-recognition in a mirror.

Self-consciousness and self-awareness would not seem to be uniquely human with what evidence we currently have in hand, but experiments with dolphins, primates and other animals provide us with less than iron-clad proof. Perhaps empathy will prove more helpful in distinguishing humans from other animals.

EMPATHY

Empathy is a projection of your own sense of a mental state onto somebody else, *were you to be in his or her situation*. But wait, is that not wrong, and exactly the reverse of a proper definition? Isn't empathy projecting someone else's mental state onto my own? No, although that is indeed a common misconception. Empathy is the ability to project yourself into your friend's head and understand what he is feeling by imagining what *your own mental state* would be like if you were in your friend's predicament. Now here is the tricky part. You then make a big mental leap: since you project that you would feel pain in his predicament based on your sense of your own mental state in that situation, you assume he too must feel pain in the same way. Therefore, you believe you understand how he feels.

If I see you suffer, I feel your pain. But I do so not by projecting your sense of pain into my head. Instead, I feel your pain by projecting my own mental image of how I would feel in your particular situation, and then imagine that you would be feeling the same. This distinction between the two ideas of empathy is a bit mind-numbing and annoying, but critical nonetheless. Think for a moment what high level representation I must have of "self" if I can mentally project that concept of self into another being, anticipate what that "projected self" would feel, and then assume that the mental state of my projected self equals the actual mental state of the other being. Wow!

A more formal definition of empathy, because we like to be complete and have an urgent need to show off, describes a situation in which the emotional state of one individual elicits a similar emotion in others, with the induced emotional state remaining objective rather than self-focused.

This academic definition excludes contagious emotions, like panic or excitement spreading among a group, in which the induced emotion indeed becomes self-focused. Empathy is outward-looking.

Empathy often is seen among those in close proximity but can occur across any distance in which the distress or emotion of one individual can be communicated to another. This ability to experience the feelings and thoughts of others is closely related to self-awareness. Empathy is only possible in animals that are self-aware: you could not hope to understand somebody else's mental state if you first could not evaluate your own. Just as self-awareness is a further refinement of self-consciousness, empathy is the ultimate refinement of self-awareness. By being self-aware, you can ask the question, how would I feel if I were in my friend's shoes? As a theoretical projection of self onto others, empathy is the most evolved manifestation of self-consciousness and self-awareness. Not only would you know whether the alpha male guarding the kill was in a good mood, you would understand his emotions and know what he felt like when he was well-disposed or angry with the world.

Logically, then, if you could show that an animal experienced empathy, you would by definition demonstrate self-awareness in that animal. Can empathy be proven experimentally? Absolutely.

As far back as 1964, rhesus monkeys were shown to stop pressing a bar to obtain a food reward if pressing the bar caused another monkey to receive a shock. The monkeys were literally willing to starve themselves rather than cause another monkey to be distressed. The experiment was replicated with rats and pigeons as well.

Primates like bonobos and macaque monkeys demonstrate what at least anecdotally looks like empathy in caring for the infirm, elderly and disabled. In the Milwaukee County Zoo, a twenty-one year old bonobo by the name of Kidogo had a serious heart condition, making him feeble and quick to exhaustion. When lost or confused in responding to handler commands, other bonobos would take Kidogo by the hand and lead him to the right spot or help him respond properly to the trainer. The same behavior was also seen spontaneously with no involvement of trainers. When Kidogo made distress calls, others would respond by guiding him hand-in-hand. Even the dominant male of the group would gently help Kidogo, a behavior not normally associated with top social status.

Another bonobo, Kuni, at the Twycross Zoo in England, showed that empathy is not restricted to fellow primates. Kuni helped a stunned bird, guarding it carefully, tenderly unfolding its wings, one in each hand, until the bird regained composure. Finally, Kuni threw the newly-conscious bird gently into the air.

Macaques apparently help the handicapped. A female known as Azalea had a mental and physical disability, leaving her with motor defects and developmental problems. While Macaques are known to be aggressive and live in highly structured groups, Azalea was accepted and assisted when necessary despite her clear infirmities and obvious vulnerabilities.

Empathy is seen in chimps. These primates understand purpose, something that requires a projection of an internal idea onto another animal or object, a strong indication that they possess a true theory of mind. Their grasp of purpose can be seen when chimps follow a functional analogy involving a single goal using different objects. For example, chimpanzees understand that a "can opener is to can as key is to padlock" (apparently better than some students on a college entrance exam). While a key and can opener are different objects, and turning a key and using a can opener are not similar actions, they share the same purpose of opening something, and chimps understand that equivalence. This talent is apparently restricted to primates.

Where do these examples of animal intelligence, self-awareness and empathy leave us? Perhaps if these traits can no longer be described as uniquely human, we might still be able to invoke other capabilities and talents to define our species. After all, chimpanzees have never been known to use a power drill or wield a pneumatic nail gun, so maybe the concept of tool use can save us from our common ancestry.

TOOL USE

Tool use at one point was indeed considered solely the providence of human ingenuity. But, in fact, nonhuman primates and birds commonly use tools, mainly to gather food. Chimpanzees, for example, regularly use stems as tools and can even pound stones with purpose, although they have never mastered flint-making. Chimps also use leaves as toilet paper. Egyptian vultures will search up to fifty yards for a rock to use to smash an ostrich egg. Green herons drop a small object onto the surface of the water to attract fish, which are fooled into thinking prey is nearby. The heron then turns the table and makes a meal of the unsuspecting fish.

If an elephant is unable to reach some itching part of his body with his trunk, the nearest tree often serves to relieve the problem. Just as often, however, an itchy elephant will pick up a long stick and give himself a good scratch with that instead. If one stick is insufficiently long he will look for one better suited to the task.

With what appears to be clear intention, elephants have been observed to throw or drop large rocks and logs on the live wires of electric fences, either breaking the wire or loosening it such that it makes contact with the Earth, thus shorting out the fence. Elephants are undoubtedly clueless about electron flow but have mastered the use of a tool to avoid its unpleasant consequences.

Some animals have graduated from tool use to tool fabrication. On the Galapagos Island, one of the many finch species made famous by Darwin uses a cactus spine as a spear to pry grubs from tree branches. Once this woodpecker finch has procured his shish kabob, he holds the skewer under foot to munch on the tasty snack. The bird will then carry the spine to another tree looking for the next meal. This finch, though, is not always happy with what nature provides, and improves the cactus spine for its purpose. One finch was observed shaping a forked spine into a single spike, and others shorten the spine to just the right length for probing and holding. Some finches can learn to use the tool by watching others do so.

These feats are noteworthy but provide only examples of one animal using one tool for one purpose. Even more impressive is the learned use of a tool set. Chimpanzees in East and West Africa sequentially use four tools to obtain honey, all gathered together for that specific purpose. They start with a battering stick, then a use a chisel-like stick, followed by a hard-pointed stick, finally ending with a long slender flexible dip stick to pull out the honey. Each tool is used in a specific sequence and sometimes made to order by clipping, peeling, stripping or splitting the wood to the desired specifications.

New Caledonian crows are famous for their ingenious tool fabrication, both in the wild and in captivity. Betty, a female crow, was filmed taking a piece of wire and trying to use it to grab some food at the bottom of a narrow tube. After several unsuccessful attempts, she removed the wire, fashioned a hook on the end, and subsequently used her new weapon to grab the food with ease. In the wild, these crows make an impressive variety of tools using a wide range of materials for diverse purposes. These birds actually shape different hooks for different tasks. This is tool use by any definition.

LANGUAGE

Examples of language are found in other animals, even perhaps with rudimentary syntax. Most famously, chimpanzees have been taught sign language, starting in the early sixties with a chimp named Washoe, who eventually learned about 100 signs. In the early 1970's, a gorilla by the name of Koko learned over 1000 signs through the patient teachings of Francine Patterson. Some experiments show that chimps can grasp the abstract idea of "categories" like dogs, giving that sign for any variety of canines seen, or a sign for "shoe" for different types of footwear. Some chimps have also been seen to combine signs in a way never taught to them to express novel ideas ("drink fruit" for watermelon for example). Scientists debate whether these primates, while impressive, can grasp syntax, which is the holy grail of language. The jury is still out. One problem is that the definition of language is itself a subject of controversy. Still, that chimps can learn sign language in the artificial environment of a lab at least raises the possibility that true language is not a uniquely human capability.

Oddly, the case for language in animals is most persuasive outside the realm of primates. Parrots are the real stars. These birds have large brains, are long-lived and are highly social. Parrots also possess tremendous vocal skills, offering the tantalizing possibility of examining their mental state directly through interspecies communication. Alex, the African gray parrot trained and studied by Irene Maxine Pepperberg, was until his death in 2008 the most famous subject, taking on the role of Hollywood celebrity. In some abstract aptitude tests, Alex performed as well as marine mammals and chimpanzees.

Alex learned labels for more than thirty-five different objects: paper, key, wood, hide (rawhide chips), grain, peg wood (clothes pins), cork, corn, nut, walnut, showah (shower), wheat, pasta, box, banana, gym, cracker, scraper (a nail file), chain, shoulder, block, rock (lava stone beak conditioner), carrot, gravel, back, chair, chalk, water, nail, grape, cup, grate, treat, cherry, wool, popcorn, citrus, green bean, and banerry (apple). He knew labels for seven colors: red, blue, green, yellow, orange, grey, and purple. He identified five different shapes by labeling them as objects with two, three, four, five, or six corners. But all that is not what is truly impressive. Alex learned to respond accurately to English questions about shape, color, material and number in any combination, meaning that he understood not only the color red, for example, but the category of color, not only the shape of a square, but the category of shapes, and could communicate in English about those categories in any randomly presented combination. Looking at a heterogeneous collection of randomly placed objects, you can ask Alex, "How many blue keys?" or "What color is the wood triangle?" or "What is the shape of the green metal object?" and he will answer accurately. Alex's mental prowess gives the avian world a proud representative in the interspecies contest for comparative smarts.

Sophisticated forms of communication in other animals, however, are not restricted to intelligent social birds and nonhuman primates. The lowly ant, ruining your sack of sugar, has amazing talents. E.O. Wilson has discovered that weaver ants possess what may be the most complex system of chemical communication in the animal kingdom. The exchange of pheromones, combined with tactile signals, provides for a "language" that can communicate distinct ideas such as "enemy close by," "enemy far away," "new territory discovered within reach," "new suitable site on which to build a new nest," and "food."

Honeybees have the famous "waggle dance," discovered by Karl von Frisch, by which scout bees return to the hive and convey to foragers where they have found nectar. With this specialized dance, the bees can provide information about the quality of the food and its direction and distance from the hive.

MUSIC

Certainly music must be unique to humans, right? No, whales appear to enjoy a good sonnet. Patricia Gray and her coworkers have shown that humpback whales compose songs using structures that are "strikingly similar to those adopted by human composers." According to these authors, humpback songs share the following with their human counterparts: they use similar length phrases to compose themes, and prefer to reiterate the material; the length of their songs fall in between that of a symphony movement and a ballad; they are capable of vocalizing over more than seven octaves, but choose to sing using musical intervals similar to or the same as in human scales; they mix percussion-like sounds and pure tones in a ratio similar to that found in symphonies; in many songs the structure would be familiar to any composer (the whale version of Mozart states a theme, elaborates the theme, then returns to a slightly modified version of the original theme); many of the sounds used are similar to human notes in tone and timbre (whales use notes familiar to us even though they could instead vocalize an almost infinite number of possible sounds, including what would be to us ugly grunts and roars); and whales repeat refrains that musicians tell us form rhymes, just the way we do. Finally, their songs are not hardwired from birth but are learned through practice with fellow pod members, and songs differ between pods and even show regional differences, not unlike that seen in different regions of the United States (think country western in Texas and punk in New York).

Whales are not the only animals aspiring to be the next Beethoven. Birds, well known for their innate vocal talents, create music beyond hardwired songs. Palm cockatoo males in North Australia and New Guinea break off a small twig from a tree, shape it carefully into what looks like a drumstick, and then search for just the right hollow log with the most desirable resonance. Once the appropriate instrument has been located, the bird holds the stick with its foot and proceeds to drum on the log like Pete Best in concert, hoping to attract the opposite sex, also much like human musicians.

CULTURE

Until recently, the transmission of information through culture, or socially learned tradition, was thought to be found only among humans. After the demise of music as ours alone in the animal world, many considered this the "last stand" in proving human uniqueness. After all, not many dolphins or elephants are seen going to the ballet. We see no ape equivalent of Ted Nugent. Culture seems to be clearly a uniquely human invention. In some human cultures, two people greeting each other will bow, where in others the two will shake hands. Some kiss once or twice on the cheek. Some societies prefer vodka over wine. Culture defines the context of our lives.

But in the 1950s, a few brave researchers demonstrated that true culture was indeed found in other species, although this conclusion was resisted for several decades.

On the small Japanese island of Koshima, researcher Kinji Imanishi observed one day that a young female macaque named Imo took some precious sweet potatoes that were inconveniently covered with sand to a nearby stream to wash them off before eating them. That alone was interesting because the behavior had never before been seen. But more impressive, over time the entire colony adopted the innovation, and their descendents wash their potatoes even today because mothers continue to pass down the new tradition to the next generation.

Imo and her colony are not just an isolated example. In 1963, in the Nagano Mountains of Japan, another young female macaque named Mukubili waded into a hot spring to get some food that had been thrown in the water. The warm water was apparently a delightful respite from the bitter cold mountain air, and a few other young monkeys climbed in. Much as in human cultures, at first the behavior caught on only with the youth, but the old folks eventually got hip. The behavior is now well established in the entire troop, and has been passed on through many generations. In another example of youth-driven culture, some juvenile macaques learned to roll and throw snowballs. That has no survival value, but is fun. The practice spread to others in the troop and is now a common play behavior.

The indisputable conclusion that other species have culture, however, is not the result of a few casual anecdotes or isolated case studies. Instead, presence of culture in other animals is seen as the result of carefully recorded observation by disparate scientists over many decades. In 1999, a group of researchers got together to compare notes from their years of field work with chimpanzees. Eventually they documented thirty-nine examples of behaviors present in one group of chimps but not another, even when the groups lived in similar environments and had access to the same foods and potential tools. Cultural differences were seen in courting behavior, hunting strategies, tool use, social grooming, medicinal plant use and vocalizations. The behaviors were passed on from one generation to the other within a social group, and not reinvented anew with each generation. More recent work with orangutans has shown similar examples of culture and social learning. The difference in behaviors between groups was even more striking in orangutans, which interact with neighboring groups less than chimpanzees.

In the final blow to the notion that culture is somehow uniquely human, various forms of social learning within and between generations have been demonstrated beyond primates, including in birds, rats, elephants, whales (in addition to composing), and perhaps even in fish.

LAUGHTER

As odd as the concept may seem, laughter and joy are not uniquely human and in fact are relatively ancient in animal history. Researchers like Jaak Panksepp at Bowling Green State University in Ohio are exploring the neural basis of humor and laughter and finding the phenomenon widespread. Scientists in this field have completed recent studies with rats, dogs and chimps, demonstrating that the source of play behavior and laughter is subcortical, embedded in the ancient portions of the mammalian brain. Chimps that are play-chasing and tickling each other vocalize with "play panting," which scientists believe is the equivalent of human laughter. Even rats laugh when tickled playfully, emitting a distinct chirp that researchers believe to be real laughter. Rats tickled playfully socially bond with the tickler, seek out tickles, and always "laugh" when successful. Human infants laugh and shriek with delight long before they have mastered any language, an indication of laughter's primitive origins. Chimps will not be headlining at the Comedy Club any time soon, but they have their own brand of humor even if the joke is lost on us.

Surprisingly, getting a handle on smiling in other species is somewhat more difficult. All primates share common neuromuscular control over facial expressions, so one would think that we could make a nice claim about smiling as a behavior seen across many animals. In fact, the "silent bared teeth display" seen in nonhuman primates is considered by some researches to be similar to a human smile. But most scientists dispute that conclusion. The meaning of displaying our pearly whites seems to have been lost in translation. A human smile typically conveys joy, but signals appeasement and fear in nonhuman primates. For other species, we simply have to conclude that smiling is tough if you have no lips.

OBSERVATIONAL LEARNING

The lowly octopus, without even the benefit of a backbone in its curriculum vitae, passes some impressive tests of intelligence, showing bursts of creativity and resourcefulness usually considered the sole providence of our primate cousins. Eugene Linden, one of a cohort of experts on animal intelligence, has detailed diverse intelligent octopus behaviors, which include escaping from "maximum security" tanks with what appears to be forethought and planning, crawling out on perfectly-timed "raids" on tanks of crustaceans, and sliding open locked tank covers by extending arms through the fact that an octopus can, according to s "observational learning," again a talent ively mammalian. What this means is tha can learn just by watching another octopus. For example, if Octopus Giuseppe learns that moving a red ball versus a white one will result in a food reward, Octopus Giovanni will learn the same lesson just by watching Giuseppe. Such observational learning is by all standards considered evidence for a higher level of intelligence.

Birds too have now been shown to be particularly good at observational learning. Working with ravens, Thomas Bugnyar showed that these observations can be keen enough to even lead to intended deception. In one experiment, a dominant and a subordinate male were given the opportunity to figure out what color-coded containers held some cheese, a raven delicacy. The subordinate male, Munin, was much better at the task; so the dominant male, Hugin, would wait for Munin to find the food, and would then muscle him out for the prize. In a blow for brains over brawn, Munin soon figured out that he could fake out Hugin by pretending to identify a container with food, open the lid and pretend to eat out of the empty container. Hugin, brute that he was, would anxiously come over to steal the food, while Hugin would return to the container truly holding food and quickly eat his fill. Hugin eventually got wise to the trick, though, and lowered himself to identifying the filled containers himself.

FARMING

What could be more defining as a human behavior than farming? After all, our species went from nomadic hunters and gatherers to builders of great cities because farming allowed for a stable food supply for a growing population. Farming is a triumph of human ingenuity. But ants beat us to it, another telling example of animal behavior brought to us by E.O. Wilson. The leaf-cutting ant lives almost entirely on the products of its own agriculture. These ants subsist on a fungus that is raised on fresh leaves and vegetation, with a supplement of other nutrients derived from plant sap. The arrangement is good for the fungus as well, since it grows only within these ant colonies.

Dedicated leaf-cutting workers prepare the agricultural center of the nest by building special gardens in which to raise the fungus, much as human farmers prepare plots of land to plant corn. Early in its life cycle, the fungus is taken from nurseries and carefully replanted in specially digested leaves until the fungus reaches maturity. Ants bringing leaf fragments to the nest for the fungus can travel as much as one mile through galleries and chambers to reach the garden. The gardens are tended by a specialized caste of workers that weed out any invading alien fungus species. Finally, the mature fungus produces an ant delicacy found in tips swollen with nectar, which are harvested to sustain the colony. Growing the fungus is no accident but is the result of a huge number of workers, organized into specialized castes, dedicated to no other task. Survival of the nest depends on a successful harvest. This is farming by any definition, even if hardwired.

Many species of ants keep livestock in the form of other insects, just as we keep other mammals as livestock. The most common commodities among ants are aphids. The ants actually herd the aphids and protect them from predators and parasites. They do this because the aphids provide the ants with drops of nourishing honeydew, equivalent to our protecting and raising cows that provide us with milk.

SOCIAL ORGANIZATION

Social organization cannot be used to define humanness. Beyond farming and raising livestock, social insects such as bees, wasps, termites and ants have degrees of social organization, specialization and coordination that can be viewed only as mind-boggling. Social systems allow animals to share labor, specialize in tasks and coordinate efforts among large numbers of individual[s toward a common goal. As a] consequence, truly social insects dominate [...] than a hundred million years, providin[g ...] cooperation has distinct advantages. M[...] are known. Even so, ants are the domi[...] net. We find over 9500 described specie[s ...] many in existence; The ubiquitous E.O. [...] in time, there are about a million billion (10^{15}) ants in the world. Ants alone weigh more than four times as much as all birds, amphibians, reptiles, and mammals combined.

The extent and types of cooperation are impressive by any standards. In most species of ant, different castes are dedicated to constructing,

[handwritten annotations:] Social insects dominate biosphere for 100,000,000 years. Ants — 9500 species. ?×3−10^{15} Ants. Weight 4× birds, amphibians, reptiles — mammals.

maintaining and repairing the nest, caring for eggs, storing seeds, foraging for food, acting as sentries to detect and announce enemies, fighting enemies, excluding waste from the nest, and protecting the queen. As a particular task requires more of the nest's attention, more workers are recruited to that task.

MATHEMATICS

Our late friend Alex the parrot offers the most direct window into the possibility of mathematics in animals. He used the labels "two," "three," "four," "five," and "sih" (six) to distinguish the number of objects up to six, including collections made up of novel objects he had never seen before. He demonstrated a rudimentary knowledge of numbers beyond some rote memorization. But Alex is not alone.

Kelly Jaakkola at the Dolphin Research Center in Miami has established that dolphins understand "numerosity," the ability to distinguish the concept of "three" versus the concept of "five" independent of the objects used to represent those numbers. Talon and Rainbow, two Atlantic bottlenose dolphins, can choose between boards with three and five dots, for example, when given the command to choose "more" or "less," even with dots of different colors and sizes randomly painted on the boards. This behavior also demonstrates a talent for recognizing that a symbol can represent a quantity, a sophisticated form of abstraction. Talon will not be helping you with your next algebra exam, but his math skill is impressive nonetheless. Rudimentary understanding of math is not uniquely human.

POSSESSING A SOUL

These disparate stories about animal self-awareness are compelling. Animals like Alex and friendly dolphins are hard to resist. Most of us believe from experience or expectation that many animals are intelligent, self-conscious and self-aware, and some brave scientists have had some success in exploring that likelihood in an experimental setting. But in reality, the preponderance of evidence for self-consciousness and self-awareness remains largely anecdotal. The current state of the art in the neurosciences simply does not yet allow for a rigorous, objective, reproducible investigation of empathy and self-awareness in other species.

Until recently, most scientists treated any study of intelligence or self-awareness as the third rail of academics – touch it and die. That attitude has changed over the past decade, however. Neuroscientists are moving beyond the old dualist arguments that posit that the mental and physical are different in kind, or that understanding the brain will not lead to an understanding of the mind. Dualism, separating mind and brain, arises from the deep human need to offer an explanation for what is not yet understood. We have difficulty just saying, "we don't yet know" while searching for the answer. From the ancients trying to explain the rising and setting sun to modern efforts to understand the beginning of the universe, humans simply make up comforting explanations when nothing more is available, with little regard to objective truth. What could be more comforting than knowing that the Earth is the center of the universe, around which everything revolves? This geocentric ("Earth-centric") view was taught as an absolute truth for almost 1500 years until Copernicus and Galileo proved instead that the Earth revolves around the sun. We don't yet know the neural mechanisms underlying consciousness, so we make up the notion that it is somehow a mysterious entity separate from the brain. Dualism is nothing more than the neurobiological equivalent of geocentrism – a false doctrine created out of a deep need to understand something that is not yet understood.

Dualism also contributes to the persistent idea that humans have souls, something beyond the body, just as the mind is something beyond the brain. By rejecting dualism, the notion of a soul becomes equally insupportable.

The concept of a human soul, even if discredited, is relevant to our views of the animal mind because the Catholic Church, and in fact most of Christianity, still teaches today that only humans have souls. There was a brief bright moment in 1990 when Pope John Paul II conceded that "animals possess a soul" and are the "fruit of the creative action of the Holy Spirit and merit respect." Those are welcomed sentiments but represent only a few words in the face of 2000 years of contrary history. Moreover, his words conflict with the Catechism of the Catholic Church, which states:

> Of all visible creatures only man is "able to know and love his creator." He is "the only creature on Earth that God has willed for its own sake," and he alone is called to share, by knowledge and love, in God's own life. It was for this end that he was created, and this is the fundamental reason for his dignity. (CCC #356)

That species-centric hubris cultivates a dangerous attitude that humans are better than other animals. If we have souls and other animals do not, if we possess a dignity conferred only upon us by our special relationship with God, if we alone were made in God's image, we have license to treat animals differently, and with less respect.

But would a chimpanzee sharing 97% of our genome not have a soul? Does this mean that the soul resides in the differential 3%? Would a chimpanzee have a soul, but not an elephant? How about Alex, our clever parrot? Even if the concept of a soul were valid, the notion that such an idea is exclusive to humans is as unsupportable as the long-held belief that we were the center of the universe. The Church was so confident about its authority on the subject that people were burned at the stake for any opposition. Yet Galileo proved them wrong, just as people today are wrong about the soul and the mind.

The materialist and reductionist approach to consciousness is triumphing, and with good reason. Consciousness is a consequence of neuronal activity. The ultimate question of how exactly consciousness arises from the physical properties of neurons will probably be solved through quantum theory, mating the classical properties of neurons with quantum properties of subatomic particles making up the neurons. But before that happens, scientists are making progress with more traditional approaches. With advances in brain imaging, scientists are beginning to correlate neuroanatomy and patterns of neuronal activity with measurements of consciousness. Progress in physics, chemistry, neurobiology, evolutionary biology and quantum mechanics combined is marching toward an understanding of consciousness at the most fundamental level.

But until the day arrives when the neurosciences can provide more definitive answers about self-consciousness, we must err on the side of caution. What little we know strongly suggests that self-awareness is widely distributed across the animal kingdom. Unless more rigorous analysis proves that wrong, we should operate under the assumption that most animals with a well-developed central nervous system are by degree self-conscious and/or self-aware. Intelligence, self-consciousness and self-awareness are adaptive traits developed in the context of sociality, which is not unique to humans, so the most parsimonious hypothesis is that such traits occur in other species. Until proven otherwise, we must assume that animals know and understand pain, fear and pleasure, and perhaps in some sense, and by degree, even joy and sadness. That understanding must guide all of our interactions with our fellow animals. That is who we are as humans: we are them and they are us.

ADVANCED TECHNOLOGY

Natural selection resulted in our large brains, which developed the capacity for language, subsequently allowing for one generation to teach the next new technologies and cultural practices. We have seen that culture exists in other animals, but certainly our advanced ability to transmit cultural information is a noteworthy if not unique human characteristic. Cultural transmission of information indeed has had consequences far beyond those normally associated with evolution. People today are identical organically and evolutionarily to those walking the Earth 30,000 years ago. The difference between then and now is a result of cultural development, quite separate from organic evolution. Culture evolves according to the rules of Lamarck, that is to inherits the acquired traits of the previous.

So as we contemplate our relationship accommodate our complex character as an ar culture and technology. We are very much but we exert pressure on the biosphere in a define our relationship with other animals and our environment while taking into account our dual role as both participants in, and external forces on, the animal kingdom and the physical world.

Current cultural norms and religious practices create within us even today a strong resistance to acknowledging our humble origin and position in the biosphere in spite of the unambiguous biological reality to the contrary. Chimpanzees and human beings share a genome that differs little, but we still insist on viewing a chimp as closer to wild game than to ourselves. If we struggle to acknowledge even our closest relative, certainly our more distant cousins will gain even less sympathy. By overcoming this chauvinism and adopting a new perspective on life, we open ourselves up to a much more enlightened, and practical, approach to interacting with our fellow creatures and the world around us. That would make us truly human.

Some critics might note that in our efforts to compare humans to other animals, we have taken a somewhat reductionist and materialist approach. We plead guilty as charged, but with extenuating circumstances. Reductionism allows complex phenomena to be broken down into more easily managed pieces, which can then be subjected to reasonable analysis. The approach is useful in ensuring that apples are being compared to similar fruit. But in taking this approach, we in no way imply that the human condition can be understood only from a materialistic perspective. The fascination, poetry, and mystery we find in nature, or within ourselves, are not in any way diminished by the facts of chemistry and physics.

PART II

RELIGION AND MORALITY

CHAPTER 4

Myths and Mysteries: The Origin of Religion

"The idea of God, as meaning an infinitely intelligent, wise, and good Being, arises from reflecting on the operations of our own mind, and augmenting, without limit, those qualities of goodness and wisdom."

– David Hume

I am sitting comfortably, dry and warm, next to a roaring campfire. I relax against the trunk of my favorite tree, fully protected from the harsh elements by a massive rock overhang guarding the entrance to a spacious cave. I don't have much to say, because I am a Neanderthal, living off the Earth 100,000 years ago. I am modern enough to have a spoken language, but the old vocabulary could use some work. I make stone tools for a living, and some of these are used to skin animals and to punch holes in hide to make clothes. I'm proudly wearing the latest fashion, a cozy bear wrap made with my own hands the previous year. I am on the cutting edge of technology.

I am gathered here with my fellow clansmen around the campfire to complete the ceremonial burial of our former leader. We are carrying on a tradition that began 200,000 years ago, when our ancestors first stored bones in a cave chamber made specifically for that purpose. But being modern, we disdain such primitive practices. We now bury our relatives and leaders in soft soil near the mouth of our home cave, gently placing the dead bodies in a fetal position for their rebirth in the next life. Before burial, we stain the bones with red dirt to anoint them in blood for the great beyond. In further preparation for their eternal journey, we place stone tools and animal bones in the grave. After all, the spirits will have to hunt. Finally, we place eight specially chosen types of flowers in the grave to help the spirits find a path to new bounty of food and medicine. Being a sophisticated clan, we understand the medicinal qualities of plants and flowers and see no reason to deprive the spirits of their healing powers.

I am particularly interested in the ceremony today because at thirty-five years old, and with only two teeth remaining, I am near the end. Those red bones will soon be mine. But I have no fear of leaving this world, because I know the spirit world awaits.

Paleontologists now widely accept the idea that our ancestors believed in an afterlife as long as 300,000 years ago. Ritualistic burial, which first appeared among Neanderthals somewhere in that time frame, is a hallmark of early religion. Burial ceremonies indicate a sophisticated concept of mortality, or at least an attempt to understand the implications of death. A real possibility exists that religion, that is, some concept of an afterlife, predates true language as one of humanity's earliest inventions.

The early rise of some belief in an afterlife is not surprising. Death is unavoidable; death raises obvious and disturbing questions. Even a primitive mind would demand some answers: What happens to my mate when she dies? Where does she go? What will happen to me? Will I see her again when I die?

Death is not, however, the only disturbing unknown. What is that big fireball in the sky? Why does the sky fire leave us to the cold dark, only to return again and again? What are those bright dots in the sky that I see when the fireball abandons me? Why does water sometimes fall from the sky? The world is one big mystery, desperately crying out for answers.

The urgent, compelling, unrelenting need for answers is a curse of the human brain's extraordinary development and complexity. The brain manages to make sense of a chaotic world by picking out patterns from the noise bombarding our senses. We don't see the trillions of photons coming into our eyes as pointillist smears of colors, we see trees and forests. We process all of that incessant sensory input and come up with a familiar scene filled with grasses, animals, lakes and mountains. In addition, we are extraordinarily good at matching cause to effect so that we can quickly learn the behaviors necessary for survival. Burning your hand quickly teaches that fire causes pain. Understanding cause and effect will save your life.

Unfortunately, this incredible talent for seeking patterns and learning cause and effect has a dark side, too. Humans see patterns where none exist, and see cause where only chance reigns supreme. We cannot seem to turn off our pattern-seeking or cause-effect neurons. Sometimes the results are benign: we identify animal shapes in cloud formations, or see a human face in a rock cliff or in _____ of Mars. A baseball player wears the _____ ng streak, believing that the underwear _____ ne. These are silly, if not smelly, manifes_____ out with no consequence.

The dark side appears when we a_____ n a way that has long-term impacts on our behavior and society. Let's go back to our sophisticated Neanderthal. We'll call him James; Zog seems too *Clan of the Cave Bear*. During one particularly bad drought, our friend draws a picture of a bear on his cave wall, something he has not done before. The next day the skies open up with a welcomed rain. James immediately sees cause and effect, and now believes that the act of drawing a bear causes rain. He knows that is the case with absolute certainty, because after all, he drew a bear, and the next day the rains came. What could possibly be clearer?

During the next drought, James of course takes matters into his own hands, and goes up to what is now a sacred cave to draw a bear. Hmmm, no rain the next day. Never does James question the causative effect of drawing bears; he knows without question that bear drawing causes water to fall from the sky. With that conviction but with no rain, the only possible conclusion is that he has somehow drawn the wrong bear, or done so at the wrong time of day, or used the wrong color. Or maybe he did not chant the right words while creating his artwork. Not sure of the problem, he develops an elaborate ritual to cover all of the possibilities. In a few days, lo and behold, water comes from above, providing yet more evidence – in fact, incontrovertible proof – that his actions cause rain. James now has developed a sophisticated ritual of drawing, dancing, and chanting as a means of ending a drought.

But lack of rain is not James' only problem. He needs to eat, and hunting has not gone too well lately. The pangs of hunger are growing stronger. He is desperate for a successful kill and his family is depending on him. Fortunately, his luck is about to change.

To ward off predators on the first night of a full moon, James dresses up in a bear suit to perform the bear dance, a tradition in his clan for many generations. While dancing, James cannot help but think how hungry he has become. Much to James's relief, the hunting party the next day kills two antelope and a hyena that had been previously wounded by a lion. Clearly, putting on the bear suit the night before not only kept predators at bay, the original purpose of the dance, but was also the cause of this huge success following almost a month of bad hunts. Cause and effect could not be more obvious.

Oddly, though, the next hunt is a complete bust in spite of the ceremony performed the previous night. Something is clearly wrong, but at no time does James question the value of the prehunt dance. That has been proven, and must not be jeopardized by doubt. Even the mere thought that the ceremony does not work might anger the invisible powers. Each night subsequent to the next series of failed hunts, small variations are added to the ritual in a hopeful attempt to find just the right mix, making for an ever-more elaborate event, with more chanting, dancing, smoke-waving and stick pounding. Finally, the newly designed dance number precedes a big kill, cementing forever the idea that a hunt will be successful only if a supremely elaborate ritual is properly performed the night before. You must get the ceremony exactly right; even the slightest variation seems to result in a bad hunt.

Life in the cave is not easy and James soon has other problems. After one good outing, James returns to camp to find his current mate, and mother to three of his eight surviving children, violently ill. Many plants and flowers are known to help cure sickness and he tries them all. None work, and his mate's health continues to decline. He feels helpless, as if some unseen force were striking down his poor companion. James then does what comes naturally: he asks this unseen force to help him, to stop torturing his woman. James beseeches this mysterious force, he begs, he pleads, every day. Then, miraculously, his partner suddenly improves. Unbeknownst to them, her attack of malaria has run its course. James, however, knows that the real explanation for his mate's recovery must be his successful connection and communication with the unseen force that had caused her so much grief. The mysterious force understood his pleas, and actually granted him his wish. His partner, smiling by his side, was all the proof he needed that his appeal to the mysterious force on her behalf has resulted in her newfound health.

Such cause and effect is so powerfully obvious that he does not question why the mysterious force would make his woman sick to begin with, only to return [...] James just knows that he is no longer a [...] *as a potent means of ma-* *nipulating and* [...] *: by requesting the inter-* *vention of a m*[...] *n* cause rain and ensure a good hunt wit[...], by soliciting the help of something vast [...] *He simply needs to ask.*

This revela[...] ely new world, giving him a tremendous sense of control over the unknown. Yes, the force is mysterious, but he can *communicate* with it, ask the force for favors. Sometimes, amazingly, the mysterious force will comply with his request. He just needs to figure out a way to please the mysterious force, to understand why his pleas are sometimes ignored, sometimes answered. The force operates in enigmatic ways.

James knows there must exist more than one force because, surely, the power that saved his mate would be different from the one ensuring a good hunt or providing a needed rain. What if he can find a way to ask

[handwritten note: Mysterious and unseen force. Sense of control.]

each force, properly and consistently, to help him maintain his health, sire more children, bring home plentiful meat, and end all droughts? How comforting that would be, how powerful the thought that he could control his fate simply by talking to these forces. Perhaps, even, a mysterious force, like the others, watches over those who died. Maybe some of those who die *become* the mysterious forces!

James now has ceremony, ritual, extravagant superstition, and an unyielding belief in the power of inexplicable forces to guide him through life, and to gain control over the unknown. James has found . . . *religion*.

Given the limited vocabulary of the Neanderthal, a monosyllabic word was probably used to describe the powerful and mysterious forces that helped control everybody's fate. Perhaps the word sounded something like gott, deus, or gud.

Religion was born of fear of the unknown, of the drive to control the uncontrollable, of the need to have mastery over one's fate in the face of an uncertain world. The first ideas of religion arose not from any awe of nature's wonder and order that would imply an invisible intelligent designer, but rather from concerns for the events of everyday life and how the vast unknown of nature affected daily existence. To allay fears of disease, death, starvation, cold, injury and pain, people fervently hoped that they could solicit the aid of greater powers, hoped deeply that they could somehow control their fate, and trusted that the ugly reality of death did not mean the end. Hope and fear combine powerfully in a frightening world of unknowns to stimulate comforting fantasies and myths about nature's plans.

The human brain is extraordinarily adept at posing questions but simply abhors the concept of leaving any unanswered. We are unable to accept "I don't know" because we cannot turn off our instinct to see patterns and to discern effect from cause. We demand that there be a pattern, that there be cause and effect, even when none exist. So we make up answers when we don't know. We develop elaborate creation myths, sun gods, rain gods, war gods, and gods of the ocean. We believe we can communicate with our ~~[illegible]~~ vior because by doing so, like James, w~~[illegible]~~ ne order, on the chaotic mysteries of the ~~[illegible]~~ dull the sting of ignorance, we fool ourse~~[illegible]~~ world. Religion was our first attempt at physics and astronomy.

[handwritten annotation: Religion — 1st Attempt at physics and astronomy.]

Of course, the biggest and most wrenching unknown served by religion is that of our fate upon dying. As a matter of survival, we are programmed to fear death but, perhaps unlike other animals, we have the cruel burden of contemplating this fear. Religion is one way we cope with our knowledge that death is inevitable. Religion diminishes the hurt of death's certainty and permanence, and the pain of losing a loved one, with the promise of reuniting in another life.

But fear of the unknown, fear of mortality, and hopes for controlling and understanding nature's course do not represent the only foundation on which religion stands. Another is social cohesion. We are social animals, gregarious by nature. Cooperation is what makes the human animal — a weak, slow and vulnerable creature — a powerful force on Earth. But cooperation becomes more difficult with increasing numbers. Some means of maintaining social order is necessary. Early societies soon learned that rules of behavior imposed in the form of rituals enabled large groups of people to live in close proximity. Rituals create norms against which people can readily judge the behavior of others in diverse social settings. Any deviation from the norm is easily spotted and can be quickly addressed. In this way, order can be maintained. Notice that modern-day teenagers express their rugged individualism by dressing identically. Any nonconforming outlier would be easy to spot. Religion offered, and offers still, an obvious means of enforcing societal rules by promising a joyous afterlife for conformers or eternal punishment for those who misbehave. Religion is used as a bribe to induce good manners.

Finally, religion was eventually transformed into an important source of raw political power, divorced from any role more benign. If religion is used as a tool to control individual behavior, someone needs to develop those rules and ensure their enforcement. Who better to act as behavior police than religious elders, shamans, or high priests? What better way is there to manipulate and bend people to your will than by making up the rules by which they must live? With that influence over the daily lives of every citizen comes power traditionally reserved for city-states and empires, with all the normal trappings, including armies, treasuries and palaces.

Fear of death, the need to explain away the unknown, hopes for controlling one's destiny, a desire for social cohesion, and the corrupting allure of power are the combined masters of all religion.

WHY ONLY ONE BIG GUY?

All early religions across all cultures worshipped multiple gods while the major faiths today pray to one. This transition from polytheism (worshiping many gods and idols) to monotheism (belief in one god) is the most important development in understanding the origin of religion. For this we must first turn to David Hume, the father of religion studies. Hume, born in Scotland in 1711 *Polytheism –* nost important figures of Western phi *across the board.* ice as a philosopher, economist and histo ent. For Hume, polytheism was the primi nkind." This is polite talk meaning "idio

Hume concluded that all ear multiple gods. All ancient records document such beliefs in all societies, without exception. The Mayans, Aztecs, Egyptians, Greeks, Romans, myriad tribes across the African continent and all early Asian sects uniformly believed in many deities, with *not a single contradictory example.* Found across cultures, continents and time, polytheism was firmly established as an early, robust and widely distributed human characteristic.

We will never know with certainty what earliest humans thought and felt, because the most ancient societies left no historic record of any kind.

But we can draw some fairly robust conclusions from archeological evidence and simple logic to suggest what our primitive ancestors believed. The further we go back in time, the greater dominance we see of polytheism. Logic would dictate that such a trend continues past the point of recorded history all the way to the beginning of the earliest human societies.

Primitive man trying to interpret the events of the world would naturally conclude he is witnessing combat among great powers with contrarian designs and intentions. The Thunder God and Sun God would not be good friends. As Hume notes:

> The province of each god is separate from that of another. Nor are the operations of the same god always certain and invariable. Today he protects; tomorrow he abandons us. Prayers and sacrifices, rites and ceremonies, well or ill-performed, are the sources of his favor or enmity, and produce all the good or ill fortune, which are to be found amongst mankind.

The power of each god is invoked individually at the appropriate moment. In Roman theism, Juno's assistance is requested at marriages, while sailors solicit the protection of Neptune before embarking on a voyage, just as soldiers pray to Mars before entering battle. This propensity to view nature's wrath and benevolence as the consequence of continuous struggle among great deities pursuing different agendas appears to be universal in all early societies. Nothing would suggest that even earlier ancestors viewed the world differently. Hunting success or failure, pestilence, availability of protective shelter, tempests, drought, birth, death, sun, darkness, success or failure in battle, the effect of medicinal plants, and all matters that influence daily life can be attributed to the disposition of the controlling gods, whether they be in a good or foul mood.

Every disaster that befalls us demands an explanation. Naturally, multiple unknown causes lead to the idea of multiple powers; polytheism is the natural state of a primitive mind. Hume has great insight here:

> We hang in perpetual suspense between life and death, health and sickness, plenty and want; which are distributed amongst the human species by secret and unknown causes, whose operation is oft unexpected, and always unaccountable. These *unknown causes*, then, become the constant object of our hope and fear.

But the idea of powerful g̶ . . . ̶ spect of our lives would not by itself be . . . e to the power; we want to be familiar v . . . fate; we want to know them so that we . . . d solicit their interventions. We are all Ꭰ . . . king to reveal the nature of the man be . . . e up a conversation with whoever is in . . .

Egoistic species
Anthropomorphize
everything!

By no coincidence then do our gods take on idealized human form. Our egoistic species has a universal tendency to transfer human-like qualities to surrounding objects, giving them characteristics that are familiar to us. This tendency to anthropomorphize everything around us has the consequence that we attribute human malice or benevolence to inanimate objects, and of course to the gods above. With their human form, gods also take on human personalities, with passions and weaknesses that make them jealous, vengeful, spiteful, fickle, wicked and foolish. How comforting to know that one's fate and fortune, tossed about by unknown causes, can be controlled by dialogue with an invisible power that possesses familiar sentiments and intelligence!

But attributing human qualities to a higher power has a paradoxical consequence, one leading inevitably to the idea of multiple gods. We raise our own estimation of ourselves as godlike, but diminish the power of the very gods we create by humanizing them. Once again, Hume is right on the money:

> They suppose their deities, however potent and invisible, to be nothing but a species of human creatures, perhaps raised from among mankind, and retaining all human passions and appetites, together with corporeal limbs and organs. Such limited beings, though m~~aster~~ ~~of~~ ~~t~~ fate, being, each of them, incap~~~~ fluence everywhere, must be vas~~t~~ answer the variety of events, ~~~~ whole face of nature. Thus eve~~r~~ crowd of local deities; and thus p

[handwritten margin note: Jesus Saints – "minor gods"]

The idea that deities are "nothing but a species of human creatures, perhaps raised from among mankind" of course applies to more than the old discarded gods of the past. The words exactly describe Jesus. The link between the one god of today and the many of the past is closer than most would assume. The characteristics that originated in polytheism continued to apply even as the number of gods diminished. One could argue, in fact, that today's religions are not truly monotheistic. Christianity has created hundreds of objects of worship in the guise of saints, who have become minor gods to many followers. Worshipers routinely solicit the intervention of saints to cope with the traumas of daily life through fervent prayer. The very act of praying to a saint elevates that figure to a type of god, even if a lesser one.

Christianity has no monopoly on polytheistic tendencies. Jews wait for the Messiah; Muslims worship Mohammad. While prophets might not themselves be conventional gods, like saints they take on a mystical quality with power and influence beyond the reach of us poor mortals. Prophets command awe and reverence, not terribly distant from how we worship god as more traditionally understood. *The notion of one god is undermined by prayer to many.* We have bravely abandoned worship of sun and thunder only to find our prayers directed instead to a cornucopia of minor gods.

As much as Hume was right, he erred fatally when he could not take the extra step of applying his treatise on many gods to one. He was so close. But we are all a product of our times and Hume was living in a religious society, in the mid-1700's, when tolerance was not a particularly well-developed trait. His times and circumstances prevented him from drawing his logic to its natural conclusion, at least explicitly. Instead of considering all gods in his sweeping natural history, he arbitrarily divided religion into two categories, a crude polytheism and a "sublime" belief in one god. This is borne out in his conclusion as he moves to discuss the origin of theism from monotheism:

> . . . it will appear, that the gods of all polytheists are not better than the elves or fairies of our ancestors, and merit as little any pious worship or veneration. These pretended religionists are really a kind of superstitious atheists, and acknowledge no being, that corresponds to our idea of deity.

To bolster this view, Hume noted that most divinities of the ancient world were supposed to have been human or humanlike, an argument he uses to diminish the actual and more sublime divine power of a real god. Yet we have Jesus, in the flesh, bleeding like a regular guy, no different from what Hume disparages in his idea of a cruder polytheistic god. Hume failed to appreciate, or perhaps coyly assumed, that his words apply with equal strength and validity to one god or many. Like many gods, one god is nothing better than the elves or fairies of our ancestors.

Although Hume was wrong at a critical point in his argument, he asked the right questions. Why did polytheism yield to belief in one god, and do so almost universally? Hume believed that the answer lay in mankind's growing appreciation for the "beauty of final causes" and nature's regularity and uniformity as strong proof of design and a single supreme intelligence. As mankind gained more control over nature's deprivations, more thought could be given to the intricacy of nature's workings. From his perspective, such contemplation must lead to the obvious conclusion that only a single designer could create the elaborate complexity that we see around us. For Hume, this was the primary distinction between polytheists and monotheists, who worshiped gods controlling an unknown fate, to monotheists understanding one god from nature's beauty and regularity.

Advances in science, which explain the mysteries of nature's wrath, remove the need for multiple gods of rain, sun and harvest. If we know the sun is a star sustained by thermonuclear reactions, we need not invoke a sun god. If we know that rain is caused by evaporation and condensation, we can discard our rain god. We understand that thunder is caused by lightning as a consequence of atmospheric ionization, relegating Thor to the pantheon of gods now myth. As gods are the child of ignorance, knowledge is a lethal potio[n] ... st powerful force.

Yet human knowledge i[s] ... ared Thor's ignoble fate. Our knowledge ... off every god but one, but stays limited e[...] the remaining survivor. The one remai[...] it is shielded from scrutiny by a failed educational system incapable of teaching students even rudimentary knowledge about their world. As a consequence, we are left with a sad "god of the gaps." As science explains evermore complex natural phenomena, the need to invoke God to understand daily events and the physical world diminishes. God becomes confined to "gaps" in scientific knowledge, diminishing in stature with each great advance of human knowledge. God is reduced to what Stephen Hawking doesn't know.

Education is this god's nemesis and greatest threat. Future generations of scientists will push human understanding deeper into astronomy, physics, and genetics, further compressing the volume left for God to occupy. Only our failure in education, leading to scientific illiteracy in the general population, allows this god to survive.

But even as the old god of the gaps shrinks in size and stature, surviving weakly on the nourishment of human ignorance, he is supplanted by a new god immune to logic and reason, rising w... ever before. Rather than fearing secular explanatio... this god simply dismisses human knowledge as irre... petuated and strengthened by humanity's darkest... ern god is called upon by the Pope to disparage th... is then called upon again by Mullahs to threaten a... anity. This god is smiting Florida with hurrica... Robertson, because the people of that state allowed gay pride flags to be flown along some streets.

So we come full circle, from multiple gods that help allay fears of the unknown, to a single god that explains the beauty and intricacy of nature, to a god reduced in stature by human knowledge, to a ridiculous and spiteful god that preys on our darkest fears, one that punishes poor Floridians for not hating gays. We have taken a long journey to go nowhere.

The time is upon us to break free from this chain of ignorance and fear.

CHAPTER 5

Why Ask Why?
The Meaning of Religion

"I do not feel obliged to believe that the same God who has endowed us with sense, reason, and intellect has intended us to forgo their use.

— *Galileo Galilei*

Every social act had a reference to the gods as well as to men, for the social body was not made up of men only, but of gods and men.

— William Robertson Smith

With apparently no appreciation for the rich irony of his statement, the Reverend Albert Mohler, Jr., president of the Southern Baptist Theological Seminary in Louisville, Kentucky, made a breathtaking observation about the recent discovery of the Gospel of Judas. As reported in the April 7, 2006, *USA Today*, Mohler said the discovery "has no bearing whatsoever on the Easter story, much less on the faith of the Christian church." He went on to dismiss the gospel as nothing but "an ancient manuscript that tells an interesting story." Really? *Really?* If the good Reverend meant what he said, and if his views are representative of his flock, the implications are astounding.

Gospels are nothing but ancient manuscripts that tell an interesting story. Well, that is exactly what *we, too,* have been saying all along! Of course, unlike Rev. Mohler, we apply that same logic to, and draw the same conclusions about, the gospels constituting today's New Testament Bible. After all, the collection of gospels of Matthew, Mark, Luke and John were accepted as canonical only at the Synod of Rome in 382 AD in the Decree of Damasus, issued, coincidentally enough, by Pope St. Damasus I. Scripture, as accepted by modern Christians, is nothing but an arbitrary collection of four gospels codified by the Christians in power in the 4th century.

Those four gospels of the modern Bible are considered special only

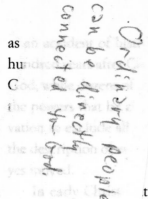

as ... because some Christians decided, nearly four
hu... ...t died, that this quartet represented the word of
G... ...er gospels were just a good read. But why would
... ...se those specific four? Did they have any moti-
... ...ers, beside the obvious contradictions buried in
... ...s found among the larger group of gospels? Well,

...ty, diversity ruled, with dozens of variations and
...s, Marcionites and Carpocratians flourishing, split-
...ing, ...ntually, from this chaos emerged two major schools
of thought. In one corner, we have the Gnostics, who believed that personal insights are the key to redemption and salvation. Gnostics were able
to hear the voice of God from within and therefore had no need for
priests to act as their go-between with God. Ordinary people could be divine, connected directly to God.

Orthodox priests in the opposing corner were none too pleased with
this idea. Gnosticism not only threatened the power structure of the Orthodox Christians, but directly contradicted their belief that faith in Jesus
and his resurrection was the sole path to personal salvation. These Christians emphasized that only the son of God was both human and divine,
making God a step removed from the man on the street. That belief conveniently ensured a role for priests, who retained the power to intercede
with God on behalf of ordinary folks.

While the two schools sparred for almost two hundred years, the
battle for dominance was never clearly won by either side. That is, until
the squabbling led to an ugly split in 180 AD, when Irenaeus, Bishop of
Lyon, formally condemned Gnostic teachings in his magnum opus
Against Heresies (who isn't?) and attacked as heretical any gospels
that differed from the mainstream church. The Decree of Damasus issued in 382 AD was really just the culmination of the movement pre-
cipitated by Irenaeus when he published his anti-Gnostic book two
centuries earlier.

We can think of the Gnostics as Democrats and the Orthodox Christians as Republicans. At the Synod of Rome in 382 AD, the Republicans were in power. Not surprisingly, the Republicans chose the four gospels that best reflected their views. Hence, we now have Matthew, Mark, Luke and John, who told a sympathetic story about Jesus' birth, life, crucifixion and resurrection. Any gospels that displeased the Republicans were conveniently neglected or declared heretical. This type of selective blindness is no different from what we experience in modern times. Witness the blind treatment of any military intelligence that did not support the war in Iraq; any gospels (intelligence) that displeased the Orthodox Christians (Republicans) was conveniently neglected or declared heretical (unpatriotic).

The selection of the four gospels was nothing but the exercise of raw political power to promote one particular belief that was much in dispute by other equally devout Christians. But Gnostic Christians, who dismissed the importance, or reality, of the resurrection, simply had less political influence and lost the election. Gnostics were the Al Gore of the 4th century. Maybe Pope Damasus I had a brother serving as an Imperial Bishop in a critical region to help throw the election his way.

More than three dozen gospels of undisputed authenticity have been known to the Church for hundreds of years, or millennia in some cases, but most did not make the canonical cut. Gospels of Thomas and Mary Magdalene, the Gospel of Truth and the Secret Book of John were denounced as heretical by the early Church but were popular enough in their day to survive in plentiful copies dearly regarded by early Christians. Even the gospels that made the team were not in complete harmony, that is to say they offered contradictory stories about the same events. Rev. Mohler could not be more right; he just needs to extend his logic to all forty gospels, *including* those of the Fab Four, Matthew, Mark, Luke and John, which are in fact, as the good Reverend states, nothing but ancient manuscripts telling an interesting story.

As an aside, the conceptual schism between Gnostics and Orthodox

Christians is analogous to the division in Islam today between Sunni and Shiite sects. Sunnis would be like the Gnostics (or like modern-day Protestants), with no one person appointed as head of the religion and with no formal clergy. Shiites, like the Orthodox Christians, have a divinely appointed religious leader and a formal hierarchy similar in structure to the Catholic Church.

In addition to its complex history of political manipulation, religion can also be understood as the winnowing of gods from many to one, as we discussed in the previous chapter. But here we want to explore a different aspect of the fact that every early religion was polytheistic, while the major religions of today are mostly monotheistic. What this means is that *all of us are atheists*, even the most devout, undoubting, dedicated priest, rabbi or mullah. Atheist means "without god," and all of us are without at least some gods. All monotheistic believers reject all gods except one. They reject all the Greek elder gods Cronus, Gaea, Uranus, Rhea, Oceanus, Tethys, Hyperion, Mnemosyne, Themis, Iapetus, Coeus, Crius, Phoebe, Thea, Prometheus, Epimetheus, Atlas, Metis, and Dione.

Muslims, Jews and Christians all deny the existence of the Greek Olympic gods Zeus, Poseidon, Hades, Hestia, Hera, Ares, Athena, Apollo, Aphrodite, Hermes, Artemis, and Hephaestus. All major religions today dismiss as nothing but myth the Roman gods Jupiter, Juno, Neptune, Pluto, Apollo, Diana, Mars, Venus, Cupid, Mercury, Minerva, Ceres, Proserpine, Vulcan, Bacchus, Saturn, Vesta, Janus, Uranus and Maia.

Yet this roster of gods was real to multiple thousands of people for thousands of years, every bit as real as the one god worshipped by Christians, Muslims and Jews today. These Greek and Roman gods were the subject of daily pleas, prayers and sacrifice, and the guiding force for much daily ritual. These mighty powers stood for millennia, ruling over their followers for a period of time that greatly exceeds all that of Christianity. Yet these gods are now demoted to nothing more glorious than a good story. What would convey upon these gods more or less legitimacy than the god of John, Matthew, Mark and Luke? *Nothing.* After all, Gospels are nothing but ancient manuscripts that spin an interesting yarn.

If asked, Christians, Jews and Muslims today would use numerous and diverse reasons to deny the existence of Greek and Roman gods who were so important to so many people for so long. *We simply extend that reasoning to include the one remaining god.* Everybody is an atheist; we, the authors, merely exclude the existence of one more god than those who consider themselves religious. Hume's disparaging conclusion about polytheists, calling them "   " perfectly to today's relig

This arg   ic sleight of hand. Any g   absurd the possibility th   do so with gusto, with n   g certainty. For identical   unyielding certainty, we   the God of the Old and   all agree in principle; we   culation resulting in one

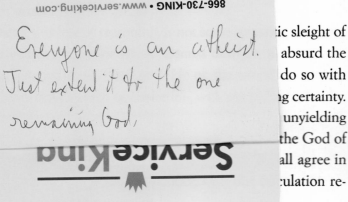

Not by any means are we first to this conclusion. In a letter to John Adams in 1823, Thomas Jefferson wrote:

> The day will come when the mystical generation of Jesus by the Supreme Being in the womb of a virgin, will be classed with the fable of the generation of Minerva in the brain of Jupiter.

But until that welcome day arrives, we should understand the deadly consequences of confusing myth with reality. That confusion cost Socrates his life in ancient Greece. He was sentenced to death in large part for his impiety in rejecting religious dogma as mere myth. He considered the story of Saturn castrating his father Uranus, or Jupiter dethroning

Saturn, as nothing but fable, much to the annoyance of religious leaders of the time. But deadly consequences of confusing myth with reality are not relics of the past; we see the impact today.

Diverse religions share a common idea that the end of days is near and that only the faithful can be saved. Of course, Religion X claims that one must be a member of Religion X to be saved, while all others – the unclean, the unchosen, the unanointed – are destined to be damned.

Predictions of the Apocalypse or its equivalent have been a common theme throughout history, often with tragic results. These are chronicled in *The Ghost Dance* by Weston La Barre, a professor of anthropology at Duke University famous for his best-selling studies in the 1950's of God and culture seen through the lens of psychoanalysis. One poignant example excised from La Barre's book tells a sad story all too familiar in the saga of religion. In South Africa in 1856, a young Xosa girl went to fetch water at a local stream. There she claimed to meet strangers from the spirit world. Excited, she returned with her uncle Umhlakaza, who spoke with the same spirit world reps. From this encounter, Uncle Umhlakaza came back with an important message. At the time of this ghostly meeting, the Xosa tribe was battling the English. The spirits told Umhlakaza that to succeed in driving out the foreigners, his tribesmen must kill every animal in their herds and destroy every kernel of corn so carefully stored in their granaries. The spirits promised him that if his tribesman followed these instructions, heaven on Earth would be theirs. Dead loved ones would return, fat cattle would rise from the Earth, corn would sprout in abundance, sickness and troubles would be banished and the old would become young and beautiful again. With such great promise, backed by the authority of the spirit world, Umhlakaza's orders were carried out, resulting in the slaughter of two thousand cattle and destruction of all grains. Instead of Earthly paradise, the Xosa experienced a famine so deadly that the tribe nearly ceased to exist.

La Barre cites many similar tragic stories derived from prophecies in which unbelievers would be punished, the dead would arise, and the faithful would be rewarded, either with eternal life in heaven or by the fulfillment of some Earthly need. Pat Robertson probably has not read La Barre. Tragedies resulting from such beliefs have wide geographic and temporal distribution, having visited the Maori in New Zealand, the Altai Turk of [...] agabuna in New Guinea [...]

The [...] long-ago places. Today, [...] ael lining up for martyr[...] several passages also sta[...] ise. That creates a looph[...] truck, as amply demons[...] nt cars and collapsed [...] le East. If a trip to parad[...] tential martyr to strap on [...] mate sacrifice is provide[...] dith, often cited as seven [...] ze awaiting a female bomber is less clear, but a stable of male virgins would not likely hold the same appeal.

In 1978, the Reverend Jim Jones, charismatic leader of the People's Temple, convinced 913 of his followers in Guyana to commit suicide by drinking cyanide-laced fruit punch, forever altering public perception of Kool-Aid. Jones claimed, and his followers believed, that he was the divine reincarnation of Jesus *and* Buddha. Citizens of Jonestown followed their divine leader's command to suffer a "revolutionary death."

In 1990, a Houston teenager by the name of Vernon Wayne Howell moved to the sleepy wind-swept town of Waco after dropping out of high school. There he changed his name to David Koresh, explaining blandly that he was the reincarnation of both King David and King Cyrus of Persia. David did not stop there, further claiming he was in fact the Messiah, appointed by God to rebuild the Temple and destroy Babylon. At least 131 of Howell's Branch Davidians were convinced enough to ensconce themselves in his compound, yielding to him their daughters as young as twelve to be impregnated by the Messiah. That episode ended badly, as we all know.

In 1997, thirty-nine members of the Heaven's Gate cult took their own lives, dying in shifts over a few days in late March. Some members helped others take a deadly mix of phenobarbital and vodka before consuming their own poisonous cocktail. Why did these people die? Members of the cult believed the prophecy of Marshall Applewhite, who claimed that the comet Hale-Bopp was the long-awaited sign to shed their Earthly bodies, which they called "containers." By leaving their containers behind, followers would be able to join a spacecraft traveling and hiding behind the comet, which would take them to a higher plane of existence.

In Uganda in March 2000, between two-hundred and five-hundred members of the Movement for the Restoration of the Ten Commandments committed suicide by setting fire to their church. The congregation apparently forgot about the Commandment concerning "thou shalt not kill." These people died because the sect anticipated the end of the world, expecting a visit by the Virgin Mary on the Friday they self-immolated. She never showed up. The prophet in this case was Credonia Mwerinde, a former prostitute.

Then we have prophets who bring with them good cheer but an odd story. In the early 1800's in Palmyra, New York, a local boy claimed he could divine the location of ground water as well as treasures buried by Indians. Persuasive as a snake-oil salesman, farmers paid him $3, a princely sum then, to find buried riches on their land. The boy, Joseph, used "magic stones" to discover the sites of this bounty. When he inevitably failed to find either water or treasure, he would leave town, often with "encouragement," and move on to other fee-based treasure-hunting activities.

After a particularly large and humiliating failure in the Susquehanna Valley near Damascus, New York, Joseph stayed on to court a local gal,

Emma Hale, in spite of community accusations that he was a charlatan. In the spring of 1826, a group of unhappy customers went further and brought formal charges against Joseph, claiming he was nothing but an imposter. He was subsequently convicted of "glass gazing," an outlawed form of fortune-telling. Emma's dad Isaac was one of the duped treasure hunters who testified against Joseph, so he was not pleased by the courtship of his daughter by this convicted criminal. He considered Joseph to be arrogant, fraudulent and lazy. Those who knew Joseph best claimed, "H⋯ ⋯r marvelous absurdity w⋯ ⋯t Joseph was "in particul⋯ ⋯cter and addicted to vi⋯ ⋯e and Emma eloped with⋯ ⋯nged father-in-law, Jose⋯ ⋯le life and to help Isaac ⋯

Instead ⋯ ⋯ ⋯seph spending all his t⋯ ⋯iscovered his son-in-law ⋯ ⋯na sitting behind a curt⋯ ⋯xplained that he had fou⋯ ⋯t to which he had been l⋯ ⋯ritten in "reformed Egyptian⋯ ⋯ly came with their own set of Rosetta stones, allowing him to translate the symbols to English, which explained his indoor activities. Joseph Smith was translating the ancient *Book of Mormon*. The "ancient" part might be in question, though, since the book agitated against such contemporary institutions as Freemasons and even Catholicism. Sadly, the plates mysteriously disappeared before the dates could be authenticated. In fact, Joseph declared that instant death would be the result for anybody but him looking at the golden plates. Nobody but Joseph, the fraudulent diviner from Palmyra, ever saw the plates. Only through the tainted word of a convicted con man do people know of the existence and content of

Christians is analogous to the division in Islam today between Sunni and Shiite sects. Sunnis would be like the Gnostics (or like modern-day Protestants), with no one person appointed as head of the religion and with no formal clergy. Shiites, like the Orthodox Christians, have a divinely appointed religious leader and a formal hierarchy similar in structure to the Catholic Church.

In addition to its complex history of political manipulation, religion can also be understood as the winnowing of gods from many to one, as we discussed in the previous chapter. But here we want to explore a different aspect of the fact that every early religion was polytheistic, while the major religions of today are mostly monotheistic. What this means is that *all of us are atheists*, even the most devout, undoubting, dedicated priest, rabbi or mullah. Atheist means "without god," and all of us are without at least some gods. All monotheistic believers reject all gods except one. They reject all the Greek elder gods Cronus, Gaea, Uranus, Rhea, Oceanus, Tethys, Hyperion, Mnemosyne, Themis, Iapetus, Coeus, Crius, Phoebe, Thea, Prometheus, Epimetheus, Atlas, Metis, and Dione.

Muslims, Jews and Christians all deny the existence of the Greek Olympic gods Zeus, Poseidon, Hades, Hestia, Hera, Ares, Athena, Apollo, Aphrodite, Hermes, Artemis, and Hephaestus. All major religions today dismiss as nothing but myth the Roman gods Jupiter, Juno, Neptune, Pluto, Apollo, Diana, Mars, Venus, Cupid, Mercury, Minerva, Ceres, Proserpine, Vulcan, Bacchus, Saturn, Vesta, Janus, Uranus and Maia.

Yet this roster of gods was real to multiple thousands of people for thousands of years, every bit as real as the one god worshipped by Christians, Muslims and Jews today. These Greek and Roman gods were the subject of daily pleas, prayers and sacrifice, and the guiding force for much daily ritual. These mighty powers stood for millennia, ruling over their followers for a period of time that greatly exceeds all that of Christianity. Yet these gods are now demoted to nothing more glorious than a good story. What would convey upon these gods more or less legitimacy

than the god of John, Matthew, Mark and Luke? *Nothing.* After all, Gospels are nothing but ancient manuscripts that spin an interesting yarn.

If asked, Christians, Jews and Muslims today would use numerous and diverse reasons to deny the existence of Greek and Roman gods who were so important to so many people for so long. *We simply extend that reasoning to include the one remaining god.* Everybody is an atheist; we, the authors, merely exclude the existence of one more god than those who consider themselves religious. Hume's disparaging conclusion about polytheists, calling them "superstitious atheists," applies perfectly to today's religious masses.

This argument, this line of reasoning, is not some semantic sleight of hand. Any good Christian or Jew would dismiss outright as absurd the possibility that Zeus exists as a real god. He or she would do so with gusto, with no inner doubts, with no hesitation, with unyielding certainty. For identical reasons, using the same logic and with the same unyielding certainty, we dismiss out of hand the absurd possibility that the God of the Old and New Testament could exist as a real god. We all agree in principle; we're just haggling about a number, with our calculation resulting in one fewer god in the equation.

Not by any means are we first to this conclusion. In a letter to John Adams in 1823, Thomas Jefferson wrote:

> The day will come when the mystical generation of Jesus by the Supreme Being in the womb of a virgin, will be classed with the fable of the generation of Minerva in the brain of Jupiter.

But until that welcome day arrives, we should understand the deadly consequences of confusing myth with reality. That confusion cost Socrates his life in ancient Greece. He was sentenced to death in large part for his impiety in rejecting religious dogma as mere myth. He considered the story of Saturn castrating his father Uranus, or Jupiter dethroning

Saturn, as nothing but fable, much to the annoyance of religious leaders of the time. But deadly consequences of confusing myth with reality are not relics of the past; we see the impact today.

Diverse religions share a common idea that the end of days is near and that only the faithful can be saved. Of course, Religion X claims that one must be a member of Religion X to be saved, while all others – the unclean, the unchosen, the unanointed – are destined to be damned.

Predictions of the Apocalypse or its equivalent have been a common theme throughout history, often with tragic results. These are chronicled in *The Ghost Dance* by Weston La Barre, a professor of anthropology at Duke University famous for his best-selling studies in the 1950's of God and culture seen through the lens of psychoanalysis. One poignant example excised from La Barre's book tells a sad story all too familiar in the saga of religion. In South Africa in 1856, a young Xosa girl went to fetch water at a local stream. There she claimed to meet strangers from the spirit world. Excited, she returned with her uncle Umhlakaza, who spoke with the same spirit world reps. From this encounter, Uncle Umhlakaza came back with an important message. At the time of this ghostly meeting, the Xosa tribe was battling the English. The spirits told Umhlakaza that to succeed in driving out the foreigners, his tribesmen must kill every animal in their herds and destroy every kernel of corn so carefully stored in their granaries. The spirits promised him that if his tribesman followed these instructions, heaven on Earth would be theirs. Dead loved ones would return, fat cattle would rise from the Earth, corn would sprout in abundance, sickness and troubles would be banished and the old would become young and beautiful again. With such great promise, backed by the authority of the spirit world, Umhlakaza's orders were carried out, resulting in the slaughter of two thousand cattle and destruction of all grains. Instead of Earthly paradise, the Xosa experienced a famine so deadly that the tribe nearly ceased to exist.

La Barre cites many similar tragic stories derived from prophecies in which unbelievers would be punished, the dead would arise, and the

faithful would be rewarded, either with eternal life in heaven or by the fulfillment of some Earthly need. Pat Robertson probably has not read La Barre. Tragedies resulting from such beliefs have wide geographic and temporal distribution, having visited the Maori in New Zealand, the Altai Turk of mid-Siberia, the Tuka in Fiji, the village of Gabagabuna in New Guinea, and the Kekesi of Papua New Guinea.

These sad tales are not restricted to far-away or long-ago places. Today, we have Islamic suicide bombers in Iraq and Israel lining up for martyrdom. While the Koran explicitly forbids suicide, several passages also state that a martyr can expect an afterlife in paradise. That creates a loophole wide enough to accommodate a bomb-laden truck, as amply demonstrated by the carcasses of twisted bodies, burnt cars and collapsed buildings now such a common sight in the Middle East. If a trip to paradise is not sufficiently attractive to convince a potential martyr to strap on some TNT, further incentive to make the ultimate sacrifice is provided by a number of virgins as promised in the Hadith, often cited as seventy-two but really of uncertain quantity. The prize awaiting a female bomber is less clear, but a stable of male virgins would not likely hold the same appeal.

In 1978, the Reverend Jim Jones, charismatic leader of the People's Temple, convinced 913 of his followers in Guyana to commit suicide by drinking cyanide-laced fruit punch, forever altering public perception of Kool-Aid. Jones claimed, and his followers believed, that he was the divine reincarnation of Jesus *and* Buddha. Citizens of Jonestown followed their divine leader's command to suffer a "revolutionary death."

In 1990, a Houston teenager by the name of Vernon Wayne Howell moved to the sleepy wind-swept town of Waco after dropping out of high school. There he changed his name to David Koresh, explaining blandly that he was the reincarnation of both King David and King Cyrus of Persia. David did not stop there, further claiming he was in fact the Messiah, appointed by God to rebuild the Temple and destroy Babylon. At least 131 of Howell's Branch Davidians were convinced enough to ensconce

themselves in his compound, yielding to him their daughters as young as twelve to be impregnated by the Messiah. That episode ended badly, as we all know.

In 1997, thirty-nine members of the Heaven's Gate cult took their own lives, dying in shifts over a few days in late March. Some members helped others take a deadly mix of phenobarbital and vodka before consuming their own poisonous cocktail. Why did these people die? Members of the cult believed the prophecy of Marshall Applewhite, who claimed that the comet Hale-Bopp was the long-awaited sign to shed their Earthly bodies, which they called "containers." By leaving their containers behind, followers would be able to join a spacecraft traveling and hiding behind the comet, which would take them to a higher plane of existence.

In Uganda in March 2000, between two-hundred and five-hundred members of the Movement for the Restoration of the Ten Commandments committed suicide by setting fire to their church. The congregation apparently forgot about the Commandment concerning "thou shalt not kill." These people died because the sect anticipated the end of the world, expecting a visit by the Virgin Mary on the Friday they self-immolated. She never showed up. The prophet in this case was Credonia Mwerinde, a former prostitute.

Then we have prophets who bring with them good cheer but an odd story. In the early 1800's in Palmyra, New York, a local boy claimed he could divine the location of ground water as well as treasures buried by Indians. Persuasive as a snake-oil salesman, farmers paid him $3, a princely sum then, to find buried riches on their land. The boy, Joseph, used "magic stones" to discover the sites of this bounty. When he inevitably failed to find either water or treasure, he would leave town, often with "encouragement," and move on to other fee-based treasure-hunting activities.

After a particularly large and humiliating failure in the Susquehanna Valley near Damascus, New York, Joseph stayed on to court a local gal,

Emma Hale, in spite of community accusations that he was a charlatan. In the spring of 1826, a group of unhappy customers went further and brought formal charges against Joseph, claiming he was nothing but an imposter. He was subsequently convicted of "glass gazing," an outlawed form of fortune-telling. Emma's dad Isaac was one of the duped treasure hunters who testified against Joseph, so he was not pleased by the courtship of his daughter by this convicted criminal. He considered Joseph to be arrogant, fraudulent and lazy. Those who knew Joseph best claimed, "He could utter the most palpable exaggeration or marvelous absurdity with the utmost apparent gravity." Others said that Joseph was "in particular considered entirely destitute of moral character and addicted to vicious habits." But Joseph was persuasive to some and Emma eloped with him in January 1827. To reconcile with his estranged father-in-law, Joseph promised to lead a more honest and honorable life and to help Isaac on his farm.

Instead of working in the field, however, Isaac found Joseph spending all his time indoors. When he finally investigated, he discovered his son-in-law muttering long phrases from the Bible, with Emma sitting behind a curtain writing down Joseph's ramblings. Joseph explained that he had found two ancient golden plates by digging in a spot to which he had been led by an angel. He claimed the plates were written in "reformed Egyptian." Fortunately, the two plates conveniently came with their own set of Rosetta stones, allowing him to translate the symbols to English, which explained his indoor activities. Joseph Smith was translating the ancient *Book of Mormon*. The "ancient" part might be in question, though, since the book agitated against such contemporary institutions as Freemasons and even Catholicism. Sadly, the plates mysteriously disappeared before the dates could be authenticated. In fact, Joseph declared that instant death would be the result for anybody but him looking at the golden plates. Nobody but Joseph, the fraudulent diviner from Palmyra, ever saw the plates. Only through the tainted word of a convicted con man do people know of the existence and content of

those disappeared golden tablets. So terribly odd that such a monumental discovery would be hidden and destroyed rather than proudly shown to the world to prove that God's word had been found at last.

Are the claims of Joseph Smith any less bizarre than those of Marshall Applewhite or David Koresh? Without large numbers, Mormonism would be considered just another lunatic cult, with a foundation little or no different from Heaven's Gate or the Branch Davidians. But the power of faith to overwhelm rational thought is not to be underestimated. Mormonism is now one of the fastest-growing religions in the world, with proselytizing mi[...] zeal in every corner of t[...]

In 1831 or t[...] Miller began predicting [...]erpretation of the Bibl[...] and redemption in Nev[...] nd west. Some claim he g[...]t of the end of the world[...]sand socalled Adventists[...]mer of 1843. Many sol[...] the big day. When the v[...]ollowers destitute and ho[...]ne date, leaving tens of t[...] their descendents still do today.

In 1966, the Jehovah's Witnesses predicted in *Life Everlasting in the Freedom of the Sons of God*, a book by the society's vice president Frederick Franz, that the world "six thousand years from man's creation will end in 1975 . . . " That prognostication must have caused some chagrin in 1976 when Armageddon was again delayed, particularly because leadership had encouraged members to sell their homes and property in 1974. The failed prophecy of 1975 continued a long tradition started by Charles T. Russell, who founded the Jehovah's Witnesses. In 1879, he claimed that 1914 was the big year in which the world would be destroyed. When

1843 - End of World
Adventists · William Miller-
Among date, Still waiting forbow,
1975 - Jehovah's Witness
End of World.

the year ended quietly, Russell changed the date to 1915. He died in 1916, when Joseph Franklin Rutherford took control of the organization. Upon taking the reins, Rutherford prophesized that in 1918, God would destroy churches and their members and that by 1920, every "kingdom would be swallowed up in anarchy." As December 31 rolled around, he reset the date to 1925. We are still here.

The consistent failure of such end-of-days predictions never seems to diminish their appeal. Here we witness first hand and up close the "hopes and fears" that David Hume cites as the driving forces of religion.

If you think Miller, Smith and Applewhite were unbalanced, how about the ridiculous apocalyptical predictions of doom in 1999 about the approaching 21st century, when computer glitches were supposed to throw mankind into chaos?

One could easily dismiss these examples of reincarnation, discovery of ancient texts with inappropriate contemporary references, or mass suicides in anticipation of the Apocalypse as the result of delusional ravings by a few nut bags. That would be a dangerous mistake. Prophets of doom and redemption, whom we find consistently across cultures and time, tell an important story.

The flocks of those many prophets predicting the Apocalypse had true faith, so strong that they were willing to die for their religion. The evidence on which they based their faith was no more or less legitimate than the myths on which any religion is based. The people of Jonestown or the congregation of the Movement for the Restoration of the Ten Commandments made the ultimate sacrifice for their religion and faith, just as soldiers of the Crusades did nine-hundred years earlier, with the same conviction that such acts would lead to an eternal place in heaven.

Let's take another look at that bug-eyed lunatic Marshall Applewhite, who commanded his followers to shed their "containers." Everybody outside of that cult would agree that the guy had a screw loose. But in fact, Applewhite had good precedent in broadly accepted religious lore. Perhaps he was not crazy after all. Gnostic Christians believed that

Jesus not only knew about but encouraged Judas to betray him so that Judas "could sacrifice the man that clothes me." *Jesus apparently wanted to shed his container.* Perhaps the Gospel of Judas has the story correct after all. Even if not, traditional Christians today, though offering multiple interpretations of what happened between Judas and Jesus, widely accept the idea that Jesus at least had knowledge of the betrayal before the fateful evening. That conclusion would be hard to deny, with passages from the Bible such as, "For Jesus knew from the first who those were that did not believe, and who it was that would betray Him." (John 6:64 in the Revised Standard Version, RSV). If that is too ambiguous, we have, "Did I not choose you, the twelve, and one of you is a devil?" The Bible speaks of "Judas the son of Simon Iscariot, for he, one of the twelve, was to betray Him." (John 6:70-71 RSV). If John is right, Jesus knew that he and his container would soon part ways and took no action to avoid the separation. Crazy like Applewhite.

Since religion is based, by definition, on faith rather than facts, no mechanism exists to arbitrate between competing ideas. Is the idea that Jesus rose from the dead any more or less silly than the notion that Joseph Smith was led by angels to golden plates in New York? As soon as logic is removed from the debate, competing positions cannot be evaluated based on relative merit but are supported as inherently right, immune to any reasonable counterarguments. The only way to support a position is simply to assert supremacy as loudly as possible, since no objective facts are available to evaluate any particular claim. We are reduced to tantrums of "I'm right, you're wrong, I win." Without logic, in the absence of facts, nobody has any basis on which to conclude that Jesus was any less crazy than Applewhite, Jim Jones, or David Koresh. Faith is faith is faith, with one having no more claim to legitimacy than another. If Koresh was nuts, then so was Jesus; there is no way to assign the label of truth to one system of belief among many. All have equal claim to the truth, with no mechanism to prove or disprove the claim. Followers of Koresh *believed* he was the Messiah as honestly as traditional Christians *believe* Jesus rose from the dead. Jews reject the idea that a dead man can be resurrected, but they believe that Moses actually parted the Red Sea, an idea no less absurd.

Cults like Koresh's can perhaps be dismissed at first because their numbers are small and their endurance short. Branch Davidians and Heaven's Gate are flashes in the pan. In contrast, mainstream religions such as Judaism, Islam and Christianity enjoy a history of long duration and boast memberships in the millions or billions. So perhaps duration and numbers of followers are one way to confer legitimacy on a belief system. No, the Greeks and Romans that we encountered earlier would disagree. As emphasized before, multiple thousands of people worshiped Greek and Roman gods for a thousand years. Greeks *believed* that Poseidon existed as a real god, with real power, with real influence over daily life. If we can dismiss Koresh, we can certainly not dismiss the Greeks or Romans. On what basis do we conclude that one god or one belief is real or true? The answer is clear and unambiguous: we cannot other than to claim that we *believe* our views to be correct. The problem with that answer is that the followers of Koresh, Jones, and Mwerinde believed *their* faith to be correct and true, too. With faith-based claims, competing ideas simply cannot be tested for truth. Therefore, to the extent that we can ever know, *all belief systems are equally true*; but, since competing beliefs contain mutually exclusive concepts, *all must be false*. Herein lies the source of religious intolerance. Since you have no way to prove your beliefs correct, you must insist that all others are wrong. Simply the existence of other belief systems is a threat.

The odd nature of competing claims with no means of arbitration was recognized long ago. In the early 1700's, Scottish-born philosopher and orthodox Christian Andrew Michael de Ramsay, known popularly as the Chevalier Ramsay, pondered "what strange ideas would an Indian or Chinese philosopher have of our holy religion . . . the God of the Jews is a most cruel, unjust, partial and fantastical being." He went on to describe how bizarre was the tale of Adam and Eve and their fall from grace:

God not only threw our first parents out of paradise, but he condemned all their posterity to temporal misery, and the greatest part of them to eternal pains, though the souls of these innocent children have no more relation to that of Adam than to those of Nero and Mahomet.

Put yourself in the position of an alien who is passing by Earth and decides to drop in for a visit. You gather the leaders of all the major religions on Earth and ask them, "Who among you can explain why your faith represents the ____" A ____ the table, you patiently listen to the Pope, th____ ____ ____ hinto priest, a Buddhist r____ ____ it denominations. (Plan____ ____ nge.) When done, what c____ ____ convincing evidence of____ ____ ition cannot offer, nor d____ ____ support port other than the____ ____ offer nothing more than____ ____ ruth. As a disinterested a____ ____ ually fanciful to you, on ____ ____ haps less compelling. Yo____ ____ o the truth, or that all ha____ ____ tales. You would draw t____ ____ it the Gospel of Judas: *claims about God from all of these religions are nothing but old myths that tell an interesting story.*

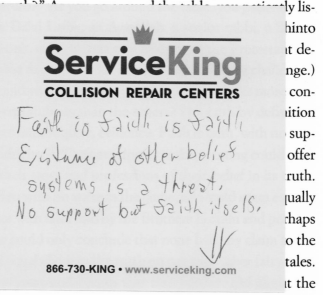

And now, let's for a moment take a look at the Tooth Fairy. No adult takes the myth seriously, of course. Yet the *evidence* for the existence of the Tooth Fairy is in fact more compelling than that for any other belief system. As a child, you put your recently yanked tooth under your pillow. The next morning, lo and behold, you have a quarter where the tooth used to be. That is concrete, real, undeniable evidence that the Tooth

Fairy came to visit during the night. What other explanation could be possible with such incontrovertible evidence? What could be more compelling: you can hold that quarter in your hand and you know for a fact that the previous night only a tooth lay beneath your head. The Tooth Fairy exists, end of story. Now, science might try to convince you, as a five-year-old, that there indeed is a more rational explanation for the nocturnal switch, such as a caring parent acting the part, but you will have none of it. You *believe* the Tooth Fairy exists, have evidence to support your belief, and dismiss the scientific explanation as heretical.

Fortunately, we all grow out of believing in the Tooth Fairy. Well, no, we don't. We just transfer that belief to something we call "God." God is the Tooth Fairy and the Tooth Fairy is God. Instead of looking for a quarter under our bed, we look to miracles as evidence to support our belief, ignoring the fact that belief cannot be supported by evidence. Yet, we insist. We see statues of the Virgin Mary crying blood, or the face of Jesus on an eggplant, or witness a healer laying hands giving ambulation to the disabled. Instead of the story involving a tooth and quarter, our narrative becomes more complex (we are adults after all), with the plot thickening to include creation and an afterlife. But both stories are made up, figments of our imagination, equally supported by "evidence." Both are valid only because we *believe*. The first impulse would be to dismiss as completely absurd any equality between God and the Tooth Fairy. But resist the temptation and ask yourself a simple question: how do the two really differ? Whatever argument you come up with to support a belief in God, can you not also apply to the Tooth Fairy or Santa Claus or trolls under a bridge in Ireland? Yes, of course, the concept that the Tooth Fairy is real is lunacy. But so, too, the belief in God. The notion that God exists is as childish and as silly as the belief that a mythical creature enters your bedroom at night to give alms for your milk teeth.

Given the historic stranglehold of religion on societies across cultures and time, this irrational and silly belief in God clearly fills a void in the human brain. In fact, religion persists in service of five different masters of human weakness: fear of death and the promise of seeing lost loved ones; the need to explain away the unknown; hope for controlling one's destiny; a desire for social cohesion; and the corrupting allure of political power.

So we create, each of us and collectively, a God who is all-powerful and all-knowing to address some combination of these five masters, or all of them. He created the universe and everything contained within, and that settles that. But this concept of the Almighty raises immediate objections. Why did he need six days to create all we see around us? With unlimited power, could he not do that creation bit in an instant, with one snap of his substantial fingers? The fact that he required six days implies limited capabilities. And why did he need to rest on the seventh day? God gets tired? Quasars and black holes must have been truly exhausting! How can God, with unlimited power and no corporeal being, get tired? Why would he need to rest? Doesn't fatigue imply fallibility and weakness? The Tooth Fairy seems much more plausible and considerably more robust: she is undaunted by the endless number of pillows she must visit each night with nary a day off.

With modern advances in technology, a greater understanding of our physical world and a growing knowledge of life's inner workings, many of the mysteries that drove early people to religion have been solved, leading to the god-of the-gaps discussed in the previous chapter. We know that the Earth is 4.5 billion years old, not six thousand. We know the Earth rotates around the sun. We know that DNA is the universal code for life. We know that malaria is caused by a parasite transmitted through the bite of a mosquito. We understand how antibiotics kill bacteria. Yet the final master of religion, political power, ensures that the myths and mysteries on which religion is founded are perpetuated, even in the face of incontrovertible contrary evidence. Religion retains its grip in the face of ever-expanding human knowledge by using political power to refocus attention on the dwindling areas of uncertainty, and by appealing to our darkest and ugliest human characteristics.

In the end, though, fear of mortality, first master of human weakness, remains and will likely always be religion's primary draw, even as the gaps between knowledge and ignorance slowly close. Science provides no comforting answers to the permanence of death. By playing to fear, religion survives as a means of manipulating people for political gain to perpetuate the power of the religious elite.

That last sentence might appear suspiciously like an endorsement of Marx and Engels, who bitterly attacked religion as a weapon in the struggle between classes. While there is some coincidental overlap in thought, our own ideas are quite distinct. Our point here is that religion seeks power as a means of self-preservation and perpetuation, not as a tool to promote one political philosophy over another. Once that power is in hand, rules and laws are promulgated that feed on fear to secure legitimacy for the religious regime. Compliance with these rules and laws is ensured by imposing upon the masses a moral code promising reward and threatening punishment here and hereafter, as we shall soon see.

If David Hume is the father of religious studies, then its grandfather is surely Baruch de Spinoza, who preceded Hume by almost one hundred years. Spinoza took on the question of ethics but in doing so, laid the foundation for a sharp look at religion. In laying this foundation, Spinoza created a path to secular enlightenment that Hume did not fully assimilate. With the publication of *Tractatus Theologico-Politicus*, Spinoza firmly established himself as a great theorist of secularism, with everlasting impact. "I believe in Spinoza's God," is how Einstein replied more than two centuries later when asked if he believed in the Almighty. Einstein was attracted to Spinoza because the philosopher was the first to describe a universe subject to natural law, with no purpose or design. Perhaps Richard Dawkins is Spinoza reincarnated? In either form, Spinoza will help guide us through the next chapter, in which we explore religious morality, built on the gossamer threads of childish dreams.

CHAPTER 6

Commandments from Above:
Exploring Religious Morality

*Wisdom denotes the pursuing
of the best ends by the best means."*
        – Francis Hutcheson

Hence the greatest crimes have been found, in many instances, compatible with a superstitious piety and devotion; hence, it is justly regarded as unsafe to draw any certain inference in favor of a man's morals, from the fervor or strictness of his religious exercises.

— David Hume

Religious morality has maintained a powerful grip on the human psyche for two millennia through the concept of "free will." Without the notion of free will granted by an omniscient and omnipotent God, religion would run into an immediate and insurmountable conundrum. Humans would be automatons, doing God's bidding with no choice. By definition, with no free will, all actions by all people would be a direct expression of God's will. That would clearly pose a problem with war atrocities, rape, torture, genocide and the full repertoire of human debauchery reflecting poorly on the Almighty. No religion would tolerate such a grim view of the creator, so there must be a way to reconcile the reality of ugly human behavior with an all-powerful, all-knowing God. Hume nicely summarized this tension between a kind God and the unkind reality of human existence:

> Our natural terrors present the notion of a devilish and malicious deity: Our propensity to adulation leads us to acknowledge an excellent and divine. And the influence of these opposite principles are various, according to the different situation of the human understanding.

Here is the central dilemma: religion must somehow explain the existence of evil in the presence of God, an endeavor known as theodicy.

Despite heroic efforts, all attempts at theodicy have failed completely. The bottom line is clear. In a world that knows evil, *an all-powerful god responsible for all creation must be evil*. That interpretation is unavoidable and certain. But given that many people will wish to dispute the claim, we will show next how no other conclusion is possible.

Some who oppose the notion of a brutish ugly deity propose that God did not intentionally create evil. If so, that begs the question of evil's origin if not from the hand of God. In one scenario, God allowed evil to flourish as an unintended consequence once his newly-minted Adam and Eve started roaming the Earth; in another, evil sprang to life without God's permission, as a rude cosmic surprise. Both scenarios would give God a pass on being evil but would at the same time mean He was not omnipotent. None of the three scenarios is looking too good for the big guy. Let's review: in the first case, an all-powerful god must be evil since evil exists and God created all, including evil; in the second case, God's work got beyond his control, a mistake not typically associated with an all-powerful thing; in the third case, God not only does not control our fate, he is incapable of peering into the future, a decidedly ungodlike attribute.

Religion solves this conundrum the old-fashioned way: by making up a silly answer with truly contorted logic. The answer in this case is free will, but only for human beings. Somehow, when God gathered his last strength to make people, before taking a one-day vacation, He decided, unlike with beavers or parrots, to give his new creation the ability to choose a path not preordained by God. This divine grant of free will solves the dilemma because people can choose to be evil without implicating God. Whew!

Unfortunately, the idea does not hold water. Even the briefest examination lays waste to the claim that free will was or could be granted by an all-powerful God. The idea is an absurd oxymoron: the very act of granting free will would destroy the power do so. Let's see why by looking at the combination of free will, evil and prayer in the presence of an omniscient God.

We can start with prayer. If God has a plan for everything and everyone, prayer could not affect His behavior. If He changed his plan according to a prayer, that would be an admission that God's original plan was flawed, making Him fallible. If only those prayers that fit into God's original plan are answered, then the purpose of praying is defeated. With preordained fate, prayer could not change any outcome, which is the very purpose of a prayer.

Aha, you might say, the trick is that god gave mankind free will – that allows for the legitimacy of prayer. But prayer cannot work in the case of free will, either. If we have the power to choose our own destiny, prayer has no role to play. If I pray to God for a certain outcome, just the act of praying is an admission that I do not determine my fate; I admit my fate is in the hands of God, that God can change the outcome of my life, making the notion of free will moot. The idea of free will is religion's version of having your cake and eating it too. You can have a God who already preordained everything *and* you can pray for a different outcome anyway *and* you have free will to change your destiny. The wishful thinking that a pastry can be consumed without being depleted is no more viable than the notion that free will and prayer are compatible.

An argument often provided to counter this line of reasoning says that God knows what every person will choose beforehand but the person does not; the person is still making a choice. How oddly tautological. Whatever we choose, our choice is according to God's plan because we chose it! But if God already knows what we will choose, already knows the outcome of every choice, that is not free will, only the cruel illusion of free will. The choice was already made at the beginning of time, meaning there never was any choice.

Another common argument is that free will allowed humans to fall from God's grace, without impugning god's character. That is simply defining away the problem without solving anything. If God is all-powerful, he *could have* created a species of humans who chose to use the gift of free will only for good. That His creations chose to behave badly means that such behavior was either God's original intent or that God is not all-knowing.

Perhaps a benevolent God created a world with evil, but He chose to do so for good reasons. He created evil, but is not evil Himself. Assuming this logic, some argue that evil and suffering are necessary in order to know God. Well, that is simply another example of solving the problem by defining it away, and ultimately contributes nothing. Since God is all-powerful, He could have just as easily designed the world such that suffering was *not* required to know Him.

Let's look at a real case of evil, that of Slobodan Milosevic and his choice of genocide: only three scenarios are possible. One, God knew beforehand the choice Milosevic would make and did nothing to prevent the outcome; two, God knew beforehand but *could* do nothing to change the outcome; or three, God did not know what choice Milosevic would make. From these three possibilities we must come to a conclusion that is irrefutable, undeniable, and logically immune to any counterargument. In a world in which evil and suffering exist, *God is either all-powerful and is responsible for that evil and suffering, through design or neglect, or God is benevolent but not all-powerful. Nothing else is possible other than the obvious conclusion that God does not exit. With evil in the world, an all-powerful God cannot be benevolent.* Whether God's power is diminished, either as an original state of being or as a consequence of voluntarily relinquishing his power to human free will, the affect is the same. If God is benevolent and not culpable of evil, He has no effect over evil. *If God is not evil, he cannot alter our fate.* No amount of twisted or convoluted logic can change that immutable conclusion.

That conclusion yields an obvious and terminal problem for prayer. If your baby is seriously ill, you pray to God for her recovery. Why? If God is all-powerful, He would already know the fate of your baby and your prayers would be for naught. Whether you prayed or not, your baby's fate is already sealed, preordained, for better or worse, by the all-powerful God. Plus, since an all-powerful God must be evil, since He is responsible for everything in the universe including evil, he might take joy in your suffering, since He has allowed so much grief to visit the human condition long before your child became ill.

Alternatively, if God is benevolent, He is not responsible for the evil and suffering in the world, meaning He has diminished powers since forces exist in the universe for which He has no responsibility and no hand in their creation. You would be praying to a being without the ability to control human fate, rendering the prayer useless. If God has no control over evil, praying to Him to stop evil and suffering makes no sense. *Prayers to an all-p[owerful but not benev]olent God are useless. Yo[u]* with the Tooth Fairy you[...]

The notion that an al[...] of the most egregious ex[...] becomes positively surr[...] powerful God can alter t[...] of the prayer. Holding th[...] a sign of insanity.

[Handwritten annotation: Cruel illusion of Free Will.]

The flip side of human free will is also important to examine; that is, does God Himself have free will? If not, can God grant what He Himself does not have? An all-powerful God is all-knowing, meaning God knows all of his future actions and all of the choices He would make. Here is the rub: God could not change those choices; otherwise, His earlier knowledge would have been wrong, meaning God would not be all-knowing! An omniscient God therefore has no free will to choose actions, since all actions must be preordained. God becomes an observer of His own omniscience since all knowledge of the future precludes any changes to that future. Any God with free will would have to be imperfect and would by definition not be all-knowing.

So an all-knowing God, who cannot possess free will, cannot grant something He Himself does not have. But a bigger problem remains. Free will implies a future with no predestination. A God who knows all, about everything past, present and future, could not create any free will that would prevent that knowledge of the future; the very act of creating free will would destroy the fact of omniscience.

These obvious arguments are not new, and in fact date all the way back to Epicurus, as summarized by Moojan Momen in 1999:

> The presence of evil and suffering in the world has ever been argued by some philosophers from Epicurus (341–270 BCE) to David Hume (1711–1776) to cast doubt on the existence of God. Other more modern writers such as Freud and Marx sought to show that religion's explanations of the presence of evil and suffering were based on delusions.

We have overstayed our welcome on this unoriginal idea that free will and evil belie the existence of a benevolent God because the idea goes to the very heart of religious morality. Philosophers from the beginning have supposed that the concept of free will, either granted by God or innate to life, is intimately connected to the concept of moral responsibility.

As others have done before us, we will show that morals are not derived from religion nor God's grant of free will, but instead arise from inherent characteristics embedded in human nature as a consequence of our sociality. What we view as moral behaviors – kindness, reciprocity, honesty, respect for others – are social norms that evolved in the context of a highly social animal living in large groups. The evolution of these social norms enabled a feeble creature to overcome physical limitations through effective cooperation. Morality is a biological necessity and a consequence of human development. Religion, however, has masked and corrupted these natural characteristics with a false morality that converts intrinsic human benevolence and generosity into cheap commodities to be purchased with coupons for heaven. Good behavior is not encouraged as a means of advancing our humanity but instead is enforced with threats of eternal damnation.

Is the concept of purchasing morality through coupons a bit harsh on religion? Consider the practice of granting "indulgences," initiated in the thirteenth century but still seen today in the Catholic Church. An indulgence is the concept that *a sinner can pay for penance.*

The idea was from the start not without controversy. One of Martin Luther's big complaints in his *95 Theses* was directed against this form of fundraising. Luther's objection was in part due to the fact that indulgences, soon after their introduction, became the subject of commercial exploitation, with "professional pardoners" selling absolution on a grand scale. Renaissance Popes Julius II and Leo X actively encouraged the practice as a way to shore up weak Church finances. Eventually, Pius V prohibited commercial trafficking of indulgences in 1567 but not their use.

Just so we are not accused of misrepresenting indulgences, here is the Church's own definition:

> An indulgence is a remission before God of the temporal punishment due to sins whose guilt has already been forgiven, which the faithful Christian who is duly disposed gains under certain defined conditions through the Church's help when, as a minister of redemption, she dispenses and applies with authority the treasury of the satisfactions won by Christ and the saints" (*Indulgentarium Doctrina 1*, CCC: 1471).

Let's be clear about what that means. A sinner can be absolved from his or her sin by *donating money.* Technically, this is not "buying forgiveness" because an indulgence only applies to a sin that has already been forgiven. But practically speaking, this is just a matter of timing. The

Church's act of forgiving a sin and the granting of an indulgence can be done in sequence with no pause, making the distinction somewhat dubious. Regardless of technical protests to the contrary, an indulgence is indeed buying forgiveness. And coupons are available for those who know where to shop! The Nordstrom coupon is obtained by kissing the ring of the Holy Father, for which the faithful earn an indulgence of three-hundred days. The Gap coupon is had by kissing the ring of a cardinal, resulting in an indulgence of one-hundred days. The coupon for Target will get you an indulgence of fifty days by kissing the ring of a patriarch, archbishop, or bishop. The exact meaning of these temporal indulgences for the absolution of sin is a source of some confusion even among the devout. An indulgence of three-hundred days apparently means, in the most common interpretation, that the recipient of the indulgences will have that many fewer days in purgatory before moving on to greener (or whiter) pastures.

Evangelical Christians engage in analogous behavior even if packaged somewhat differently; a lubricious evangelical minister piously urging his television viewers to donate to his ministry is perpetrating the idea of indulgences. Some are blatant about the correlation between donation and absolution while others try to put a patina of respectability on the solicitation. That is, some ministers will make viewers feel as if the contribution is to help others while hinting strongly that the donor will benefit directly, usually in proportion to the magnitude of the largess. In either case, the effect is the same as an indulgence: the faithful are buying their way into heaven.

For us to understand this powerful grip that religion maintains on morality, we must look to early times when God and morality first become confused as common subjects. And for that journey, Baruch de Spinoza will be our guide. But before we can appreciate Spinoza's contribution, we must first put moral theory in context.

PART III

A NEW
NATURAL
ETHIC

CHAPTER 7

Off the Beaten Path: Moral Theory

*The highest activity a human being can attain
is learning for understanding, because to understand
is to be free.*

— *Baruch de Spinoza*

The universe we observe has precisely the properties we should expect if there is, at bottom, no design, no purpose, no evil and no good, nothing but blind, pitiless indifference.

– Richard Dawkins

The most important and fundamental consequence of evolution is that life has no design, purpose or inherent meaning. But the notion is not yet widely accepted outside of academia. While authors such as Richard Dawkins and Stephen J. Gould have written elegantly and convincingly about this point, contemplating the lack of meaning is too dangerous and fearful for most people in the context of today's religious teachings. But "blind pitiless indifference" need not be frightening when viewed as an opportunity to understand the wonder of life in all of its diverse glory shed of any pretense. Embracing pitiless indifference removes the blinding shackles of false hope and empty promises of religion, and creates in its place an opportunity to see the world with clear eyes and to define ourselves meaningfully on the solid ground of natural history. Only when we can define ourselves honestly can we develop and adopt a legitimate and meaningful code of ethics for our species. Only when free from fables and fallacies can we develop and adopt a legitimate code of ethics as a rightful consequence of our humanness. This new code of ethics is neither a gift from above nor an immutable law of nature waiting to be discovered, but one derived from and informed by our natural place in the biosphere.

Embracing blind pitiless indifference does not mean accepting an uncaring mechanistic world devoid of warmth and fellowship. By releasing our tenacious white-knuckled grip on the futile hope for design, purpose and meaning, we become free to move beyond the cold reality of a random world. We can create a new and deeper sense of self and community based on our biology and our evolution as rational social creatures. A newly trained skydiver cannot feel the pleasure of free flying if he clings stubbornly to the airplane. Similarly, we must first let go of false hopes and myths about divine purpose before we can enjoy the fruits of a natural ethic.

With a natural ethic, any questions concerning the meaning of life become inconsequential. In a world with no design and no purpose, there can be no questions about meaning. The question "why" simply is not valid when the answer sought involves higher purpose. One can ask why the Earth rotates counterclockwise when viewed from above, looking down at the North Pole. The answer involves the history of rotating gases that eventually coalesced to form the planet. That explanation provides an answer to why as a matter of history rather than as one implying purpose. Asking why in search of something beyond history, as in what purpose did God have in making the Earth rotate west to east, is meaningless in a world with no design. Just the act of posing the question "why" implies the presence of purpose, so in the absence of purpose the question vanishes. A natural ethic can be understood only in the context of a world in which the question why vaporizes into nothingness.

Admittedly, this chapter is not a barrel of laughs. Perhaps watching grass grow will seem stimulating afterward. But this dose of theory is necessary medicine, so grab a strong cup of coffee, suck it up, and plow through to the other side.

With java in hand, consider that we suffer this chapter because establishing that a natural ethic can be valid only in a world of blind pitiless indifference is necessary as a first condition, but not sufficient to justify any claim to novelty. And we desperately want to prove we are saying something new. So a natural ethic must be distinguished as truly unique, and substantially different from seemingly related concepts of moral philosophy that began emerging in the 1500's.

A brief review of the major moral theories that shaped the debate about good and evil over the past five-hundred years will allow for a comparison of each to our very own natural ethic, enabling us to follow the intellectual heritage of this new ethic while points of divergence are highlighted in the analysis. Hold on; here we go.

MORAL SENSE THEORY

In the eighteenth century, a group of prominent philosophers led by Anthony Ashley Cooper (third Earl of Shaftesbury) promoted moral sense theory as the appropriate guide for human interaction. They held that moral life does not depend on knowledge of natural laws, eternal truths or self-interest. Instead, humans were said to have an innate, non-rational capacity to make moral judgments. Cooper proposed that self-interest and fear of either human or divine authority are improper motives in moral life. Not all humans are virtuous by nature, but ordinary people have natural capacities to act virtuously and to distinguish right from wrong. Cooper's ideas were further developed by Presbyterian preacher Francis Hutcheson, who argued that people have an internal sense of morality, just as we have a sense of smell and touch. Hutcheson also argued that actions are virtuous because the *motives* that produce the actions please observers of the action, irrespective of self-advantage.

Even before describing how a natural ethic is distinct from these ideas, serious problems with moral sense theory should be noted. First one must conclude logically from Hutcheson's philosophy that if actions (or motives) are virtuous because we approve of them, then any motive or action that we approve is virtuous. That has obvious flaws. Second, Hutcheson states that we aim to be virtuous because virtuous acts please us. Problematically, this implies that a person not pleased by virtuous acts will not be motivated to act virtuously. This contradicts the underlying concept that self-interest is an improper motive for morality. Yes, this is why a strong cup of coffee was recommended before delving into the chapter.

In the end, a natural ethic is fundamentally distinct from moral sense theory, independent of that theory's inherent flaws. The concept of improper motives from fear or self-interest in moral life proposed by Cooper is fully consistent with a natural ethic, but the two ideas diverge from this common ground. The claim that people have an innate, *nonrational* capacity to make moral judgments or that moral judgment is innate like touch or smell is counter to the central claim of *moral choice* on which a natural ethic is based. Moral sense theory is also incompatible with a natural ethic's primary claim that morality is, *by degree*, a human invention, albeit one constrained by evolution, our biology and our current place in the biosphere.

A natural ethic requires no claim that people are born with a sense of morality like a sense of taste or sight. As explained in annoying detail below, humans are born with the unique capacity (in degree) to *develop* a sense of morality and the ability to *choose* a moral life. It is *the choice* to be moral that is critical: our humanness is partly defined by our choice to be moral simply because we can be, not because we are born as inherently moral creatures like dolphins are born as inherently good swimmers. Equally important, the idea that we aim to be virtuous because virtuous acts please us is not compatible with a natural ethic. This concept is close to the idea embedded in Utilitarianism that actions are right in proportion as they tend to promote happiness, a perspective we have already examined and rejected.

RATIONALISM

Rationalism, supported by philosophers such as Descartes, Spinoza, and Leibniz, as well as Ralph Cudworth, Samuel Clarke, William Wollaston, and John Balguy, is the belief that actions are in themselves either right or wrong. These philosophers argued that reason and logic alone are powerful enough to understand fundamental truths about goodness and virtue, just as reason can grasp mathematical theory. Rather than being born with a sense of morality, people must use reason to understand right and wrong. As opposed to empiricists, rationalists believe it possible to construct knowledge of the external world, the self, God, and ethics from innate ideas derived naturally of the mind or from derivations of logic.

In spite of the fundamental difference between rationalism and moral sense theory, both camps agree on the presence of benevolence in humans, and both oppose egoism. Just as the long-standing and tired "nature versus nurture" argument missed the point because the answer lies in both, here too elements of both philosophies of moral sense theory and rationalism can be supported. The question is not one of either/or. Humans, like all social animals, are born with an ability to learn how to function in society (sharing certain common concepts of acceptable behavior typically found in social animals) and can apply reason to understand more complex and subtle concepts of morality. The debate between rationalism and moral sense theory is unenlightening because neither philosophy is adequate. Both bring critical but incomplete elements to the discussion.

EGOISM

Ethical egoism is in sharp contrast to rationalism and moral sense theory. This is the theory that humans do only what pleases them or what is in their perceived self-interest. The argument is that humans are neither sociable nor benevolent, but that self-interested motivation has positive results because society benefits from the economic activity of those who attempt to improve their circumstances. As a moral theory, egoism states that we each *should* as a moral imperative pursue our own best interests without regard to others. That leaves undefined what constitutes our own best interest, but presumably that would include the pursuit of wealth, power or pleasure. Oddly, egoism allows for altruism, if such behavior is viewed by the altruist as being in his best long-term self-interest.

As a moral theory, egoism has serious problems even if self-interest could be precisely defined. First, actions promoting self-interest in the short term are sometimes counter to one's long-term interests, and the theory does not specify the timeframe for judging the personal consequences of any action. Mary could study tonight and forgo an evening of partying with friends, clearly a decision that would promote her long-term self-interest, or she could party tonight to promote her immediate self-interest at the risk of failing her class. What option is consistent with egoism and her self-interest? Second, an egoist cannot openly advocate his theory because logically he would be best served as the only egoist in a world of altruists. As more egoists are recruited, followers would have greater difficulty reaping the rewards of acting in self-interest or, at a minimum, calculating the consequences of an action would become more complicated. That calls into question the validity of ethical egoism as a normative theory of morality. Finally, ethical egoism is inconsistent and incompatible with most commonly held views of justice, fairness, love and honest companionship. That alone does not make egoism wrong, just highly suspect.

Instead of acknowledging the unique human capacity for choosing to be moral in pursuit of a natural ethic, egoism proposes that each person acts selfishly for personal betterment, and in doing so inadvertently promotes the general welfare. Egoism may even be an accurate assessment of the current human condition, and may explain the popularity of religious morality. For example, someone acting morally in fear of God is doing what is in his perceived best interest, as the egoists would predict. But the results of ethical egoistic are not as positive as the theory would imply and the theory does not advance understanding much because it is primarily descriptive.

Once again, Plato had the early and final word, this time on egoism through his words on justice. In Plato's *The Republic*, Thrasymachus,

Adeimantus and Glaucon set up the premise that being unjust is superior to being just, arguing with Socrates that contemplating the welfare of others should not even be a consideration if an action advances one's self-interest. Plato then convincingly refutes this concept through his typical wit and logic. While the focus is on justice, everything said in this classic dialogue can be applied directly to egoism. Plato shows that one fatal flaw of egoism is that support for the theory ultimately must rely on a circular argument. To see this point, let us move forward two millennia and observe as Tom sees Bob fixing a flat tire by the side of the road. Tom stops to help his friend even though his support will make him late for work. An egoist would say that Tom is motivated only by the desire to feel good about himself, rather than by any altruistic desire to help Bob. In other words, Tom derives self-satisfaction from helping Bob and Tom is motivated only by the selfish desire to feel good about himself. Is that not, though, the very definition of an unselfish person? Being motivated to help somebody and feeling good about it makes one unselfish, not selfish. A selfish person would not derive that same satisfaction from helping a friend. While extreme versions of ethical egoism can be constructed to be internally consistent, and therefore theoretically defensible, the logic of egoism does not hold up under the scrutiny of common sense.

KANT'S ETHICAL THEORY

Of all the philosophies articulated previously to which a natural ethic must be compared, the most subtle and complex is Kantianism. Immanuel Kant proposed an ethical theory derived from human obligations based on laws that hold for all rational beings. Kant restricted the category of rational beings to include only humans, although he refers generically to rational beings as if other creatures could theoretically be included. He claimed that acts can be judged as moral based on the principle on which the action was taken, rather than on the action's consequences (in direct opposition to utilitarianism). Fundamental to Kant's philosophy is the principle that "rational nature exists as an end in itself" and the idea of "humanity as an end in itself." From this he derives the notion that "all rational beings come under the law that each of them must treat itself and all others never merely as means, but in every case at the same time as end in themselves." As a consequence, Kant states that one should "Act as if the maxim of thy action were to become by thy will a universal law of nature."

All of this, crudely summarized, means that one can judge an act as moral by asking two questions: could the action, if adopted by everybody in the particular circumstance in which the action was taken, be sustainable if codified as a universal law of nature, and does the action have a consequence or objective possessing a worth as an end in itself? The latter question is a way to emphasize that the ends do not justify the means, and that one cannot use another rational being as a means to a desired end without that party's knowledgeable consent. For beings that are ends-in-themselves (humans), the means must be considered so that not only the goal but the means are consistent with a universal natural law. With means-to-ends objects (everything but humans, really), we need not worry about distinguishing between goals and means to achieve them. For these, the end could justify the means with no moral qualms.

In reading that, our head hurts as much as yours. And we're not done yet. But these concepts are critical to understand if we wish to grasp the true meaning of a natural ethic.

Kant's odd terminology of "end-in-himself" is meant to emphasize that a person is autonomous, requiring no further justification for moral behavior toward that person. Kant contrasts this concept of "end-in-itself" to a "phenomenon," which is what appears to an observer rather than the thing itself. Being a person is in and of itself reason to expect moral behavior from others. A person is not merely a means to an end but the end itself or the *primary consideration* when we contemplate the consequences of an act such that we do not interfere with another person's ability to reason or act as an independent agent.

Kant's approach to morality is subtle, and he recognized that human beings are not entirely rational and sometimes behave on impulse in ways inconsistent with their own best interests or those around them. This is the animalistic side of our dual nature. But even when we behave in a way that is fully rational, the other side of our nature, we must choose among many possible actions, without knowing which is best among alternatives. Defining best becomes a further complication because the definition will depend on the criteria we use.

Important elements of a natural ethic are consistent with Kant's philosophy. As rational beings, our behavior is not entirely dictated by natural impulse. We have the ability to reason and as a consequence have a special burden to apply that reason to behave morally. Motivation is important in determining morality. Kant rightly points out a moral difference between a shopkeeper who refrains from overcharging a child because he fears losing customers who view him badly, versus a shopkeeper who refrains from such behavior from a principle of honesty.

While intent and motivation are also important to a natural ethic, the two philosophies are quite distinct despite this confluence. Kant creates a clear dichotomy between beings that are ends-in-themselves and those that are means-to-ends. As a consequence, Kant places humans on an arbitrary and artificial pedestal, assuming that rationality is really a uniquely human trait. (This assumption has a long history, dating back to Aristotle's *Nicomachean Ethics*.) A natural ethic is based on the contrary notion that humans are not any more unique than any other species and that traits that define humanness, including rationality, can be found in degree throughout the animal kingdom. Within the logic of a natural ethic, the line between beings that are ends-in-themselves and those that are means-to-ends has no inherent meaning, which if true, would undermine the basic premise of Kant's ethics.

One final distinction must be made between Kant and a natural ethic. Kant's "search for and establishment of the supreme principle of morality" implies that a supreme principle is waiting to be discovered like a new planet or new element in the periodic table. True, the supreme principle is a creation of rationality and so is dependent on humans for its existence, unlike plants or elements. But the notion of discovery is still implied by Kant, whereas in a natural ethic, moral principles are not discovered, they are *created* by humans through choice, and those choices are informed by our biology and evolution.

NATURAL LAW THEORY

In older versions of natural law, derived originally from Thomas Aquinas, moral guidelines were interpreted as an integral part of nature. A set of moral guidelines exists in nature and if you happen to know those guidelines, you are free to judge morality in others against this objective criterion. Not surprisingly, this philosophy was popular with the Anglican and Catholic churches because God provided them with the set of moral guidelines against which everybody could be judged.

But later natural-law philosophers (from Hugo Grotius to Samuel Pufendorf) believed that morality is created in human communities and that the only means of understanding ethics was to study human nature. The central idea behind natural law theory is to use studies of human nature to develop moral guidelines that transcend local customs and traditions. These generalized guidelines are the "laws of nature" that give the theory its name. Natural law theorists fall into two camps – those that emphasize the rights of people and those that stress their fundamental obligations. But all believe in some form of underlying universality of moral standards. The implication of natural law theory, then, is that humans have an innate idea of morality shared across all cultures that simply must be discovered through study. While the "idea" of morality is different from the "sense" of morality (like touch or taste) discussed under moral sense theory, the two concepts are not as far apart as old proponents of the two schools would have implied. Both view morality as innate. The same distinctions between a natural ethic and moral sense theory apply equally here. By the standards of a natural ethic, what is universal is the ability of people to develop a moral code, and the ability to choose to be moral. In this sense a natural ethic is quite distinct from natural law theory.

In a more modern twist on natural law theory, Hayden Ramsay in *Beyond Virtue* argues against the traditional concept of virtue as a commitment to objective human good. Instead, Ramsay describes the natural law theory of virtue as bringing its own rewards. Ramsay also applies the concept of personal integrity to analyze Aquinas' ethics, including the place of the emotions in morality. The idea that morality brings its own rewards could be interpreted as being aligned with the concept that morality is its own obligation (being moral because we can be), taking Hayden a step closer to a natural ethic. But the fundamental flaws of natural law theory remain.

RELATIVISM

Unlike natural law theory, a natural ethic accepts that culture influences moral practices, without accepting the notion of moral relativism. Differences among societies can exist that fall more into the category of tradition than ethics, where societies can agree to disagree without any moral quandary. For example, Jane lives in a society in which eating dog meat is considered immoral whereas Tom's society encourages the consumption of canine flesh as a means of culling excess unwanted dogs from society. An impartial observer not from either society would be hard-pressed to render judgment that one approach is moral and the other immoral. In some limited cases, morality relative to society is indeed plausible when moral variance remains within reasonable bounds. Recognizing cultural imposition of differences in moral codes does not, however, imply any support for moral relativism, either at the level of the individual or society.

Moral relativism fails completely at any significant level, as it must if a natural ethic can be supported as a human characteristic informed by our species' evolution and biology. To a relativist, no moral code can be criticized because whatever a society deems morally right is so by definition, and cannot be condemned by another society. But that raises some questions that, when answered, prove the fallacy of relativism. Does morality within a society get determined by majority rule? What if abortion is approved by 51% of the population one year and 49% the next? That would mean abortion is moral one year and immoral the next, clearly an untenable position. And what constitutes the unit called "society" that approves of a given moral code? Is a society defined by nationality or ethnicity? Is the United States one society, or is it made up of multiple societies of Hispanics, gays, Wall Street bankers and bikers? If so, does each of those societies have a unique moral code? How would conflict between them be resolved? Any reasonable answer to any of these questions dictates that ethical relativism must be false as a theory. Torturing children for fun would be universally condemned, regardless of how right a particular society found that practice. Relativism fails completely, which means that some elements of morality must be basic to humanity across time and across cultures.

But the failure of relativism does not yield a triumph for natural law theory. "Don't randomly kill people" would probably be an example of a moral concept that almost everybody could support. A society that lacks such fundamental codes cannot be excused because of cultural differences. Obvious admonitions such as "don't kill randomly" are the human equivalent of the code governing wolf societies as described in K. Lorenz's *King Solomon's Ring*. Social rules prevent dominant wolves from harming subordinates, and these behaviors are hard-wired.

These fundamentals are basic behavioral traits found in social animals generally and are necessary for social behavior to develop successfully. While such fundamental behavioral codes can be considered laws of nature, they do not shed much light on the complexity of human conduct. Ultimately, little is gained by searching for core moral values shared by all humans in every culture because such concepts are so basic as to be unrevealing, and constitute social norms common to most animals living cooperatively in large groups or societies.

NATURALISM

Evolution is fundamental to the foundation of a natural ethic. As such, a natural ethic might easily be confused with naturalism or be considered an offspring of that moral theory. However, naturalism makes no important contribution to a natural ethic and the two are entirely unrelated in spite of the common link through evolution.

In prescient anticipation of Charles Darwin's great work, Herbert Spencer developed an evolutionary theory of ethics almost ten years before the publication of *On the Origin of Species*. The central idea is that ethics can be understood on the basis of natural laws discovered through natural science. Moral properties are identical to "natural" properties and susceptible to the same type of objective study.

Spencer proposed that human societies and biological organisms depend fundamentally on the same evolutionary principles for their development, not as an analogy but as a homology. Consequently, human institutions, as a product of evolution, can function on their own without external guidance just like other products of evolution such as independent organisms or even the internal organs or systems of an animal. From this perspective, Spencer's ideas are consistent with natural law theory. Science can deduce morality by studying natural laws that promote life and happiness.

On this basis, Spencer defines "good" as that which satisfies our interests from an evolutionary perspective. "Interests" therefore are defined as those objectives that contribute to the life, development and reproduction of the organism. Success in meeting those objectives results in happiness. Happiness is achieved with the complete adaptation of an individual organism to its environment. Biology (survival instincts) would dictate then that happiness is what each person naturally seeks. From this, Spencer concluded that humans possess, as a matter of basic biology, a natural mechanism or an innate sense to drive individuals toward moral behavior. Here Spencer's ideas are consistent with moral sense theory.

But naturalism is seriously flawed. A collection of pure facts (gathered through the objective study of natural science), no matter how vast or comprehensive, will not logically entail an *evaluation* of those facts. Morality is ultimately evaluative, so naturalism fails at the most basic level. Naturalism falls in the gap between "is" and "ought" that Hume earlier emphasized. "Morals excite passions, and produce or prevent actions. Reason of itself is utterly impotent in this particular." The bottom line is that naturalism is at best descriptive rather than explanatory, and that is insufficient for any moral theory.

EXISTENTIALISM

A natural ethic is based on the notion that life has no meaning, purpose or design, and from this perspective a natural ethic could be considered a descendent of existentialism. Existential atheists hold that life has no inherent meaning, while existential theists believe life is without meaning that we can understand. In either case, humans are forced to define their own meaning in an irrational universe, and that is precisely aligned with a natural ethic.

Further, existentialists view the freedom to choose as the essence of the human condition. Freedom burdens each individual with being fully responsible for his own actions and beliefs. Freedom to choose entails risk because one can make the *wrong* choice. Consequently, freedom, choice and responsibility can be frightening and too much to bear, and the result is that people escape to religion or other worldviews that provide the comfort of external guidelines and rules for behavior. Existentialism rejects this self-deception and flight from reality and demands that each individual fully embrace personal responsibility.

Up to this point, the existentialist emphasis on choice and personal responsibility would indicate that a natural ethic is simply a version of existentialism. But the two are vastly different, and the divergence is most evident on the question of objective truth.

Existentialists believe that individuals make choices based on personal experiences, beliefs, and biases. Those choices are unique to each individual, made in a vacuum, in the absence of any form of objective truth. As a consequence, the most important questions in life, including those of right and wrong, are not accessible to reason or science. Truth is not universal but unique to each individual and can be discovered only through personal experience. Truth is restricted to whatever can be perceived by human senses. In stark contrast to rationalist and empiricist views that moral choice involves an objective judgment of right and wrong, existentialists believe that moral decisions have no objective or rational basis.

The existentialist idea that truth is subjective could not be further from the principles of a natural ethic. Every glance through a microscope revealing the teaming microbial masses in a drop of water defies the basic premise of existentialism. Prior to the invention of the microscope, that hidden world was not part of the human sensory experience and therefore, according to existentialism, was not real and in fact did not exist. Existial truth can only be discovered through personal experience and without the microscope, nobody could have the experience of seeing a protozoan swimming frenetically in a water drop. Somehow, with the arbitrary invention of a device consisting of ground glass and metal, an entirely new reality suddenly popped into existence.

But the fundamental flaw in existentialism is not that scientists can create technical means of extending our senses to greater distances and smaller spaces previously inaccessible to earlier generations. Instead, the flaw is in discounting the human ability to expand and modify concepts of reality long before our senses catch up. Atoms and electrons were discovered decades before technology allowed for their direct measurement.

Atoms are outside the human experience but are no less real as a consequence of our inadequacies. Superstring theory and M-theory suggest that our concept of three dimensions is only a gross approximation of a world really existing in nine or ten dimensions. For now, those dimensions are as inaccessible and bizarre as atoms once were, but those too might eventually yield to human ingenuity. Perhaps the wiring of a brain that evolved in a world approximated in three dimensions under the conditions found on Earth precludes any ability to comprehend nine dimensions. If so, and if superstring theory is right, those nine or ten dimensions nevertheless exist, independent of the structural limitations of the human brain.

Claiming that there is no objective truth is a form of incredible arrogance akin to the religious claim that humans are made in God's image. To accept the claim of subjectivity, one would have to agree that if no human beings were alive to contemplate truth, none would exist, that truth is only the creation of the human mind. Truth is a human fabrication. That concept places humanity on a pedestal with no foundation or justification, giving humans a special role in the biosphere no different from the Old Testament. Imagine a virus that killed only humans, and one so effective that every last human being died in a week's time. The remaining primates, birds, tigers, bees and bacteria would carry on just fine without us, actually much better without us, with no warping of time and space. The bonds between a mother chimpanzee and her daughter and sisters would remain unchanged. The pain experienced by a gazelle as the claws of a lion took her down would be no different than before. Humans hold no special place in the biosphere. Yes, life is random, absurd, meaningless, indifferent, but in no way does that imply the absence of an objective truth independent of human life.

Existentialists are disturbed by the fact the God does not exist, giving humans nothing to cling to, whereas natural ethicists revel in and embrace that reality. Jean-Paul Sartre said, "Thus there is no human nature, since there is no god to conceive it." That ultimately is an absurd position;

human nature exists as a consequence of our evolution and biology, just as all species have a unique nature.

The maddening aspect about existentialism is that it came tantalizingly close to a natural ethic with its emphasis on personal choice, the claim that life has no inherent meaning and the notion that are we are responsible for creating our own meaning. But the failure to recognize an objective truth fatally wounds the theory and undermines all of the theory's claims.

A NATURAL ETHIC AS A "META-ETHIC NORMATIVE AND PRACTICAL THEORY"

Traditionally, the academic study of ethics has been divided into three distinct fields: meta-ethics, normative ethics and practical ethics. Meta-ethics is based on the belief that moral claims are objective, capable of being true and false, but that some are true. Normative ethics explores the best way to live using general principles, rules and guidelines. Practical ethics asks how we should behave in particular circumstances. A natural ethic cannot be neatly placed in any of these fields. Moral principles of a natural ethic are objective and true but are not immutable truths to be discovered. The principles of a natural ethic are human creations but remain objective and true as the product of our evolution, biology and place in the world. From these principles are derived both rules and guidelines for living a moral life, and for applying those rules to practical everyday circumstances at the level of individuals and society. A natural ethic is all three categories of ethics and none of them.

All major ethical theories, whether utilitarian (focusing on the morality of an action itself) or deontological (emphasizing the morality of an action's consequences), begin with a basic notion of a fundamental "good" and "right" as a foundation on which the remainder of the theory is built. Similarly, virtue ethics assume a fundamental morally good person as a foundation for the theory.

A natural ethic takes a different approach by eschewing the concept of a natural good or right. Instead, what is fundamental is the human ability to choose to be moral, with that choice being informed by our biology as rational social creatures. Our biology limits our choices, puts boundaries on our choices, so that humanity collectively agrees on certain principles that others have confused as fundamental or set down by natural law or God. Those principles are real and important but not fundamental or embedded as a law of nature; they are a creation of ours as a species, not something to be discovered or gifted to us by God. These principles are not immutable, can change over time with human experience, and can in some cases differ among different groups of humans. *We have freedom to choose, but not unlimited freedom nor unlimited choice.* We have freedom to choose but are constrained by our evolutionary history, by our nature as social animals, by our ability to transmit culture and technology across generations, and by our ability to contemplate the fate of future generations.

A natural ethic states that we must be moral because we have the capacity to be moral. The ability to choose to be moral brings with it the obligation to behave morally, but that obligation is not the obligation of other moral theories. That mandate is made up, is strictly a human invention, is not a law of nature, and in fact is quite arbitrary. *No external force conveys legitimacy on that mandate.* But the choice to be moral because we can be is what ultimately defines us as human. That is us. The mandate is arbitrary but also powerful when properly understood. We have the power to define ourselves, free of any myths, in the full light of our potential and limitations.

A NATURAL ETHIC VERSUS RELIGIOUS MORALITY

A natural ethic is distinct from other moral theories but certainly is informed by them. With over two millennia of thought on the subject of ethics, it would be fair to say that any single element embedded within a natural ethic has been previously debated to some degree within the major categories of consequentialism, nonconsequentialism, natural law, naturalism, moral sense, egoism, rationalism, relativism or existentialism. But the common parts have been assembled to create a unique theory with little resemblance to any prior invention. The exception is Divine Command Theory, with which a natural ethic has no overlap and no shared history.

Pursuit of a natural ethic is completely removed from reward as a *motivating* force. But that does not imply the absence of unintended positive consequences for society and for the species as a whole, even if no benefit is derived by the individual or even that individual's distant future relatives. A clear distinction must be made between motivation and ultimate effect.

Note that this last statement should not be confused with the concept proposed by Hutcheson that actions are virtuous because the motives that produce the actions please observers of the action, irrespective of self-advantage. With a natural ethic, virtue relies on the choice to be moral, not on the pleasure an observer derives from one's actions. If I shoot a robber to protect my mother, that action might be virtuous to society in general but not pleasurable to the robber's colleagues in crime as they watch him die.

One could argue that achieving a positive consequence for our species in the distant future is a type of reward, and that such reward is sufficient motivation to act morally for some individuals. If true, one could further argue that pursuit of a natural ethic would be little different than common morality derived from or linked to religious practice or the moral philosophies just discussed, i.e., all types of morality would be driven by hopes for personal gain (at varying levels of subtlety and distance depending on the moral theory).

At some fundamental level, pursuit of a natural ethic may indeed be motivated by a sense of personal satisfaction, even if abstract from any practical benefit or gain. But this creates no meaningful equivalency between religious morality, other forms of moral philosophy, and a natural ethic. The primary practical benefits of pursuing a natural ethic are sufficiently long-term and diffuse to make such benefits qualitatively different from those that could benefit an individual now or his descendents in a few generations. Achieving a positive consequence for our species in the distant future is not a type of reward in the usual sense of that word, but perhaps instead is an awareness that provides further reinforcement to an already existing trait.

As suggested by the discussion of motivation, no moral theory is entirely mutually exclusive of all others, and even widely divergent theories will overlap. Many of the daily behaviors consistent with a natural ethic also will be compatible with religious or other moral behavior. Commandments four through ten of the Ten Commandments basically offer a minimum standard for good behavior that would be common to any ethical code, at least in the western world. (Commandments one through three relate directly to a belief in God and therefore do not address issues concerned with the pursuit of a natural ethic.) Also, certain tenants of the Christian faith, such as the mandate to love your neighbor, can be seen only as a positive moral incitement.

However, this mandate is put into practice sporadically at best. Mother Theresa of Calcutta was, after all, not the average Christian believer. Exceptional individuals, whether believers in God or not, are just that — exceptional — and therefore one cannot draw general conclusions about humanity from their behavior. In Mother Theresa's individual case, for example, the linkage to morality and her religion is clear, and commendable, but her example bears little weight in countering our argument about the role of religion in promoting a false morality in general. Furthermore, even an extreme example like Mother Theresa has no monopoly on doing good and others strive in that direction outside of any religious content, as evidenced by hundreds of secular charities.

While even divergent moral systems can share some common ground, in many important cases, discussed in the next chapter, moral behavior and the consequences thereof are more often mutually exclusive when comparing a natural ethic to religious morality. Like religion itself, morality based on religious belief is founded on the "incessant hopes and fears which actuate the human mind." Unreasonable hopes and fears, and extravagant superstition and credulity, have played and continue to play a part in the religious *and moral* behavior of mankind. Pursuit of a natural ethic, in contrast, is motivated simply by a desire to be distinctly human, to take a defining characteristic of humanness and refine and enhance that trait to the maximum extent possible.

This desire to be distinctly human, not by consequence of some fundamental law but by choice, must not be confused with Aristotle's *eudemonia*. Aristotle suggested that rationality makes humans unique from other animals and that, as a consequence, living in accordance with reason is the only way for humans to flourish. A natural ethic rejects the notion that rationality is a uniquely human characteristic, as earlier explained.

Pursuing morality simply because we can, even in the absence of any personal gain, has the potential for shifting the balance between favorable and unfavorable consequences of moral behavior. The remainder of this book explores the potential long-term global benefits of a natural ethic, if widely adopted.

CHAPTER 8

God, Greed and Glory: Motivations for Moral Behavior

*For a man to conquer himself is the first
and noblest of all victories.*

– Plato

We are taught from an early age that moral behavior is desirable as a ticket to heaven and God as a means of avoiding the agony of eternal damnation. This much has been explored in detail in previous chapters. Morality, according to these teachings, is not an obligation or a characteristic inherent to humankind but something to be cynically manipulated for other gains or bartered in exchange for bad behavior. This concept of morality for sale is now so deeply embedded into the fabric of our society that the underlying premise is rarely challenged, and may at great risk to those who dare. Along with that unquestioning acceptance comes the notion that the Bible is the primary if not sole source for this moral guidance. Yet the Bible is nothing of the sort. Only the most selective reading of the text could ignore the preponderance of jealous, hateful, wrathful, bloody, murderous, spiteful, mean-spirited and vengeful proclamations from God. *He is not a good role model.* That statement requires some explanation and background.

Religious morality is based on the idea that God reveals to humankind how to live through His word as laid down in the Holy Book. The Bible is the instruction manual to life. Just as one would expect the captain of a Boeing 747 to have read the operations manual for his airplane before departing with three-hundred passengers in tow, one would assume that most Jews and Christians would have read cover to cover the source document on how to live a good life. Not so. Surprisingly, few people professing a belief in God have read the entire collection of sixty-six books constituting the Bible. Anecdotally, the number is well under 10%, although the actual number is notoriously difficult to pin down.

That ignorance of the actual text might explain why a 2006 Gallup poll revealed that more than 30% of Americans believe the Bible to be the literal word of God. Only by *not reading* the document could the glaring inconsistencies and incongruities be readily ignored, which they must be if God is to remain an infallible moral counselor. Nevertheless, whether based on reading the Bible or not, a substantial number of the faithful believe the book to be literally true. So let's look at what the God of Abraham has to say about morality, in His own words.

Perhaps most striking is that slavery, incest, rape, polygamy and misogyny are fully condoned and encouraged by God. Literally. In *Genesis 4:19*, we are told that Jacob had two wives; Solomon was busier with seven hundred. In *Genesis 16:2*, Sarah gave permission to Abraham, her husband, to have sex with her maid, Hagar. Of course since Hagar was a maid, she did not need to consent to this relationship; so Sarah gave Abraham permission to rape Hagar so that she could act as a surrogate egg source. *Genesis 19:8* tells the story of how some friends of Lot, men from Sodom, were sitting around his house when those friends decided they would like to gang rape two female guests that Lot was hosting. But no, having a sense of decorum, Lot instead offered up his two daughters for the evening's activities: "I have two daughters which have not known man; let me I pray you, bring them unto you, and do ye to them as is good in your eyes." Such an action was perfectly acceptable because women were nothing but property to be used at will. Note that Lot said "which" and not "who" in reference to his daughters. *Genesis 19:30* goes on to tell us more about Lot, who was not satisfied with serving up his daughters for rape. Lot himself subsequently had sex with both. Each became pregnant as a result, each giving birth to a son. None of this is condemned in any way by God.

God makes clear throughout the Bible his view that women are unclean and the source of man's biggest woes. God's brutal treatment of women must bring into question His judgment if the Bible is the direct word of the Almighty. *Ecclesiastes 25:18* claims, "Sin began with a woman and thanks to her we all must die."

Leviticus 15:19-30 contains a series of long passages that condemn a woman as filthy while menstruating and only clean again spiritually and physically seven days after her period started. *Leviticus 15:28* gets quite specific, noting that on the 8th day, a woman can return to society, but only after she goes to a priest and sacrifices two pigeons or two doves (or turtledoves according to the King James Version). This sacrifice is necessary to atone for her sin of being unclean. *Leviticus 20:18* and *Ezekiel 18:5* continue the obsession with vaginal bleeding, basically equating that biological function with immorality.

God also has some quaint ideas about punishment for moral backsliding. *Exodus 21:16* tells us that if a man seduces a virgin, the crime is not against the woman but instead is considered theft of the father's property. *Deuteronomy 22:13* calmly demands that if a woman presents herself as a virgin but is not, on her wedding night she is to be taken to her father's house and stoned to death. Again, *stoned to death*, for those believing the Bible is the literal word of God. For all others, one must wonder what the passage is meant to signify if not literally true.

The admonition to kill morally errant women is difficult to fathom in modern times but makes sense in the context of women as chattel. We cannot accommodate shifts in values in more modern times, however, if the Bible represents His word. God's word would know no time boundaries between past and present, so his proclamations are as good now as then. God says that women are dirty property with little commercial value. He even offers a comparative price for a female specimen. The Ten Commandments make clear that a woman has no more value than an ax or a mule. We see this in what is perhaps the most frequently misquoted phrase of all time: the Commandment not to covet a neighbor's wife says nothing of the kind. The prohibition against adultery is covered elsewhere on the list. No, this Commandment reads:

> "Thou shalt not covet thy neighbour's house, thou shalt not covet thy neighbour's wife, nor his manservant (male slave), nor his maidservant (female slave), nor his ox, nor his ass, nor any thing that is thy neighbour's."

God simply tells us here that we should not covet our neighbor's *possessions*, one of which happens to be his wife, of no greater value than his oxen. If the idea of women as property is still not clear enough, *Exodus 21:7* allows a father to sell his daughter for cash if he needs extra income. By any standard, the sale of women is immoral, but that is exactly what the Bible encourages, explicitly, not as an allegory.

Much is made in modern society about the immorality of homosexuality. But if we draw that inspiration from the Good Book, a few adjustments are needed if we accept the text as divine. Christians point to the destruction of Sodom as described in *Genesis 19* as proof that God does not condone homosexuality. But not one passage in *Genesis 19* supports that conclusion. Yes, a mob was intent on gang rape, and some interpret that to include a demand for gay sex. But Lot would hardly offer up his daughters to gay men. In fact, the Bible contains only one unambiguous condemnation of homosexuality in *Leviticus 18:22*, which proffers the odd language, "and with a male you shall not lay lyings of a woman." Note what is missing here: the passage contains no prohibition against women having sex with other women. Lesbianism is never condemned in the Bible. Modern Bibles have expanded the original language to state that all homosexual acts by both men and women are forbidden, but that is just a contemporary fig leaf. The original language clearly refers to males only.

While killing is said to be prohibited as immoral, God-sanctioned murder is found throughout the Good Book. Fear of God's wrath is the main reason for the multiple dozens of ceremonies leading to animal sacrifice, which are meant to prevent God from striking down sinners. *Leviticus 16,* in chapters 1–34, describes in great procedural detail how to sacrifice bulls, rams and goats to atone for sins in order to avoid a premature death from a vengeful and jealous God. This is yet another passage where literal interpretation presents a dilemma. We do not see many churches today hosting goat sacrifices on Sunday, but that is exactly what the Bible tells us to do.

Perhaps all of this blood and guts is restricted to the Old Testament? No, violence is found throughout the New Testament as well. *Matthew 10:34* declares that Jesus is no man of peace. In his own words, Jesus says, "Think not that I am come to send peace on Earth; I come not to send peace but a sword." Some Christians try to explain that away as an anomaly, or to claim a meaning discordant with the words. But a violent Jesus is no fluke. In *Matthew 11:20–24,* Jesus condemns entire cities to dreadful deaths and eternal damnation because the hapless citizens did not appreciate his sermons. In *Mark 7:9–10,* Jesus makes known that he supports the idea of killing children who disobey their parents. If sacrificing goats and bulls presented a problem for literalists, the admonition to bump off rambunctious children creates an even bigger conundrum. "Kill your disobedient kid day" is not a common event at most houses of worship. And yet that is the word of God, something literalists cannot explain away. For all others, any alternative interpretation of the words from Jesus will require considerable creativity to avoid the harsh reality of his utterances.

Family values, beyond the tenuous survival of children, suffer a violent end as well upon close scrutiny of God's word. *Matthew 10:21* informs us that Jesus will tear families apart, so that brother will kill brother, father will kill child, and children will kill parents, all of which is perfectly acceptable because loving Jesus is more important than loving family. In a final blow to family values, in *Matthew 10:36,* we learn that "a man's foe shall be they of his own household." Jesus tells us here that if we love our mother and father more than him, we are not worthy of his love. This does not exactly describe the Brady Bunch.

God does not offer Himself up as a moral guiding light, but instead presents himself as wrathful and mean, a force to be feared rather than respected. That point is made repeatedly in Matthew, Mark, Luke and John. *Luke 12:5* admonishes us to fear God specifically because He has the power to kill and torture us. *John 3:36* emphasizes the point further, noting that if you do not believe in God, you will feel His wrath forever in hell.

Any document from which we derive moral guidance should at least be internally consistent, but the Bible is replete with contradictory statements. Obvious problems such as "an eye for an eye" and "turn the other cheek" are often explained away as being a difference between Old and New Testament. But that fails completely as a clarification if the Bible is the word of God unless we now want to claim that only the New Testament is His word. That is not tenable, though, because Genesis would be left hanging in the breeze and we cannot excise the story of origin from God's narrative.

But "coming in peace" in one passage, and then "not coming in peace but with a sword" in another is not even the most egregious type of inconsistency. The facts of the underlying story do not align. The Bible cannot even get straight when Jesus was born. *Matthew 2:1* and *Luke 2:1–5* tell stories with completely different timelines about the birth of Jesus. If the Bible were the word of God, would He not know the story of his own son's birth?

This religious narrative of murder, rape, incest, fratricide, polygamy and sacrifice provides the rationale for moral behavior in modern society. We can do better. Myths of a primitive nomadic society piled on empty threats and false promise, and then piled further atop crude fables, are no basis for human morality in the 21st century. *Whether the literal word of God, some form of allegory or a type of metaphor, the Bible offers no credible advice on daily life and how to live our lives well.* The Bible is not a viable source document for moral teachings. Even the most cursory reading of the text reveals the Bible to be nothing but a badly written story full of factual errors, inconsistencies and incongruities. The foundation on which religious morality is built is obviously fundamentally and fatally flawed. But religious leaders have a clever ploy to prevent close scrutiny by claiming blasphemy for any dissent or, in modern times, accusing doubters of intolerance. They must do so because the edifice will crumble if the founding document is examined too closely.

We are fortunate that these tactics did not stop the great inquiring minds emerging from the Dark Ages, who knew well that the Bible, and religion more broadly, offered no useful advice on human behavior. Those times did not tolerate heresy well, so the pioneers of enlightenment had to tread carefully. Those who did not paid the ultimate price. In 1619, the Italian philosopher Lucilio Vanini was burned at the stake for merely suggesting that humans derived from apes, 250 years ahead of his time.

Leading the charge to redefine human morality in this dangerous environment of the seventeenth century was Baruch de Spinoza. In spite of the obvious risk, he denounced religion and its moral philosophy as a fraud perpetrated on the superstitious by exploiting fear and ignorance.

Spinoza's primary contribution, among many, was to explain what being human means in a world without purpose or divine design and in which humans hold no special place. He created a viable and robust alternative to religion to explain the motivation for moral behavior.

His contributions deserve close study as an effective push against the tyranny of religious thought in defining human goodness. Others such as René Descartes and Frans van den Enden came before and influenced Spinoza, but all had considerably less impact on redefining western philosophy.

Early on, Spinoza rejected Descartes' philosophy based on the French philosopher's own famous words. "That nothing ought to be admitted as True, but that which has been proven by good and solid reasons." Spinoza took this sentiment to heart and felt that Descartes had not met his own test of validity. Unlike Descartes, Spinoza believed the Bible to be nothing but a tale told by man, and that the soul dies with the body.

Spinoza was excommunicated from his religious community, a pre-dictable outcome, because religion offers absolute truth about life, about morality, brooking no dissent. In dismissing that, Spinoza looked for truth from within, using only his internal resources. He reached all the way back to Socrates in his belief that "knowledge of the union that the mind has with the whole of Nature" is the primary basis for understanding the human condition. The mind and brain are one, and God plays no role in life, or death.

In publishing his seminal work, the *Tractatus Theologico-Politicus*, in 1670, Spinoza established himself as the first modern philosopher. He further developed his philosophy in his five-part *Ethics*, published three years later in 1673. The Church quickly denounced *Tractatus* as "the most vile and sacrilegious book the world has ever seen." The battle was joined, and today we still fight.

Spinoza's primary offense in the eyes of the Church was confusing God with Nature. That "confusion" becomes most alarmingly evident in Spinoza's view of the resurrection. "The passion, death and burial of Christ I accept literally, but His resurrection I understand in an allegori-cal sense." Church officials reacted in horror, rebutting that anything but literal belief in the rebirth of Jesus would call into question the validity and truth of the canonical Gospels. That in fact was Spinoza's explicit in-tent, couched in terms appropriate to the 1600's.

The principles of our natural ethic have a lineage that traces back directly to this moment when Spinoza drew "first blood" in 1670 upon publication of *Tractatus*. Spinoza turned to rationality instead of miracles to understand the world's mysteries, the first modern philosopher to do so. He believed that with sufficient time and study, the universe could be fully understood as a "self-sufficient machine" with no role, place or room for God. Through objective study, man could comprehend the ultimate mechanical principles of the universe without invoking the mysterious powers of an unknowable God. Knowledge would relegate the Almighty to the sidelines, unemployed. Spinoza boldly demoted the God of Abraham, who would finally join the venerable pantheon of discarded deities from the Incas, Mayans, Egyptians, Romans and Greeks, leaving none in His place.

Great modern thinkers like Richard Dawkins, Richard Feynman and Steven Weinberg continue that tradition by further strengthening the argument against purpose and design. Feynman in his usual understatement notes that "the theory that [the cosmos] is arranged as a stage for God to watch man's struggle for good and evil seems inadequate." Like Dawkins, Weinberg notes that the more we know, the more pointless the universe is revealed to be.

Let's summarize what we know. The Bible offers no guidance on morality and is nothing but a badly narrated story told in order to extract obedience from gullible masses. God either does not exist or if He does, He is irrelevant. The universe is unguided, uncaring and without purpose or design.

Where does that leave us? How can we be moral in a godless, pointless world? What is our motivation to be moral if not to please the Almighty?

Those questions rest upon the false premises that morality derives from God and that something has been lost by letting go of God. The book up to this point has been largely devoted to proving that neither premise is true. Still, faith is persistent and demands an answer even if the questions are flawed. And the legitimate query remains: what guides human morality?

Morality is our biological destiny. Traits that we view as moral are deeply embedded in the human psyche. Honesty, fidelity, trustworthiness, kindness to others, and reciprocity are primeval characteristics that helped our ancestors survive. Good behavior strengthened the tribal bonds that were essential to survival. What we now call morality is really a suite of behaviors favored by natural selection in an animal weak alone but strong in numbers.

Our inherent good, however, has been corrupted by the false morality of religion that has manipulated us with divine carrots and sticks. If we misbehave, we are threatened with the hot flames of hell. If we please God, we are promised the comforting embrace of eternal bliss. Under the burden of religion, morality has become nothing but a response to bribery and fear, and a cynical tool of manipulation for ministers and gurus. We have forsaken our biological heritage in exchange for a ticket to heaven.

By shedding the burden of a wrathful God, we reveal the power to create our own meaning, our own sense of purpose, our own destiny. By rejecting the false premises of religion we are free to move beyond the random hand we are dealt at birth to pave our own road to a better life. Neither birth nor God defines our fate. Imagine for a moment this world in which no invisible man hangs in the sky using magical powers in "mysterious ways" to control our life. Imagine that we can toss away the crutch of false hope and bad myth to walk unhindered down the path of personal responsibility.

By walking this path, we collectively have the opportunity to enhance our humanness, to further define who and what we are, by choosing to behave morally because we can.

> A natural ethic is based on the principle that with the ability to choose to be good comes the obligation to make that choice; *choosing* to be moral is what makes us special. The act of choosing to live a good life is the foundation for all pleasure, peace and happiness.

Whereas religion claims that happiness is found from submission to a higher power, a natural ethic defines happiness as the freedom to discover within ourselves our inherent good and then to act on that better instinct, not because of any mandate from God but simply because that choice makes us more human, more special. Happiness, virtue and morality are possible with nothing more than what is within each of us. We need not and cannot appeal to any other authority.

Virtue is its own reward, yes, but in a deeper sense than is often meant with that idea. Spinoza wrote in *Ethics*, " . . . men believe they are free in as much as they are conscious of their volitions and desires, yet ignorant of the causes that have determined them to desire and will." But we are not ignorant of those causes; we know, and we are each truly free. Our causes are our biology, our evolutionary history, our sociality. That the reward of pleasure, peace and happiness is achieved through the freedom to discover and act on our virtuous instincts is only half the story, though, the proximate half. Virtue is its own reward, too, as an essential element of humankind's nature that allows for our survival in large groups, the ultimate half.

With this personal freedom, of course, comes also the obligation for each of us to act wisely and responsibly. We fulfill this duty first by taking a more modest view of our place in the world. When we see that humans are a natural part of the ecosystem, not above or separate from the environment, we will protect the resources that sustain us. When we reject the hubris and conceit of religion, we will redefine our relationship with each other without calling upon God to smite our enemies. When we understand that true morality is independent of religious doctrine, we will create a path toward a just society. A natural ethic is our guide to a full life in which we no longer accept the arbitrary and destructive constraints of divine interference.

CHAPTER 9

Reflections in the Pond: Redefining Who We Are

It is impossible to live a pleasant life without living wisely and well and justly. And it is impossible to live wisely and well and justly without living a pleasant life.

– Epicurus

Modern man is the missing link between
apes and human beings.

– Stuart Caesar

We have reached a point where the theories underlying a natural ethic can be applied to everyday life, moving finally from ideal to real world. While this step is necessary, we approach the task with some reluctance and discomfort. First, a great danger exists in trivializing fundamental concepts by applying them to mundane concerns. Second, sometimes only a fine line delineates dogmatic preaching from an open presentation of ideas.

With these two deep concerns as a constant companion, what follows is a description of our personal odysseys and struggles to live by the guidelines of a natural ethic. Under no circumstances do we intend to impose our views on others. We are not attempting to replace one religion with another. We would serve badly as priests. No, the goal instead is to present to the world the principles of a new moral theory and to demonstrate how those principles can apply to life's difficult realities. Our hope is that among those who are listening, some will discover that a natural ethic resonates as a foundation for living a moral life.

CONCEPTUAL FOUNDATION FOR A NATURAL ETHIC: A RECAPITULATION

The freedom to discover and choice to act on our innate virtues free from divine influence defines our philosophy, but the definition did not appear from thin air. The idea is derived from set of fundamental truths and underlying assumptions about the human condition. These founding principles create the context in which a natural ethic can be fully understood, just as trigonometry and algebra create a path to understanding the elegance of calculus. So before we go further in applying a natural ethic to the complexities of daily life, let's review the conceptual framework on which a natural ethic is built.

• Life on Earth began as a contingent event (possible, but not certain), based on standard laws of physics and chemistry.

• Life is an arbitrary designation along a continuum of complexity; no sharp boundary separates life from nonlife. The living and nonliving share a wide margin of ambiguity. There exists no magic or divine spark of life.

• Evolution is an undirected process with no purpose, intelligence, or foresight.

• As with any species, human beings can be defined by a suite of evolved characteristics, the most prominent being the development of a large brain. But humans, who evolved under the same laws of nature as all other creatures on Earth, hold no exalted status in the pantheon of life.

In addition to these four primary concepts, a natural ethic rests on another seven critical ideas that together complete the foundation on which all subsequent claims are based.

1. All species exploit the environment to the maximum extent possible until either competition, resource depletion, predation, disease or other constraints limit growth and expansion. Social animals, from

insects to people, fin _____ cooperation and comp _____

2. Like every oth _____ h of
using all available _____ ical
difference, however _____ has
successfully co-opte _____ y as
we fight to pass our _____

3. This unique _____ ent,
and to threaten each _____ ects
over a short period. _____ an-
imals in pursuit of survival, our actions may cause our extinction, either
through the degradation of the resources on which we depend or, more
directly, through the use of weapons of mass destruction.

4. Advances in technology have not been matched by developments
in a moral code adequate to limit the destructive behavior of *Homo sapiens*. Inherent morality in the species, which would have an ameliorating
impact, has been corrupted by millennia of religious teachings, which
offer a false morality based on promises of eternal reward and threats of
damnation. War, overpopulation, unrelenting poverty, destruction of the
environment, and intolerance among fellow humans are all exacerbated,
to an important extent, by a false and obsolete religious moral code. A
new morality is needed to promote greater respect for each other and the
resources on which people depend, and to compensate for our species'
well-established destructive tendencies.

5. The large brains that gave us technology, prosperity, religion and
war also give us the ability to choose, personally and collectively, to be
concerned with the fate of distant generations and to behave for the
greater good.

[Handwritten note overlays text:] Choose a new secular morality or we will be no more than bacteria with e-mail accounts. We can control our own destiny and that is joyous

6 ... in God's image and told ... the amazing ability to ch ... op in a just society while ... ans fail to seize this oppo ... e than bacteria with e-ma ... be, if we ourselves decic ... tionships with each othe ...

... ng a future in which all of ... ich we depend, we have ... other species. The choi ...

BEYOND COSMIC DICE: A PERSONAL ODYSSEY

Understanding and embracing a natural ethic required us, the two authors, to adopt a new worldview. The greatest leap from the common human perspective was for us to recognize that life has no conferred meaning and that God is a false concept. At first this discovery might seem depressing and nihilistic. But the exact opposite is true. Understanding that life has no grand plan or conferred meaning was for us amazingly liberating when fully embraced. There is great emotional satisfaction in recognizing that all life is contingent, that is, possible but not inevitable. The question "why" becomes irrelevant and silly, and the burden of trying to find the answer to an impossible question is lifted. Asking "why" about life is as futile and meaningless as asking why a roll of the dice came up six on the first throw and three the next. Asking why simply is not a valid question. There is no why.

How do we find comfort and solace in a natural ethic, then, with no guiding hand from above, and if we cannot ask why? The two of us find solace in knowing that, *within the limits of chance*, we can take full control over our own lives and can be fully responsible for our own actions. We do not fear some horrible deity above that we are unable to understand, one with unlimited powers and acting for unknown reasons. Being alive is an amazing roll of the cosmic dice, not a directive from God. Only we are responsible for our lives, not an invisible man in the sky with magical powers. We can control our own destiny, and that is joyous.

But what exactly is meant by that caveat "limits of chance?" In daily life, we routinely make decisions that affect ourselves, our family and friends. The outcome from those many choices is much in our own hands, independent of surrounding circumstances: we can create opportunity for advancing our life and we can mitigate risk; we can choose to be moral; we ourselves can create meaning and purpose in our lives. We have tremendous power to create our own path. We are masters of our own thoughts.

But we occupy a world in which *randomness plays a role.* Some events in life, both trivial and grand, are simply beyond our control. Getting hit by a drunk driver while strolling on a sidewalk cannot be avoided by careful planning or by becoming a better person. Such a sad fate is not an act of God but an act of randomness, without any meaning. This is the limit of chance. The dice rolled six instead of three. There is no secular version of divine justification, because there is no justification of any kind.

So we must acknowledge that we live in a contingent world. But that is no excuse for shirking responsibility, or for not taking control of, and responsibility for, our lives. Randomness exists in the background but most events in our daily life are under our direct command. Taking control of our lives is joyous. Our inner life, our own thoughts, our acts of kindness, our responsibility and honesty, are all immune to the random events in the world around us. We can, with a natural ethic, move beyond the randomness of cosmic dice. The choice to be moral is a prime example.

NATURAL ETHIC GUIDELINES:
PERSONAL MORALITY

A natural ethic clearly does not offer the equivalent of biblical proclamations, or the proscriptions of the Qur'an mandating precise details of personal hygiene. Instead, the central tenets of a natural ethic offer a common understanding of our obligations to the environment, to our neighbors and to ourselves.

The guidelines presented here are personal, not universal. These guidelines represent our attempt to apply the principles of a natural ethic to our own daily lives. As emphasized earlier, we have no intention of imposing our views or creating mandates for others. Each individual must derive his or her own set of personal mandates. The admonitions that we articulate are solely for ourselves.

On the other hand, others might find our list a good starting point for applying a natural ethic to their own circumstances. Each person will develop a unique approach tailored to personal need. While there will certainly be variation in individual lists, each will share the common characteristic of being consistent with the underlying philosophy.

Variation should not be understood, however, to mean that everybody has free reign. Our mutual obligations create boundaries around individual moral codes. That is analogous to free speech being defended up to the point where speech creates injury to others, such as falsely yelling, "Fire!" in a crowded theater. As emphasized in our discussion of moral relativism, free speech, yes, but within responsible confines. Personal choice has limits.

The individual nature and personal character of these guidelines are demonstrated clearly by the fact that we, the authors, do not fully share a common list. We come from different cultures and backgrounds and therefore, like many others, cannot be expected to view life from the same perspective at all times. For example, we both agree that we should be completely honest, but we disagree on implementation. One of us (JS) takes the extreme view that honesty is mandatory in all matters at all times in all circumstances and that no form of deceit of any kind is acceptable, regardless of intent or impact. GNS, on the other hand, believes that intention and impact can allow for some forms of deceit that are fully consistent with our admonition to be honest. Our differences become clear in the example of throwing a surprise party for a loved one. GNS believes that such harmless and fun deceit falls well within the boundaries of the guideline, whereas JS does not.

Another difference is illustrated in our respective response to a gift that we find undesirable, although given with the best intentions. JS would, with as much tact as possible, be quite open about the gift's undesirability, whereas GNS would have no qualms, in this particular circumstance, about telling a white lie.

The interesting point here, however, is not so much divergence but commonality in spite of our different upbringing. Our small differences simply reflect natural variation in individual experiences. The large areas of overlap in our perspectives, in contrast, are a consequence of the natural basis of our moral code, shared as an inherent human characteristic. Building on this common foundation, we have developed a shared list of guidelines, presented in no order of priority, which appropriately reflects our attempts to apply a natural ethic to our daily lives.

Respect the environment

If humanity fails to use vulnerable natural resources sustainably, all that follows here has little meaning, for *Homo sapiens* will no longer roam the Earth. Human morality obviously has little meaning in the absence of any humans. Respecting the environment is therefore a primary tenet of a natural ethic, preceding all others.

The vast majority of people in the western world now live in highly industrialized societies. While this migration to urban and suburban living has conferred

"Commandments"

...traordinary advantages and comforts to millions of individuals, one consequence is that people have become
removed from the natural resources on which society depends. Daily lives are not typically affected by nature
other than by weather. But even in this setting, positive
environmental impact can result from small acts, such as
personal efforts to conserve energy, recycle and minimize
wasteful consumption. Equally important is public support for environmental laws that reduce greenhouse gas
emissions, promote sustainable use of renewable
resources, reduce or eliminate pollution and protect
critical habitat and endangered species.

Be honest

Be completely honest in all aspects of life. That
means no easy answers to avoid embarrassment, no half-
truths, no deceit through either omission or commission,
and no perjury. Certain social or professional situations
might require deft handling with grace or humor, but be
honest always.

Be reliable

Always mean what is said, and say only what is
meant. Always do what is promised. Never promise what
cannot be delivered. A person's word should be so sound
that once uttered, all who hear know the deed is done,
without question.

Be responsible

Assume full responsibility for each and every action
taken and every commitment made. Make no casual commitments; treat each commitment, no matter how small,

as a trust never to be violated. If that is not possible, then do not make the commitment. While chance plays a role in life, rarely is somebody a victim of circumstance. Any reasonable commitment will account for the normal vagaries of life and potential obstacles that must be overcome. Any failure to meet a commitment or to fulfill a responsibility must not be passed to others or excused as a result of unforeseen hurdles.

Be faithful

Honesty, reliability, and responsibility all demand that partners in a monogamous relationship remain absolutely faithful, assuming a sex life compatible with the explicitly stated and reasonable needs of both partners. Nobody would deny the occasional urge and temptation to stray at least at some point during a long relationship. The desire is normal but the obligation to resist temptation is not negotiable. Monogamy is based on trust, which once lost is lost forever.

Respect and be tolerant of others

Recognize and welcome the tremendous diversity of human thought and culture. Take the best from diverse views encountered. Avoid senseless distinctions between the sexes. In spite of obvious anatomical and physiological differences, the two sexes are equally well adapted to life and equally deserving of all rights. Some of the world's greatest ills result from intolerance, the numerous forms of "isms," and a false sense of righteousness. These sentiments should be strongly resisted. Be open to the idea that long-held convictions may be wrong.

Question assumptions. Allow for emotional and intellectual growth by nurturing and welcoming variety.

Do no harm to others

Except in self-defense, or in the case of national defense in times of hostility, no justification exists for harming another person. The premeditated taking of another life is perhaps the ultimate immoral act. But this guideline applies to emotional as well as physical harm. Verbal or behavioral abuse is unacceptable. Strive to ensure that every interaction is positive, to the degree possible. Always assume the best in others until proven differently, but mount a strong defense when necessary. Do not attack first, but defend vigorously against personal assault, because pacifism in the face of aggression encourages further attack.

Be happy for the success of others

Avoid the destructive emotion of envy by striving to be self-content. Evaluate if a longing is healthy and reasonable. If so, devote creative energies to obtaining the object of desire. If not, relinquish that particular dream, and wish well to those who have what was earlier coveted.

Cherish family and friends

Contemplate just for a moment life without friends and family, and the importance of both quickly becomes evident. Without family and friends, life would be intolerably lonely and empty, no matter the degree of inner strength or personal wealth. Nourish these relationships and be available for family or friends whenever needed.

Enjoy safe and responsible sex

Sex between consenting adults is normal, healthy, exciting and fun. But because of the risks of disease and unwanted pregnancy, sex is in a category different than eating ice cream and demands a high degree of adult responsibility. Practice birth control appropriate to personal reproductive goals, using any suitable method. Enjoy sex, in whatever variety is appealing. For those not in a stable, monogamous relationship, use protection to avoid venereal disease. Avoid promiscuity, which is counter to the guidelines counseling moderation and balance. Promiscuity comes with no concise definition, but sex should be well balanced with all of life's other pleasures.

Nourish good health

Promote good health through proper habits of eating, drinking and exercise. Identify a weight not to be exceeded and do whatever necessary, within healthy bounds, to remain below that weight. Moderation and balance are essential. Ensure proper monitoring of health and fitness through appropriate medical examinations. Every body should be treated with the respect and caring deserving the precious opportunity of life. The very value of life is diminished when the body is neglected.

Be true to yourself

Given any choice at all, take no action that will cause shame in public or private. Even with highly personal matters, act only in a way that would be proudly discussed publicly, using the concept of exposure as a guiding principle in evaluating if a contemplated action is desirable.

Be moderate in all things, including moderation

Moderation in eating, drinking, sex, exercise, work and play is a virtue, and should be the norm in daily life. But moderation can itself be taken to an inappropriate extreme. Exploring limits occasionally requires some excess so that the boundaries of reasonableness can be defined, and redefined, with growth and learning.

Be consistent

Remain on the path appropriate to personal goals, but adapt flexibly to new circumstances. Consistency in views, perspectives and behaviors provides a stable platform for growth and personal relationships. However, in an ever-changing world, consistency should not be dogmatic and should allow for flexibility in the face of compelling evidence for change.

Disdain mediocrity

Aim high, think big, and push to the extreme limits of natural ability. Mediocrity is a powerful enemy of self-improvement and personal ambition. Once mediocrity is accepted at work, home or play, and in any personal relationships, motivation to strive harder is severely diminished. Life is too short and precious to waste toiling for mediocre results. Having tried to achieve greatness and failed is better than the alternative.

Find balance in life

Excess in any one area of life for an extended period is usually detrimental to overall quality of life. Happiness and peace can be found by properly balancing focus on family, time with friends, career development, and recreation. An inordinate focus on a narrow interest diminishes pleasure and reward in areas neglected. Finding balance enables more of life's rich and disparate offerings to be sampled. Even Olympic athletes, who perhaps have the clearest justification for excessive focus, must at some point develop other aspects of their lives. Avoid obsessions and fetishes. Excessive focus is not necessary to fight mediocrity. Do not take life too seriously.

Live for today, plan for tomorrow

Acknowledge each day the joy of being alive and live each day to the fullest, to a degree that is responsible. Find a healthy balance in extracting the most from life every day, and the prudence of delaying rewards when necessary to plan for a productive and happy future. Sacrifice and self-discipline are necessary to achieve greatness in life, but a little indulgence each day honors the pleasure of being alive.

At different life stages, the balance between these opposing forces will tend to shift. With age, experience and accomplishment comes a natural tendency toward reaping the rewards from past sacrifice. A serious student will devote years of hard study toward the benefits of a degree, while others during that time are enjoying more of life on a daily basis. But that sacrifice once made yields a commensurate reward in future pleasures. No formula exits to balance self-indulgence and self-sacrifice. The best approach is to incorporate a clear recognition of the dilemma into life's daily decisions.

Be curious

Always continue to learn; read; expand and challenge the mind. Learn something new every day. Study political science and natural history in order to understand current circumstances, events, other cultures, and sense of place in the world. Watch less television or, better yet, none at all, play fewer video games, and spend less time surfing the Internet.

Use time wisely

Accomplishing good is a complex task and requires a high degree of efficiency because life seems short. As a consequence, a number of practical tools needs to be adopted in order to integrate a natural ethic into daily life:

Be organized. Good planning requires good organization, in both personal and professional spheres. Keeping home and office neat and clean is essential to maintaining an uncluttered and organized mind free for more creative pursuits.

Practice good time management. Time is a valuable and scarce commodity that requires careful management in a world growing increasingly complex. How to achieve that goal is highly personal. Here are some basic suggestions: write down a list of tasks each day, and cross them out when done; diligently mark on a calendar all commitments as they are made. While seemingly trivial, these simple acts are in fact the foundation for an organized and productive life.

Plan ahead. Responsibility and reliability are not magical qualities that appear from nothing. These require diligence, dedication and planning. Reliable and responsible behavior can be achieved only by planning sufficiently far ahead.

Take calculated risk. Any worthwhile achievement in life will entail some risk in some form. Do not shy from risk, for that is necessary to conquer mediocrity. But practice sound risk management. Risk does not imply recklessness. Understand the potential costs and benefits of any risk, and work to minimize the former and enhance the latter. Risk tolerance should be commensurate with the potential gain and appropriate to circumstances.

Never procrastinate. "Never put off until tomorrow what can be done today" seems trite, but the admonition is essential to a life fulfilled. Do difficult tasks first. Procrastination is a sign either of weakness or that an action being contemplating should not be. If the former, gather strength to do what is necessary, even if unpleasant. If the latter, take heed and reevaluate.

Donate to charity

Share good fortune with others by donating to worthy causes. Donate money or time to the degree that is prudent and appropriate to personal circumstances at the time of giving. Social, cultural and environmental causes all present ample opportunity for charity.

Respect animal rights

All domesticated animals should be treated humanely, given adequate food and veterinary treatment, and placed in an environment supportive of both physiological and psychological needs. Animals raised for food should be slaughtered as humanely and painlessly as possible. Pets deserve yet an additional layer of protection and care because pets have been elevated by human intervention to the status of friend or family member. That the animal might be unaware of this special status matters not.

Leave the world a better place

Have a net positive effect on the world. Strive to contribute positively to family, friends and society through a lifetime of good deeds. Be more prone to give than to take, but do not be selfless to a degree that endangers the ability to enjoy the gift of life.

NATURAL ETHIC GUIDELINES AND THE TEN COMMANDMENTS

In reading these guidelines, a question might arise among Jews and Christians as to how the guidelines relate to the Ten Commandments. People generally believe, incorrectly, that all of the Commandments govern moral behavior in society. But as mentioned earlier, the first four Commandments relate directly to the belief in God and have nothing to say about moral behavior.

All the Commandments, starting at *Exodus 20:2–17*, and found in other versions in the Old Testament in *Exodus 34:12–26* and *Deuteronomy 5:6–2*, actually contain twenty-five instructions, generally arranged into the ten sections most familiar from the *Exodus 20* version. In addition, the Commandments are supplemented throughout the Old

Testament with over six-hundred additional rules and regulations. Even with this extensive coverage, the Commandments and supplemental decrees ignore, treat superficially or are now entirely irrelevant to many morally sensitive issues. Thorny questions, for example about abortion and euthanasia, which some may believe are encompassed under "Thou shalt not kill," are not adequately nor appropriately addressed by the Ten Commandments.

While the Commandments, in their various forms, are accepted by Jews and Christians, two are consistently broken by most Christian denominations regardless of any justification, rationalization or subsequent interpretation offered by the religious hierarchy. The second Commandment states that a "jealous God" prohibits making "any graven image, or any likeness of any thing that is in heaven above, or that is in the Earth beneath, or that is in the water under the Earth." Yet Eastern Orthodox churches are densely decorated with ornate icons, Roman Catholic and most Protestant churches depict Jesus, the Virgin Mary and the Saints in paintings, stained glass and statues, and virtually every church has an image of a crucified Jesus displayed prominently at the altar. Commandment #4, proclaiming that the Sabbath should be remembered and kept holy, is also routinely ignored by many practicing Jews and Christians.

Natural ethic guidelines include, but go well beyond, the remaining six Commandments. Honor thy mother and father (#5) is included in "cherish family and friends." Thou shalt not kill (#6) has the same sense in prohibiting murder as "do no harm to others." The guideline to "be honest" includes commandment #7, thou shalt not commit adultery, commandment #8, thou shalt not steal, and commandment #9, thou shalt not bear false witness against thy neighbor. Of course the prohibition against adultery, commandment #8, also falls under the guideline to be faithful to a spouse or significant other. Thou shalt not covet thy neighbor's house, thou shalt not covet thy neighbor's wife (#10) is encompassed under "be happy for the success of others." Just three of the natural ethic guidelines, therefore, capture the six Commandments from the Bible that touch on morality. The remaining personal guidelines are clearly distinct from the ten biblical Commandments and offer a significantly different set of individual moral standards.

Implicit in the pursuit of a natural ethic is the existence of "sinners," because humans often fail to fulfill their own best intentions. Exceeding the limits of personal guidelines is as easy as violating any other set of social expectations. The difference between sinning against religious morals and a natural ethic is great, however, because in the case a natural ethic, a person sins against his or her own free conviction, not a divine authority. Therefore, the punishment of guilt is potentially much stronger and deeper as a violation against self, and perhaps a much greater motivating factor in preventing future transgressions.

CHAPTER 10

Getting Our Act Together:
A New Morality

As is a tale, so is life: not how long it is,
but how good it is, is what matters.

– Lucius Annaeus Seneca

An ethical man is a Christian holding four aces.
                                              – Mark Twain

Divine morality is the absolute negation of human morality.
                                              – Mikhail Bakunin

Human beings are above all social creatures. We belong to many communities, from our immediate families and local neighborhoods to larger groups in our surrounding counties, cities, and states. We also inhabit a global human society increasingly connected across national boundaries. As productive members of these disparate societies, people living a natural ethic on a daily basis can have an important impact beyond self at different levels of social and political organization. The cumulative effects of many people acting individually will have broad consequences. But people acting together toward a defined political agenda accelerate the effect. A common agenda creates a social climate more conducive to the wider and more rapid adoption of a natural ethic.

Because personal actions can lead to political consequences, the two areas have considerable overlap. Some topics are therefore discussed in the context of both personal and cultural morality.

The political agenda that derives from a natural ethic does not fall easily within typically defined political parties of western democracies. The agenda is defined by issues, not rigid ideology, and would probably be considered liberal by conservatives, conservative by liberals, and too extreme by moderates. By evaluating issues from the perspective of a natural ethic, rather than viewing them through the lens of party ideology, the hypocrisy and misguided actions resulting from political excess can be largely avoided.

Political positions often result from adopting, without deep thought, a party platform that may be defined by left or right extremists, and party loyalty can lead to an agenda that might be rejected on even the most cursory personal reflection. With a focus on a natural ethic, politics becomes more local and more personal, but more selfless at the same time as each individual considers the greater good.

The list of issues provided in the next section is an example of how we apply the central tenets of a natural ethic to the political arena. The list is not comprehensive and does not attempt to create a set of mandatory political positions that must be adopted, because a single, universal platform does not exist. As with personal moral guidelines, each person must develop his or her own sense of the political implications of a natural ethic.

NATURAL ETHIC GUIDELINES: CULTURAL MORALITY

- EDUCATION

A society that is largely scientifically illiterate will be ill equipped to survive in the 21st century, unable to guide advances in science and technology toward the greater good. Although understanding basic science is critical to everyday life in a technology-driven world, the subject is given inadequate treatment in most public schools today. As a result, people are often poorly equipped to understand the complexities of an issue before forming an opinion about the costs and benefits of adopting or restricting a particular technology.

Nearly all the great ethical challenges facing society today are exacerbated to some extent by rapid advances in science and technology. Current political, religious and educational institutions are improperly armed to address the moral consequences ensuing from scientific achievements.

In any society dominated by religion and religious morality, technology often proceeds at a pace greater than society's ability to address the associated moral dilemmas. The issue of therapeutic cloning offers a prime example. Religious bias and scientific illiteracy combine powerfully to restrict a technology with extraordinary potential for good and with little associated risk.

The solution is not to retard technologic advances, from which people benefit greatly, but to adapt school curricula accordingly and accelerate the adoption of an ethical code capable of addressing these challenges.

The urgent need to reform our system of education is made evident by the sad state of public schools in America. Nowhere is this better illustrated than by the issue of evolution as taught in the United States. Evolution is one of the most successful, thoroughly documented scientific discoveries in human history. However, more than seventy-five years after the trial of State of Tennessee *v* John Scopes and despite incredible advances in biology, many public school boards strive to eliminate the teaching of evolution from the curriculum.

Rather than keeping apace of scientific advances, the U.S. system of education has fallen woefully behind. If a scientific discovery as important, mainstream, and established as evolution can be a source of controversy for school curricula, even if only in a few states and only sporadically, society is extraordinarily vulnerable to the results of a general decline in science education.

A brief history of evolution and education reveals the depth of the problem. More than forty years elapsed after the Scopes trial before the Supreme Court ruled in 1968 that banning the teaching of evolution was unconstitutional (Epperson *v* Arkansas). The antievolutionists then changed tactics by attempting to equate evolution with a religious belief, arguing that evolution was not an established fact. The word *theory* associated with the discovery was grossly misunderstood or intentionally twisted by those seeking to force on public school students a single religious view of creation. Creationists and their allies express no reservations about teaching the Theory of Relativity as fact, but they attempt to sow confusion by absurdly calling evolution a belief on equal standing with the Theory of Creation.

Teaching evolution is equal to teaching that the Earth is a sphere or that the sun is the center of the solar system. All are established facts. Some may still believe that the sun revolves around the Earth as the Bible implies, but including such an idea in a school curriculum is unacceptable. Teaching creation according to Genesis also would require the science curriculum in public schools to include the notion that a great fish swallowed Jonah, that Joshua made the sun stand still, that Noah put a breeding pair of every animal species on a boat, and that the Earth was created in six days, along with a host of other literal interpretations of the Bible.

How can society hope to teach children the basics of science, which are essential for being able to evaluate the moral implications of technical issues, when forced to fight this primitive battle? The public education system is broken and desperately needs focused attention, but civil society is forced to divert time and resources to a ridiculous battle more appropriate to the 1600's. But fight we must. The religious right must be stopped to ensure that children receive an education that prepares them for modern life in a technologically advanced society.

Without winning the battle on teaching evolution, there is no hope of conquering scientific illiteracy in general. Failure to do so has serious consequences. Ignorance of scientific principles prevents the public from distinguishing the dangerous from the harmless and from preventing the abuse of science for malevolent purposes. On the basis of bad science, governments support costly efforts to enforce ill-conceived laws to protect consumers from nonexistent or negligible risk, while draining resources from areas of critical need.

Ignorance of science allows the public to be deceived by a barrage of dubious claims. The antivaccine movement is a classic case. Vaccines are one of the greatest achievements of modern medicine, saving hundreds of millions of lives and improving the quality of life for countless others, but because of medical illiteracy and misplaced religious zeal, some parents are, in a display of dangerous ignorance, forcing school boards across the country to accept students with no vaccination history.

Vaccinations, however, are only the tip of a dangerous iceberg. Scientific illiteracy is pervasive and the list of consequences almost endless. The public is unable to filter exaggerated claims by environmental groups (Alar in apples) from legitimate concerns (global climate change). People opposed to irradiated food ignore the existence of more than fifty known strains of *E coli* that can cause bloody diarrhea, kidney failure, and death. This is a typical case of poor risk-benefit analysis. People are duped by claims of harmful emissions from cell phones. Life-saving diagnostic x-rays are eschewed from fear of radiation and vulnerable people are persuaded to rely on crystals and astrology for guidance.

Without an ability to reason critically, people believe in weeping statues of the Virgin Mary, the existence of a carved face on Mars, out-of-body experiences, and Christ's image captured on the Shroud of Turin. Among the most notable miraculous relics of Catholicism is the much publicized "blood" of San Gennaro, patron saint of Naples. Since the fourteenth century, a substance said to be the dried blood of the martyred saint periodically liquefies and reddens indicating good years and bad, according to legend. Virtually the entire metropolitan congregation turns out once a year to wait anxiously as the miracle proclaims the city's fate. The explanation is absolutely trivial. Many substances, including mixtures readily available to medieval chemists, have the property exhibited by the purported blood.

Religion has no monopoly on uncritical thinking. Former NASA administrator Dan Goldin, while defending funding for the space agency, was famously asked, "Why are we building meteorological satellites when we have the Weather Channel?"

To fight this scourge of illiteracy, people must move beyond silly controversy, such as whether to teach evolution, and emphasize the basics of reading, language proficiency, history, math, and science from the early grades, and build on that foundation through to graduation. To combat scientific illiteracy, middle-school students should be required to demonstrate a minimal level of scientific knowledge against a national or international standard as a requirement for graduation. Society does no service to the student or to itself by graduating children ill-prepared for today's world.

- ### ENVIRONMENT

Responsible and careful stewardship for the environment is a direct consequence of a natural moral code. With the realization that each person has control of his or her own destiny comes a strong sense of personal responsibility and a collective sense of stewardship for our host planet, home to everything we know.

Sustainable use of resources and respect for the environment have become moral imperatives because of mankind's global dominance and capacity for large-scale destruction. Earth is the extraordinary product of billions of years of transformations and balanced interactions between the physical world and biosphere. This balance is at risk because of mankind's inability to reconcile its needs with environmental conservation. Only humans can restore balance and steer away from global destruction with careful management. The future of life on Earth will be affected to an important degree by how well we respond to this challenge.

The challenge can be met successfully only with a change in attitude. The world was not created by God in six days and given to humans for their sole benefit. People are part of the environment, not separate from their sustaining resources. Destruction of the environment is a direct attack on humankind because it threatens the materials that sustain life, assaults human heritage, and directly fouls our own nest.

The change in attitude toward the environment must also recognize legitimate human needs. The radical environmental movement must be rejected as inconsistent with a natural ethic and harmful to environmental protection. Extremists fail to recognize that all animals naturally impact the environment, and all require use of the Earth's resources. Humans are no different. Radicalism can cause harm directly, such as in terrorist attacks on research facilities, as well as indirectly by creating adverse publicity for more necessary efforts to protect the environment. Arguments put forth without proper scientific rigor have confused the issue, undermined otherwise legitimate basic assumptions, and cast doubts on the credibility of the movement as a whole.

Even more detrimental to a serious commitment to sustainability is the so-called wise use movement promoted by industry to justify degrading the environment. The term *wise use* is a sinister means of co-opting and confusing the well-established principle of sustainability. Both extremes of radical environmentalism and blind industrialization harm legitimate efforts to promote responsible conservation.

A natural ethic requires, as a moral imperative, prudent stewardship of the environment and sound resource management. Humans possess the means to flourish over countless generations in a stable, high-quality environment. To do so, society must pass and enforce laws that promote improvement in quality of life while indefinitely preserving a healthy environment. The two goals are not incompatible and can be mutually reinforcing when wisely pursued.

• POPULATION

The Bible promotes unrestrained growth of the human population. The Roman Catholic Church teaches that, with the exception of abstinence, any form of contraception is seen as an affront to God. This position demonstrates the pernicious effects of religious extremism and directly contradicts a natural ethic.

The argument against these religious teachings on population control is distinct from the contentious issue of abortion. Preventing a sperm from fertilizing an egg can hardly be seen as murder, because nothing yet has been conceived. Abstinence or a physical barrier between sperm and egg are equally forms of prevention. The only remaining justification for abstinence, as opposed to the use of contraception, is that sex without the intent to procreate is a sin.

Despite lessons from the Song of Solomon, the Pope confirms this view in stating unequivocally that sex must serve only the purpose of creating life. Pope John Paul II supported Paul VI's earlier stand in *Humanae Vitae*, the 1968 encyclical that condemned abortion and banned use of contraceptives. In 1981, in *Familiaris Consortio* (The Role of the Christian Family in the Modern World), Pope John Paul II wrote that couples "manipulate and degrade human sexuality" when practicing contraception leading not only to "positive refusal to be open to life but also to a falsification of the inner truth of conjugal love." Although convoluted, the meaning is unambiguous.

Martin Luther, in rare agreement with the Pope, said that contraception is a sin "worse than adultery or incest" in language not difficult to understand. Most modern Protestants and many practicing Catholics no longer hold this view. As the Pope's words make clear, though, leaders of at least some mainstream religions teach unambiguously that any form of contraception is a sin, *including within marriage*, even if the laity tend to ignore the teachings. The official view completely disregards the positive effect of protected sex in strengthening the bond between a loving couple. Teaching that sex without the intent to procreate is a sin is a classic example of moral and religious overreach.

These extremist religious teachings cannot be defended on the basis that only humans have sex without the intent to procreate, implying that the act must therefore be unnatural. The pursuit of sex for the sake of pleasure is not a uniquely human predilection. Nature presents many examples of animals that enjoy recreational sex, including bottlenose dolphins and many nonhuman primates. Bonobos, who along with chimpanzees are our closest cousins among the apes, frequently engage in sex and do so in virtually every partner combination imaginable, although close family members tend to avoid sexual contact. Despite this high degree of promiscuity, bonobos reproduce at a rate no greater than other closely related primates with more sedate sex habits.

Although having no basis in biology or reason, extreme religious mandates do have unfortunate consequences for the human condition. Unprotected sex leads to overpopulation, which contributes to poverty, disease, lack of educational opportunities, unsustainable resource use, and a host of other ills. The poor and vulnerable are preyed on to promote a Catholic Church policy that is rejected overwhelmingly by those with even modest levels of education. By no coincidence, the use of contraception and the reduction in average number of children women bear are directly related to the general level of female education in a society.

Adopting a natural ethic can ameliorate the negative consequences of this long history of promoting unfettered population growth. A natural moral code promotes responsible sex between consenting partners who use contraception or protection as they deem appropriate to achieve their own reproductive goals and good health. Having personal control of reproductive choices is an important step in helping families rise above subsistence-level poverty. Reproductive choice diminishes human suffering and has positive effects on the environment: striving to use scarce resources sustainably is a much more realistic goal when not fighting each day to stay alive.

INSTITUTIONAL INTRUSION ON PERSONAL CHOICE

The institutions of the church and state have a long history of denying individuals the right of personal choice. Although the problem of inappropriate imposition of institutional mandates is noticeably minimized in modern western democracies, invasive policies still intrude on personal freedoms. The problem of institutional intolerance is illustrated by three issues vexing modern society: abortion, euthanasia, and divorce.

Abortion

Prevention, not abortion, is the vastly preferred method of family planning. Abortion is an invasive surgical technique, physically and psychologically traumatic, expensive, and potentially dangerous. Whereas sex should be as frequent as desired, unwanted pregnancy should be exceptional rather than routine. Part of the adult responsibility commensurate with having an active sex life is prudent and careful use of contraception. Abortion should not be viewed as a population control issue, because the procedure should not be a primary tool for reproductive choice. However, if an unwanted pregnancy occurs, a women's right to choose must be strongly supported within the constraints of a natural ethic.

Abortion foes claim that the procedure is murder, based on the notion that a fertilized egg has the same suite of rights enjoyed by all humans. The belief that a few cells derived from a fertilized egg is a human being is a sad example of good intentions based on misguided notions of biology. The small ball of cells is *potentially* a human being, but so are eggs and sperm, even if to an unequal degree. All require certain conditions to realize the potential to become human. Ovulation and male masturbation would be acts of murder by the same logic that confers the status of humanness on a fertilized egg or early-stage embryo.

Somewhere between a just-fertilized egg and a baby about to exit the birth canal lies a distinction between potentially human and human. Because that line is difficult to draw does not mean that the line does not exist. Clearly, the division between potentially human and human is increasingly difficult to distinguish with time from conception, but even later stages of the embryo pass milestones that offer important guidelines.

In the absence of a central nervous system, the embryo is incapable of any sensation. Until a brain is formed with a functioning cortex, the embryo has no ability to form any conscious thought. Neural development begins early, but the process is slow relative to other organ systems. The three main lobes that will become the brain form by the twenty-ninth day. About six to eight weeks after fertilization, the first detectable brain waves can be recorded, but the brain is not nearly fully formed and the cortex is little distinguished. Before eight weeks, in the absence of any brain function, the growing embryo is little different in its human potential from a fertilized egg. Abortion at this stage is therefore fully acceptable.

Later stages of growth do not offer a sign as clear as brain development but the fetus provides another point of determination, although one involving a higher emotional and ethical cost in the hierarchy of decision-making. Before a fetus is capable of living outside the womb at week twenty-three, even with invasive medical intervention, the line from potential to actual human has not been crossed. Before week twenty-three, a premature baby cannot survive. Viability between weeks twenty-three and twenty-six is uncertain. After week twenty-six, survival is possible, although lungs do not reach maturity until week thirty-four and a suite of lifetime medical problems can be expected. Medical advances can only push this point of viability so far back toward conception because functioning lungs, even if not mature, must be present for a fetus to survive outside the womb. No amount of medical intervention before that point of development will change this fundamental fact of biology, which establishes a second threshold for abortion at twenty-three weeks. A science-fiction scenario of an artificial womb in the far future would not change this calculation of natural embryogenesis.

Beyond the point of viability outside the uterus, the threshold for when an abortion is a reasonable choice becomes significantly higher. Late-term abortions are difficult to justify except in the extreme case of rape or incest in which the victim had no access to medical care earlier in the pregnancy.

Euthanasia

Although sanctioned mercy killing is a difficult subject fraught with terrible moral peril, a patient's right to die under carefully controlled circumstances is fully consistent with a natural ethic. The issue requires careful consideration because euthanasia brings into sharp relief two competing principles: protection of human life and the right to decisional autonomy. The Roman Catholic Church firmly rejects any form of assisted suicide and euthanasia, as articulated in the 1980 *Vatican Declaration on Euthanasia* and affirmed in subsequent speeches by Pope John Paul II. In this, the Pope is aligned with Judaism and most Protestant denominations. In contrast, a natural ethic stresses respect for an individual's dignity and rights of autonomy. Because arguments of abuse are often used to oppose euthanasia, considerable attention is given here to ways of addressing and preventing such abuse.

Dr. C. Everett Koop, a former Surgeon General of the United States, said that " . . . we must be wary of those who are too willing to end the lives of the elderly and the ill. If we ever decide that a poor quality of life justifies ending that life, we have taken a step down a slippery slope that places all of us in danger." The underlying sentiment is sound but the conclusion is not. Fear of abuse is always legitimate but is not an adequate argument against meeting urgent societal needs. Rather than paralyze society with inaction, the proper approach is diligence and appropriate regulation to prevent abuse.

Almost 85% of Americans die in a professional health care facility. Of that group, about 70% choose to withhold some form of life-saving intervention, according to Dr. Lawrence M. Hinman at the University of California, San Diego. Nearly 60% of the total U.S. population, therefore, has already taken a step onto Dr. Koop's slippery slope. The danger to individuals and society feared by Dr. Koop has not materialized.

A patient's wish to withhold treatment to sustain life or his desire to accelerate an advanced stage of illness toward death is not a black and white distinction. Advances in medical technologies continue to enhance our ability to postpone death and increasingly force us to decide whether to allow ourselves to die. When does allowing ourselves to die differ from taking an active part in the process of dying? Does a distinction exist between a physician writing a prescription that he or she knows will be used by the patient for suicide and a situation in which the physician is present to facilitate the death at the patient's request?

The critical difference between what Dr. Koop said and what is advocated here is who makes the decision to die. His statement implies that somebody other than the patient makes the decision to die based on a subjective, arbitrary conclusion about the patient's quality of life. Dr. Koop is arguing against the utilitarian model in which euthanasia is seen as a tool to benefit society rather than the individual. That approach is indeed unacceptable.

Opponents of euthanasia and most historical debates on the topic often confuse the issue by assuming that the utilitarian model is the basis for discussion. They then argue that when society gives someone the power of life or death, we invite abuse, which is true, but not what most proponents of euthanasia are contemplating. Euthanasia consistent with a natural ethic advocates the *patient's* right to be allowed to die or to request the end to his or her own life.

A wall of safeguards must be erected to ensure that the patient's true wishes are respected and to ensure that nobody but the patient makes the decision to die. Procedures can be established to prevent abuse. For example, a patient would have to make his or her wishes known in a living will (an advance directive or power of attorney for healthcare), signed in the presence of multiple witnesses, at least one of whom is not related to nor has any financial relationship with the patient, when no doubt exists about the patient's sound state of mind. At a time near death, in circumstances in which the patient is no longer capable of communicating, the instructions in the advance directive should be carefully followed. Such instructions can include clear guidelines for a patient's wish for active or passive euthanasia.

Certain minimum criteria must be met, regardless of the patient's instructions. Delineating the boundaries of appropriate medical conduct by articulating these minimal criteria, although difficult, is no different from developing typical professional standards that provide guidance to physicians on their obligations to patients more generally. Criteria may include a doctor's certification that the patient would likely die in the near future, that prolonging the patient's life would cause significant suffering, and that the patient's wish to die cannot be accomplished without some assistance (if active euthanasia is the patient's wish). In the case of an infant or small child, both parents (if living) and three doctors from three different institutions should be allowed to make a unanimous decision on behalf of the patient if the minimal criteria are satisfied.

Even with the patient's instructions clearly articulated and a doctor's certification that the minimum requirements have been satisfied, any action facilitating the death of a patient according to that patient's instructions should require the written approval of at least three people, including the patient's physician, a family member, and an unrelated friend. Not everybody will meet the criteria or have family, friends, or doctors willing to sign the necessary documents. Not everybody can pass the eye examination for a driver's license, either, but society places certain limits on individual rights balanced against societal needs. Strict safeguards place a heavy burden on patients to plan ahead, but that is a necessary impediment to prevent abuse and to allow the freedom of choice in a society rightfully leery of ending life. Guidelines developed for assisted suicide in Oregon and for the euthanasia law in the Netherlands offer salient examples of how the competing need to respect life and autonomy can be addressed reasonably.

With proper safeguards in place, society should not prevent a patient from experiencing a peaceful and painless death, surrounded by family and friends. The bottom line is that euthanasia should be allowed by society, but barriers for implementation must be extraordinarily high.

Divorce

The decision to divorce must solely rest with the couple involved, not some external authority of church or state. If children are involved, society clearly has an interest in their well-being to prevent neglect and abuse. A community therefore has a role in ensuring that the *process* of divorce is consistent with basic standards, but not in the *fact* of the divorce.

For the sake of children innocently affected and for the benefit of the disputing adults, divorce should be pursued with careful consideration and only after all reasonable attempts at reconciliation have failed. However, divorce is not inherently immoral, and when sought with the appropriate intentions, divorce is fully consistent with a natural ethic. Any institutional intrusion with this decision, whether religious or secular, is grossly inappropriate. External constraint on a couple's choice about any aspect of their relationship is unacceptable.

Divorce is not the only decision at risk from invasive institutional interest. Any effort by a community to prohibit premarital sex between consenting adults, force prearranged marriage, or deny the possibility of divorce is fundamentally incompatible with the tenets of a natural ethic. These inappropriate intrusions of institutions into personal decisions can cause considerable cross-generational unhappiness and harm, not only to the affected individuals but to society at large. Personal choices must remain private, free from the prying eye of society.

• ARMED CONFLICT

War will continue to be embedded in the human condition for the foreseeable future. A strong defense against inevitable enemies is therefore essential to freedom and democracy, and that reality must be considered in setting national priorities. But a long-term, evolutionary view of the potential benefits of a natural ethic must also be considered. Although pursuit of a new moral code will not prevent conflict any time soon, society has to start somewhere. Pursuing a natural ethic would necessarily prevent one human from harming another without just provocation. Wiser environmental management brought about by a new moral perspective would reduce or avoid many conflicts now fought over scarce resources. Over time, enough people may adopt a natural ethic such that conflict would become less common or perhaps rare. In the meantime, maintaining a healthy and intelligently applied defense budget is critical. This is not a cynical position, but one that recognizes a difference between short-term needs and long-term objectives.

• GLOBALIZATION

For better or worse, globalization appears to be inevitable. Both potential costs and benefits are well understood. On the negative side of the ledger, globalization will increase homogenization and irreversibly destroy invaluable cultural diversity. Economic decision-making will become further removed from the individual and local interests. Globalization may lead to an even greater disparity of wealth among nations.

Despite these dangers, not all is gloom and doom. Globalization may have significant and positive impacts. Cultural and economic homogenization creates a climate less conducive to conflict. Moreover, an increase in global economic efficiency can result in more rational resource use and a more equitable distribution of lower-cost goods.

Globalization should be guided toward its positive consequences. Whether people reap the benefits of globalization or suffer its negative impacts will depend to some extent on how effectively the principles of a natural ethic are applied to the process.

• GENETICALLY MODIFIED FOODS

Poverty and hunger continue to plague humankind and the benefits of the first Green Revolution are reaching a limit to alleviate problems of food production. Genetically modified (GM) foods are a critical means of extending the Green Revolution, although not the only one. Changes in food distribution systems and the elimination of starvation as a tool of war also play a critical role in eliminating hunger. Yet despite the enormous potential benefit of GM foods, the technology faces fierce opposition. Some skepticism is justified but many of the risks are greatly exaggerated and legitimate concerns are often poorly understood by the general public.

For millennia, plants have been artificially selected through traditional breeding programs and introduced into the environment. As crop genetics became more amenable to laboratory manipulation, the process has become more accelerated and controlled. The novel combinations that can be created now present opportunities and dangers. The environmental and health risks are real and must be carefully managed and regulated closely. The damage caused by the unintentional spread of a novel genetic trait can be serious and irreversible and therefore requires a high degree of diligence. The transfer of pest resistance to weedy relatives of crop plants is an example of potential harm. Current regulations and enforcement are largely inadequate and should be strengthened to ensure uniform compliance at the global level.

The best way to address these dangers is to responsibly acknowledge them. Proper planting techniques and scheduled crop rotations, combined with careful regulation, can prevent the risk of spreading undesirable genomic traits from becoming a serious problem.

Another concern is that nontarget organisms, notably insects, will be harmed indirectly from genetically modified plants. Scientists were initially concerned, for example, that pollen from corn altered to kill moth larvae was also a threat to monarch butterflies. The fear was that pollen from the gene-altered corn was landing on milkweeds around farms and killing monarchs, which eat that plant. A dispassionate examination of the issue, however, reveals that butterflies and other insects are placed in greater danger by pesticides used on conventionally bred corn than by the pollen from modified corn crops. The legitimate issue is that unintended consequences must be anticipated to the extent possible (recognizing the potential irony) when introducing a modified crop into commercial production.

In the health arena, the threat of allergic reactions is a concern, but simple testing can prevent this from becoming an issue. Scientists genetically engineered soybeans to contain a Brazil nut gene in an attempt to make soy more nutritious. Tests showed that people allergic to these nuts also reacted to the modified soy. As was done in this case, known allergens can and should be tested when used in genetic engineering. In another twist on this technology, rather than introducing a foreign gene, many plants are modified by enhancing a gene already present. For example, gene sequences from cold-water fish have been inserted in some fruits to help them withstand colder temperatures. Those same genes, isolated from arctic flounders, are found naturally in fruit and perform the same function, offering protection against cold. An allergic reaction to fish, for those sensitive to seafood, would therefore not be likely when eating such modified fruit. In any case, the potential for the modified fruit to generate an allergic reaction can be tested, and an allergen should be tested in any application, independent of the underlying technology.

The other risk of using modified crops is political. Care must be taken to ensure that the benefits of crop modification accrue to local farmers and developing country economies, not exclusively to multinational corporations that presently control most genetically modified seeds.

Despite risks, the benefits of genetically modified food to global society are too great to ignore. Crops are modified to enhance nutritional value, increase abundance, promote resistance to pests, and create the ability to grow in harsh conditions of drought or high salinity. For example, the U.S. Department of Agriculture is working on wheat genes that will allow the crop to grow in conditions now too hostile. Rice enriched with vitamin A, such as Golden Rice, would help alleviate a widespread nutritional deficiency in Asia that has serious health consequences, including some forms of blindness. Golden Rice is a step in the right direction but greater advances in improving the nutritional quality of rice are needed. Pest-resistant crops reduce the environmental assault of pesticides, lower the cost of production, and raise productivity.

Genetically modified crops should not be used as an excuse to use herbicides indiscriminately by developing herbicide-resistant plants. Herbicide resistance was a useful trait to engineer as an early test bed for crop modification, but it is not the most desirable characteristic to pursue as the science matures. Unlike pest resistance, which can significantly reduce the application of farm chemicals, herbicide resistance may encourage environmentally unsound practices by augmenting the use of herbicides. The focus for genetically modified foods should be on improving nutritional quality, enhancing hardiness to allow crops to grow in hostile environments, and reducing the use of pesticides by harvesting insect-resistant plants.

With the important assumption that proper and rigorous management and regulations can be put in place internationally, genetically modified crops can be introduced safely and can significantly benefit the environment, reduce hunger and suffering, and create financial opportunities for poor farmers in areas currently unsuitable for crops.

• THERAPEUTIC CLONING

Efforts to prevent therapeutic cloning are seriously misguided and result from perhaps the most egregious example of scientific illiteracy in society. The intellectual deficit is particularly acute in our political leaders.

Any design to thwart advances in carefully regulated therapeutic cloning is highly immoral, because this research has the potential to relieve horrible suffering in millions of lives without presenting any threat or danger to society. Cardiovascular and nervous system diseases, diabetes, autoimmune diseases, and blood disorders are all targets for treatment through advances in therapeutic cloning. With the creation of stem cells from cloning, cures may be found for Parkinson's disease, Alzheimer's disease, stroke, epilepsy, multiple sclerosis, rheumatoid arthritis, and even paralysis caused by spinal cord damage.

Some who oppose therapeutic cloning maintain that creating human life only to destroy the resulting embryo is immoral. This argument misses the point that human life has in fact not been created and therefore is not being destroyed in this process. A cloned group of cells (blastocyst) is the product of an unfertilized egg artificially inserted with the nucleus of another cell, not the product of fertilization of an egg by a sperm. An attempt to represent this construct artificially created outside a womb as human is again analogous to calling an egg or a sperm a human being. All have some potential to become human, a capacity that is extraordinarily limited without further human intervention. In therapeutic cloning, the ball of cells created in the lab is typically teased apart to generate an embryonic stem cell line at the blastocyst stage. This detail is important. An embryo attaches to the wall of the uterus and begins developing *after* the blastocyst stage; stem cells are therefore created from an embryo before it has any potential for further growth. Steel beams lying on the ground have the potential to become a skyscraper with human intervention, but nobody would claim that the beams *are* the skyscraper.

All efforts to clone humans for reproductive purposes should be opposed. Although therapeutic cloning is fully consistent with a natural ethic, reproductive cloning is not and must be prevented through appropriate legislation and enforcement, independently of any issues concerning therapeutic cloning. A ban on therapeutic cloning will not reduce the likelihood of abuses leading to reproductive cloning and may have the opposite effect. Criminals intent on pursuit of reproductive cloning would not be swayed by a ban on something much more benign.

• ANIMAL RIGHTS

Just as the agenda of the radical environmental movement is not reasonable, extremism in protecting animal rights should be equally rejected.
This extremism is based on a flawed morality and overzealous application
of the sound and correct principle that animals have fundamental rights.

Carnivorous animals eat other animals, and the predator-prey relationships of this world are a natural component of healthy ecosystems.
Denying that relationship is foolhardy. Eating another animal is not immoral; predation is an act of nature. However, in pursing a natural ethic,
much more must be done to ensure that all animals in our care, including those used for meat, milk or eggs, are treated humanely and with dignity and respect, in conditions suitable to their physiological and
psychological well-being.

The picture fades into shades of gray and becomes more complicated
when animals are used for purposes other than nutrition. The use of animals in research is potentially not immoral as long as no reasonable sub-
stitute is available, the research animals are treated well and with respect,
suffering is avoided at all costs, the fewest number of animals are used to
complete the research, and the research addresses a topic that could generally be deemed important in advancing human knowledge. Research
should be completed using the most appropriate species having the least
developed central nervous system.

The threshold for using apes, dogs and cats in particular, or mammals in general, should be extraordinarily high, no matter how important
the underlying research may be. For primates, the rules regulating research should be identical to those applied to humans. The one exception
would be informed consent, which obviously is not possible to obtain.
Instead, a committee comprised of community leaders, scientists and animals rights advocates could by unanimous vote provide consent if extraordinary circumstances so warranted. That such consent would be
terribly difficult to achieve is appropriate and offers at least some

reasonable protection to any potential primate research subject.

Proper treatment must ensure that all possible means are used to minimize or eliminate pain and that physical and mental needs are adequately met. Even so, the goal should be a continuing effort to develop alternatives to the use of animals in research and, in the meantime, to reduce to the greatest extent possible the number of animals used. Any research proposing to experiment on animals should meet a significantly higher standard in funding requirements to ensure that these conditions are satisfied. Any abuse of the privilege of using animals for research should be severely punished.

Egregious examples of animal abuse, such as cockfights or dog races, are not acceptable. Frivolous use of animals, such as for fur in modern societies where superior materials are available, is also counter to the pursuit of a natural ethic and even more so when animals raised or used in this way suffer in inhumane conditions. Other immoral uses of animals include illegal trade of exotic and endangered species or parts thereof.

Some use of captive animals to promote education and the further protection of wildlife can be justified in certain well-defined and well-regulated conditions, but use of animals solely for entertainment for profit is not consistent with a natural ethic. Our humanness is diminished every time an animal is abused or used frivolously.

Destruction of habitat is also a serious threat to animals and as such is a form of misuse and abuse. The issue is one of degree, not absolutes. Humans, like other animals, have a natural need for territory and resources. Our actions become immoral when habitat is destroyed recklessly, with no thought or care to sustainable use. In some cases, the act is immoral *collectively*. A subsistence farmer burning virgin rain forest to plant a crop to survive and support his family is doing what anyone else would do in similar circumstances. Our obligation as a human society is to create conditions in which those actions are unnecessary, thereby creating an opportunity both for habitat use and preservation.

In any discussion of animals, the role of pets in human life must be considered. Elevation of individuals from other species to a status in which they are respected, loved, and accepted as family members is perfectly normal and a common practice across many cultures.

Western culture's revulsion of killing a dog for food, while condoning slaughter of cattle for beef, offers an example in which pets are morally distinct from other critters. Nothing in nature distinguishes these two sources of protein, only our own perception of hoof and paw. Because dog meat is as nutritionally valuable as beef, our sharp distinction between beef and dog is strictly a social and moral one. We disdain consuming dog meat because we attribute a certain level of sentience to our canine friends. Cows should be treated humanely while alive and in our care, but the expectation of killing the cow for food is the modern expression of a normal predator-prey relationship.

The social and moral distinctions that we construct around our pets impose on us certain responsibilities. This includes a duty to treat dogs, cat, birds and other animal friends with an extra degree of respect and dignity, even if the pet remains unaware of any special status. Mistreating or abandoning pets is unacceptable because we ourselves have raised the pet to an elevated status. Our own actions obligate us to ensure the well-being of all adopted animals.

• DEATH PENALTY

No country in the world uses the death penalty in a way that is morally acceptable. As a practical consequence, the death penalty is not consistent with a natural ethic as practiced today. As with all human institutions, the criminal justice system suffers in various degrees from corruption, incompetence, or malfeasance. Even the most ardent supporter of the death penalty would agree that, in some cases, innocent people are convicted, and the guilty walk free. Advances in DNA testing have proved that in the last ten years, at least 170 prisoners in the United States, innocent of the crime for which they have been convicted, have been sentenced to death. Dennis Williams and Verneal Jimerson spent eighteen years on death row in Illinois for a crime they did not commit. Kirk Bloodsworth wasted nine years on death row as a child killer while the murderer roamed free. There are more than 170 other known examples, and these are the "lucky" ones who were eventually freed before execution.

The penalty of death is too permanent to account for inevitable errors or willful misconduct on the part of police, judges, or prosecutors. The danger of executing an innocent person is greater than the societal benefit derived from putting a guilty prisoner to death, particularly when reasonable alternatives exist, such as life in prison with no possibility of parole.

These practical considerations and barriers lead to the question of whether use of the death penalty, if properly implemented, could ever in theory be consistent with a natural ethic. With such an emotionally charged and complex issue, no universally accepted answer can be given. As with honesty, divergent views, within boundaries, can be compatible with a natural ethic. These boundaries can be defined by understanding the goals of incarceration and punishment.

The rationale for imprisoning a convicted criminal is threefold: to protect society from future harm, to deter other would-be criminals, and to punish the offender. Given these objectives, a person can take the position, fully consistent with a natural ethic, that no circumstances warrant use of the death penalty, because nothing derived from the three purposes of incarceration can justify state-sanctioned infliction of physical harm. On the other hand, a natural ethic could also encompass the view that, in extreme cases, involving particularly heinous crimes in which guilt is certain (such as with war crimes and crimes against humanity), the use of the death penalty with proper implementation could be justified. However, these theoretical considerations, while accommodating divergent views, do not diminish the practical conclusion that use of the death penalty anywhere in the world today is not compatible with a natural ethic.

• PUBLIC INVESTMENT

The allocation of public funds immediately raises the question of relative priorities, which inherently contain an important moral dilemma. With finite financial resources, equally worthy needs cannot all be fully met. Society must therefore make difficult choices. In wrestling with this dilemma, a common mistake is made that urgent social needs, such as homelessness, hunger, and medical treatment for the poor, always take precedence in a moral hierarchy of competing demands.

In the competition for public funding, the false belief that human suffering is sacrificed to any cause not addressing an immediate human concern usually results in inappropriately low levels of support for other critical needs, such as environmental protection and scientific research. The underlying logic responsible for this paucity of funding is flawed on two accounts.

First, the vagaries of government funding create a different reality of opportunity cost. Deciding on appropriations is not a zero-sum process (adding money to one account does not necessarily mean taking funds from another), particularly when deficit funding is allowed. Although poverty and hunger have no place in a prosperous democracy, funding levels for those urgent problems do not suffer when other programs are supported. Let's look at a highly visible program of research and technology: space exploration. In the United States, the thirteen appropriations bills are passed largely independently of each other. If all funding for space exploration were terminated today, not a single penny would be transferred to another account for social services. In constant dollars, NASA's budget is now about half of its peak in 1966. That savings of nearly $14 billion per year has not gone to social programs or tax reduction.

Second, science and technology, including space exploration, are important enough that funding would deserve support even if at the expense of some social services. Just imagine the world today if Prince

Henry the Navigator had not initiated costly maritime expeditions from Portugal to the west coast of Africa in 1419, inaugurating the Age of Exploration. The motivation then was as it should be now: to advance human knowledge and reap the economic and technologic rewards of advanced exploration. Curiosity is one of humankind's defining characteristics. The quest to understand the universe is a powerful driving force in the world's collective psyche. By exploring space and supporting science, we have an incredible opportunity to answer the ultimate questions concerning our existence.

Similar arguments to those made for space exploration and scientific research can be applied to protecting the Earth's environment. The irony of opposition to environmental funding is that a healthy and well-functioning ecosystem is essential to meeting the very human needs that some people fear are being neglected to support "frivolous" causes. Degradation of the environment can cause significant economic loss, which contributes to poverty and suffering at the local level. Wetlands, for example, provide numerous economically important functions, such as water filtration, physical barriers against erosion, and breeding grounds for commercially important species that support local fisheries. Their destruction has serious immediate economic consequences as well as long-term social effects. Funding to protect the environment and to mitigate pollution should be afforded high priority in the distribution of public monies.

A NATURAL ETHIC:
BECAUSE WE CAN, BECAUSE WE MUST

A natural ethic has a strong basis in biology and a clear distinction from religious morality. One prominent characteristic of humans is sociality. Functioning as a group in many circumstances conveys significant advantages on members of the group. Associated with sociality is altruism, which is sacrificial behavior that in some way promotes the propagation of the genes of the altruistic individual, usually by aiding the survival of a close relative sharing some common genetic stock. The ultimate altruistic behavior would be dying for the sake of another's survival. An uncle getting in harm's way to protect a nephew is an example. Social cooperation and altruism are significant factors in the success of our species, a fact that underlines the biological basis for a natural ethic as a defining *and adaptive* human characteristic.

In contrast, a religious code of ethics based on personal reward for behaving morally or eternal punishment for not doing so leads to a flawed morality with long-term and serious consequences for humankind. Many of society's ills, including violent intolerance of our fellow humans, result to a considerable degree from religious morality based on fear of the unknown and hopes for immortality. If we are to survive, an alternative approach must be found. Pursuit of a natural ethic is one possibility. Behaving morally for no reward and in no fear of punishment, but because we have the capability of being moral creatures, is one of the traits that can define humanity. Pursuit of a natural ethic is a means of augmenting what is good in humans and minimizing elements of our darker side.

We can choose a path unique to humans by elevating ourselves above the common fate of other species. We can choose a natural ethic. Those who do embrace a natural ethic will find a certain satisfaction derived from knowing one's place in the universe. Amazing clarity is achieved in realizing that life is not controlled by some unseen and mysterious god but by an individual's power to make decisions and a personal choice to be moral. There is tremendous joy in understanding that purpose and meaning in life are self-derived, and that these precious commodities are not some gift from above that can be taken away arbitrarily by a wrathful deity working in mysterious ways. With a natural ethic, we are the masters of our own fate. Nothing is more powerful, or more satisfying.

CHRONOLOGY OF MAJOR
ETHICAL THEORIES

Moral theories evolve, with new ideas incorporating and modifying earlier innovations. The moral theory pie can therefore be divided arbitrarily many ways, and the distinct categories presented below could be recombined legitimately into other groupings. The world could be viewed with equal validity as primarily Cartesian versus non-Cartesian, or through the filter of empiricism versus rationalism, or through historic periods such as the Enlightenment and Industrialization.

Indeed, the major categories depicted here are often not mutually exclusive, and principal proponents in one category may have contributed significantly to another. For example, Francis Hutcheson is primarily associated with moral sense but much of his logic is consistent with natural law theory. Spinoza falls across multiple categories, from rationalism to the latter development of utilitarianism. Thomas Hobbes is associated with egoism and natural law.

In addition to philosophers, a few scientists have been included in this chronology, not because they necessarily belong to a particular school of philosophical thought but because they have made contributions so vital or so radically different from previously held worldviews that their ideas forever altered all subsequent discussions of philosophy.

The chronology is not comprehensive; rather, its purpose is to provide a global overview of how moral theory evolved broadly over time.

CLASSICAL ETHICS

CLASSICAL GREEK ETHICS

THEORY	DATES
Pythagoras	560–500 BCE
Socrates	470–399 BCE
Democritus	460–370 BCE
Plato (*Platonic Ethics*)	430–347 BCE
Aristotle (*Nicomachean Ethics*)	384–322 BCE

HELLENISTIC ETHICS

Theophrastus	372–386 BCE
Pyrrho of Elis (*Pyrrhonism*)	365–275 BCE
Epicurus (*Epicureanism*)	341–270 BCE
Zeno (*Stoicism*)	342–270 BCE

ROMAN ETHICS

(Variations of and modifications to Greek and Hellenistic Ethics)

Cicero	106-43 BCE
Lucretius	95-55 BCE
Seneca	4 BCE–65 AD
Epictetus	55–135 AD

RELIGIOUS ETHICS AND DIVINE COMMAND

MEDIEVAL ETHICS

(All of the following philosophers adhered to some form of Divine Command Theory, even when pursuing and modifying Platonism, Stoicism and other classical theories; some Christian thinkers fully rejected all forms of classical traditions of ethics.)

THEORY	DATES
Augustine of Hippo	354–430
St. Benedict	480–547
Boethius	480–524

THEORY	DATES
Gregory the Great (Pope Gregory I)	540–604
Alcuin	735–804
Aselm of Bec (Archbishop of Canterbury)	1033–1109
Peter Abelard	1079–1142
Alan of Lille	1120–1203
William of Auxerre	1150–1231
Albert the Great	1200–1280
Thomas Aquinas *(early Natural Law)*	1225–1274
John Duns Scotus	1266–1308
Walter Burley	1275–1345
William of Ockham	1285–1349

RENAISSANCE ETHICS

(Divine Command Theory still dominated as a foundation throughout this period.)

THEORY	DATES
John Buridan	1300-1358
Francesco Petrarca *(Humanism)*	1304–1374
Giovanni Dominici	1356–1419
Guillaume Budé	1467–1540
Phillip Melanchthon	1497–1560
Lambert Daneau	1530–1595
Justus Lipsius *(Neostoicism)*	1547–1606

RENAISSANCE SCIENCE

THEORY	DATES
Nicolas Copernicus	1473–1543
Giordano Bruno	1548–1600
Richard Hooker	1554–1600
Francis Bacon	1561–1626
Galileo Galilei	1564–1642
Isaac Newton	1643–1727

NATURAL LAW

THEORY	DATES
Francis Suarez	1548–1617
Hugo Grotius	1583–1645
Thomas Hobbes	1588–1679
Richard Cumberland	1632–1718
Samuel Pufendorf	1632–1694
John Locke	1632–1704

DUALISM

THEORY	DATES
René Descartes (natural law/rationalism)	596–1650

NATURAL RELIGION

THEORY	DATES
Pierre Bayle	1647–1706
William Wollaston	1659–1724

RATIONALISM

THEORY	DATES
Ralph Cudworth	1617–1688
Baruch de Spinoza	1632–1677
Nicholas Malebranche	1638–1715
Gottfried Wilhelm von Leibniz	1649–1716
Samuel Clarke	1675–1729
Christian Wolff	1679–1754
John Balguy	1686–1748
William Whewell	1794–1866

EGOISM

THEORY	DATES
Bernard de Mandeville	1670–1733
Helvetius	1715–1771
Paul–Henri Thiry (Baron) d'Holbach	1723–1789
William Paley	1743–1805

MORAL SENSE

THEORY	DATES
Lord Shaftesbury	1671–1713
Francis Hutcheson	1694–1746
David Hume (a category by himself)	1711–1776

STATISM
(Political and Economic Ethics)

THEORY	DATES
Jean–Jacques Rousseau	1712–1778
Adam Smith	1723–1790
G.F.W. Hegel	1770–1831

NONCONSEQUENTIALISM (DEONTOLOGICAL THEORIES)

KANTIANISM

THEORY	DATES
Immanuel Kant	1724–1804

INTUITIONISM

THEORY	DATES
H.A. Prichard	1871–1947
William David Ross	1877–1971
George Edward Moore	1873–1958

CONSEQUENTIALISM

ACT-UTILITARIANISM

THEORY	DATES
Jeremy Bentham	1748–1832
James Mill	1733–1836
John Stuart Mill (act and rule)	1806–1873

RULE-UTILITARIANISM

THEORY	DATES
John Austin	1790–1859
Henry Sidgwick	1838–1900

NIHILISM

THEORY	DATES
Demosthenes	371–322 BCE.
Max Stirner	1806–1856
Mikhail Bakunin	1814–1876
Friedrich Nietzsche	1844–1900

NATURALISM

THEORY	DATES
Herbert Spencer	1820–1903
John Dewey	1859–1952
Ralph B. Perry	1876–1957
Clarence Irving Lewis	1883–1964

EXISTENTIALISM

THEORY	DATES
Blaise Pascal	1623–1662
Søren Kierkegaard	1813–1855
Frenz Brento	1838–1917
Edmund Husserl	1859–1938
Karl Jaspers	1883–1969
Martin Heidegger	1889–1979
Jean–Paul Sartre	1905–1980
Simone de Beauvoir	1908–1986
Albert Camus	1913–1960

RELATIVISM

THEORY	DATES
Protagoras	490–421 BCE
George Santayana	1863–1952

REFERENCES

CHAPTER 1

Davies, Paul
    1999 *The 5th Miracle: The Search for the Origin and Meaning of Life.* New York: Touchstone.
Dawkins, Richard
    1996 *The Blind Watchmaker: Why the Evidence of Evolution Reveals a Universe Without Design.* W.W. Norton & Company.
Gribbin, John
    1993 *In the Beginning: The Birth of the Living Universe.* New York: Little, Brown & Company.
Horowitz, N.H.
    1955 *On Defining Life. In The Origin of Life on Earth.* A.I. Oparin, ed. New York: Pergamon.
Keosian, John
    1964 *The Origin of Life.* New York: Reinhold.
Marquand, Josephine
    1968 *Life: Its Nature, Origins and Disribution.* Edinburgh: Oliver & Boyd.
Orgel, Leslie E., Stanley Miller
    1974 *Origins of Life on Earth (Concepts of Modern Biology).* Upper Saddle River, NJ: Prentice Hall.
Schrodinger, Erwin
    1944 *What is Life?* Melbourne: Press Syndicate, University of Cambridge.
Shklovskii, I.S., and Carl Sagan
    1998 *Intelligent Life in the Universe.* Boca Raton, Florida: Emerson-Adams Press, Inc.
von Neumann, J.
    1966 *Theory of Self-Reproducing Automata.* A.W. Burks, ed. Illinois: University of Illinois Press.
Wohler, Friedrich
    1828 *On the Artificial Production of Urea.* Annalen der Physik und Chemie 88:253-256.

CHAPTER 2

Cech, T.R.
    1990 *Self-Splicing and Enzymatic Activity of an Intervening Sequence RNA from Tetrahymenia.* Bioscience Reports 10:239–260.
    1993 *Structure and Mechansims of the Large Catalytic RNAs: Group I and Group II Introns and Ribonuclease P. In The RNA World.* R.F.

Gesteland and J.F. Atkins, eds. Pp. 239–269. Cold Springs Harbor, New York: Cold Springs Harbor Laboratory Press.

Clack, Jennifer A.
2005 *Getting A Leg Up on Land.* Scientific American, December:100–107.

Clark, R.W.
1984 *JBS: The Life and Work of JBS Haldane.* Oxford: Oxford Paperbacks.

Darwin, Charles
1995 [1859] *On the Origin of Species.* Grammercy.

Darwin, Charles
1997[1871] *The Descent of Man.* P. 698. Amherst, New York: Prometheus Books.

Davies, Paul
1999 *The 5th Miracle: The Search for the Origin and Meaning of Life.* New York: Touchstone.

Dawkins, Richard
1996 *The Blind Watchmaker: Why the Evidence of Evolution Reveals a Universe Without Design.* W.W. Norton & Company.
2000 *Unweaving the Rainbow: Science, Delusion and the Appetite for Wonder.* Houghton Mifflin Co.

Gilbert, Walter
1986 *The RNA World.* Nature 319:618.

Gould, Stephen J.
1996 *Full House.* New York: Harmony Books.

Gray, Patricia M., Bernie Krause, Jelle Atema, Roger Payne, Carol Krumhansi, and Luis Baptista
2001 *The Music of Nature and the Nature of Music.* Science 291:52–54.

LaFree, Scott
2000 *Meet Me at the Goo.* New Scientist November:44–47.

Miller, S.L, and C. Chyba
1992 *Whence Came Life? Sky and Telescope June*: 604–605.

Semendeferi, Katerina, A. Lu, N. Schenker, and H. Damaiso
2002 *Humans and Great Apes Share a Large Frontal Cortex.* Nature Neuroscience 5(3):272–276.

Tattersall, Ian, and Jeffrey H. Schwartz
2001 *Extinct Humans.* Boulder, Colorado: Westview Press.

Tully, Timothy P.
1999 *In Brief.* Scientific American, November.

Wills, Christopher, and Jeffrey Bada
2001 *The Spark of Life.* New York: Perseus Publishing.

Woese, Carl
1967 *The Genetic Code.* New York: Harper and Row.

CHAPTER 3

Beck, B.B.
1980 *Animal Tool Behavior.* New York: Garland STPM Press.

Bugnyar, T., and K. Kotrschal
2002 *Observational Learning and the Raiding of Food Caches in Ravens, Corvus Corax: Is It "Tactical" Deception?* Animal Behavior 64:185–195.

Dally, Joanna M., Nathan J. Emery
2006 *Food-Catching Western Scrub-Jays Keep Track of Who Was Watching When.* Science 312 (June): 1662–1665.

de Waal, F.B.M.
  1996 *Good Natured: The Origins of Right and Wrong in Humans and Other Animals*. Cambridge: Harvard University Press.
  1997 *Bonobo: The Forgotten Ape*. Berkeley: University of California Press.
Emery, Nathan J., Nicola S. Clayton
  2004 *The Mentality of Crows: Convergent Evolution of Intelligence in Corvids and Apes*. Science 306 (December):1903–1907.
Gallup, G.G. Jr.
  1970 *Chimpanzees: Self-Recognition*. Science 167:86–87.
Gillan, D.J., D. Premack, and G Woodruff
  1981 *Reasoning in the Chimpanzee: I. Analogical Reasoning*. Journal of Experimental Psychology: Animal Behavior Processes 7:1–17.
Gould, Stephen Jay
  1997 *Foreword: The Positive Power of Skepticism*. In *Why People Believe Weird Things*. Michael Shermer, ed. P. ix. New York: W.H. Freeman.
Gray, Patricia M., Bernie Krause, Jelle Atema, Roger Payne, Carol Krumhansi, and Luis Baptista
  2001 *The Music of Nature and the Nature of Music*. Science 291:52–54.
  Hare, Brian, Michael Tomasello
  2005 *Human-Like Social Skills in Dogs?* TRENDS in Cognitive Science 9(9):439–444.
Hermann, Esther, J. Call, M. V. Hernandez-Lloreda, B. Hare, and M. Tomasello
  2007 *Humans Have Evolved Specialized Skills of Social Cognition: The Cultural Intelligence Hypothesis*. Science 317:1360–1362.
Hofstadter, Douglas
  2007 *I Am a Strange Loop*. New York: Basic Books.
Holdrege, Craig
  2001 *Elephantine Intelligence*. Electronic document. The Nature Institute Spring.http://natureinstitute.org/pub/ic/ic5/elephant.htm.
  Imanishi, Kinji
  1963 *Social Behavior in Japanese Monkeys*. Charles A. Southwick, ed. Primate Social Behavior. Toronto: Van Nostrand.
Jaakkola, Kelly
  2005 *Understanding of the Concept of Numerically "Less" by Bottlenose Dolphins (Tursiops Truncatus)*. Journal of Comparative Psychology 119(3):296–303.
Linden, Eugene
  2002 *Octopus and the Orangutan: More True Tales of Animal Intrigue, Intelligence, and Ingenuity*. New York: Dutton Books.
Lock, Andrew, and Charles R. Peters
  1996 *Handbook of Human Symbolic Evolution*. Oxford: Clarendon Press.
  Masserman, J., S. Wechkin, and W. Terris
  1964 *'Altruistic' Behavior in Rhesus Monkeys*. American Journal of Psychiatry 121:584–585.
Millikan, G.C., and R.I. Bowman
  1967 *Observations on Galapagos Tool-Using Finches in Captivity*. Living Bird 6:23–41.
O'Hear, Anthony
  1997 *Beyond Evolution: Human Nature and the Limits of Evolutionary Explanation*. New York: Oxford University Press.
Panksepp, Jaak
  2000 *The Riddle of Laughter: Neural and Psychoevolutionary Underpin nings of Joy*. Current Directions in Psychological Sciences:183–186.

Pepperberg, Irene M.
  1990 *Cognition in an African Grey Parrot*. Journal of Comparitive
        Psychology 104:41–52.
  1995 *Studies to Determine the Intelligence of African Grey Parrots*.
        Proceedings of the International Aviculturists Society January 11–15.
Premack, David, Ann Premack
  2003 *Unlocking the Mystery of Who We Are*. New York: McGraw-Hill.
        Premack, David, G. Woodruff
  1978 *Does the Chimpanzee Have a Theory of Mind?* Behavioral and Brain
        Sciences 4:515526.
Preuschoft, S., J.A. van Hooff
  1995 *Homologizing Primate Facial Displays: A Critical Review of Methods*.
        Folia Primatol 65(3):121–137.
Reiss, D., Marino L.
  2001 *Mirror Self-Recognition in the Bottlenose Dolphin*. Proceedings of
        the National Academy of Science 98:5937–5942.
Rice, G.E. Jr., and P. Gainer
  1962 *'Altruism' in the Albino Rat*. Journal of Comparative & Physiologi
        cal Psychology 55(1):123–125.
Semendeferi, Katerina, A. Lu, N. Schenker, and H. Damaiso
  2002 *Humans and Great Apes Share a Large Frontal Cortex*. Nature Neu-
        roscience 5(3):272–276.
Tully, Timothy P.
  1999 *In Brief*. Scientific American, November.
Watanabe, S., and K. Ono
  1986 *An Experimental Analysis of "Emphatic" Response: Effects of Pain
        Reactions of Pigeon Upon Other Pigeon's Operant Behavior*. Behav-
        ioral Processes 13(3):269–277.
Weir, A.A.S., J. Chappell, and A. Kacelnik
  2002 *Shaping of Hooks in New Caledonian Crows*. Science 297:981.
Wilson, E.O.
  1996 *In Search of Nature*. Washington, D.C.: Island Press.
Woodruff, G., D. Premack
  1979 *Intentional Communication in the Chimpanzee: The Development of
        Deception*. Cognition 7:333–362.

CHAPTER 4
Curley, Edwin
  1994 *The Ethics and Other Works: Benedict de Spinoza*. Princeton, NJ:
        Princeton University Press.
Feuerbach, Ludwig
  1957 *The Essence of Christianity*. New York: Harper Torchbook.
Hauser, Marc
  2006 *Moral Minds: How Nature Designed Our Universal Sense of Right
        and Wrong*. New York: Ecco Press.
Hume, David
  1888 [1739]   *A Treatise of Human Nature*. L.A. Selby-Bigge, ed. Oxford:
        Clarendon Press.
Hume, David
  1998 [1751]   *An Enquiry Concerning the Principles of Morals*. Tom L.
        Beauchamp, ed. Oxford: Oxford University Press.
Hume, David
  1957 [1757]   *The Natural History of Religion*. H.E. Root, ed. P. 76.

Stanford: Stanford University Press.
Jensen, Gary
   2003   *Religious Cosmologies and Homicide Rates Among Nations: A Closer
          Look.* Journal of Religion and Society 8:1.
La Barre, Weston
          The Ghost Dance: The Origins of Religion. New York: Dell Publish
          ing Co., Inc.
Paul, Greg
   2005   *Cross-National Correlations of Quantifiable Societal Health with Pop
          ular Religiosity and Secularism in the Prosperous Democracies, A First
          Look.* Journal of Religion and Society 7:1.
Stark, Rodney, and William Sims Bainbridge
   1996   *A Theory of Religion.* New Jersey: Rutgers University Press.
Stewart, Matthew
   2006   *The Courtier and the Heretic: Leibniz, Spinoza, and the Fate of God.*
          New York, NY: W.W. Norton & Company, Inc.

CHAPTER 5
Curley, Edwin
   1994   *The Ethics and Other Works: Benedict de Spinoza.* Princeton, NJ:
          Princeton University Press.
de Ramsay, Andrew Michael
   2001 [1728]   *The Travels of Cyrus, to Which is Annexed a Discourse Upon
          the Theology and Mythology of Pagans*: Volume 2. P. 475. Adament
          Media Corporation.
Feuer, Lewis S.
   1959   *Marx & Engels: Basic Writings on Politics & Philosophy.* New York:
          Doubleday.
Feuerbach, Ludwig
   1957   *The Essence of Christianity.* New York: Harper Torchbook.
Franz, Frederick
   1966   *Life Everlasting in Freedom of the Sons of God.* New York: Watch-
          tower Bible and Tract Society.
Galanter, Marc
   1989   *Cults: Faith, Healing and Coercion.* New York: Oxford University
          Press.
Hume, David
   1888 [1739]   *A Treatise of Human Nature.* L.A. Selby-Bigge, ed. Oxford:
          Clarendon Press.
Hume, David
   1998 [1751]   *An Enquiry Concerning the Principles of Morals.* Tom L.
          Beauchamp, ed. Oxford: Oxford University Press.
Hume, David
   1957 [1757]   *The Natural History of Religion.* H.E. Root, ed. P. 76. Stan-
          ford: Stanford University Press.
La Barre, Weston
   1970   *The Ghost Dance: The Origins of Religion.* New York: Dell Pub-
          lishing Co., Inc.
Lawrence, Bruce B.
   1998   *Shattering the Myth: Islam Beyond Violence.* Princeton: Princeton
          University Press.
Plato, 380 BCE
   1995   *The Last Days of Socrates: Euthyphro, Apology, Crito, Phaedo.* Harold

Tarrant, ed. Hugh Tredennick, trans. Penguin USA.

Stewart, Matthew
2006 *The Courtier and the Heretic: Leibniz, Spinoza, and the Fate of God.* New York, NY: W.W. Norton & Company, Inc.

Tucker, Pomeroy
1867 *Origin, Rise, and Progress of Mormonism: Biography of Its Founders and History of Its Church.* New York: Utah Lighthouse Ministry.

CHAPTER 6

Catholic Church
2003 *Catechism of the Catholic Church.* New York: Doubleday.

Cross, F.L., E.A. Livingstone
1977 *Oxford Dictionary of the Christian Church.* Oxford: Oxford University Press.

Curley, Edwin
1994 *The Ethics and Other Works: Benedict de Spinoza.* Princeton, NJ: Princeton University Press.

Hume, David
1888 [1739] *A Treatise of Human Nature.* L.A. Selby-Bigge, ed. Oxford: Clarendon Press.

Hume, David
1998 [1751] *An Enquiry Concerning the Principles of Morals.* Tom L. Beauchamp, ed. Oxford: Oxford University Press.

Hume, David
1957 [1757] *The Natural History of Religion.* H.E. Root, ed. P. 76. Stanford: Stanford University Press.

Latourette, Kenneth Scott
1975 *A History of Christianity, Volume 2: Reformation to the Present.* San Francisco: Harper.
1975 *A History of Christianity, Volume 1: Beginnings to 1500 (Revised).* San Francisco: Harper.

Luther, Martin
1957 [1517] *Luther's Ninety-Five Theses.* Minneapolis: Augsburg Fortress Publishers.

Momen, Moojan
1999 The Phenomenon of Religion: A Thematic Approach. Oxford, England: Oneworld Publications.

Stewart, Matthew
2006 *The Courtier and the Heretic: Leibniz, Spinoza, and the Fate of God.* New York, NY: W.W. Norton & Company, Inc.

CHAPTER 7

Aristotle, 350 BCE
1998 *The Nicomachean Ethics* (Oxford World's Classics). Preprint edition. J.L. Ackrill and J.O. Urmson, eds. W.D. Ross, trans. Oxford University Press.

Beauchamp, Tom L. (ed.), David Hume
1998 *An Equiry Concerning the Principles of Morals.* Oxford: Oxford University Press.

Black, Max
1964 *The Gap Between 'Is' and 'Should.'* The Philosophical Review 73:165–181.

Dawkins, Richard
  1996 *The Blind Watchmaker: Why the Evidence of Evolution Reveals a Universe Without Design.* W.W. Norton & Company.
George, Robert P.
  2001 *In Defense of Natural Law.* Oxford University Press.
Hume, David
  1888 [1739] *A Treatise of Human Nature.* L.A. Selby–Bigge, ed. Oxford: Clarendon Press.
Hume, David
  1998 [1751] *An Enquiry Concerning the Principles of Morals.* Tom L. Beauchamp, ed. Oxford: Oxford University Press.
Jensen, Henning
  1971 *Motivation and Moral Sense in Francis Hutchinson's Ethical Theory.* Kluwer Print on Demand.
Kant, Immanual
  1989 [1785] *The Foundations of the Metaphysics of Morals.* Lewis White Beck, ed. Prentice Hall.
LaFollette, Hugh
  2000 *The Blackwell Guide to Ethical Theory.* Hugh LaFollette, ed. Oxford, UK: Blackwell Publishers Inc.
Leibniz, Gottfried Wilhelm
  1998 [1686] *Philosophical Texts.* Richard Franks and R.S. Woolhouse, eds. Oxford Press.
Lorenz, Konrad
  1988 *King Solomon's Ring: New Light on Animals' Ways.* Plume.
Mill, John Stuart
  2002 [1863] *The Basic Writings of John Stuart Mill: On Liberty, the Subjection of Women and Utilitarianism.* J.B. Schneewind (Introduction), ed. Modern Library.
Osterberg, Jan
  1988 *Self and Others: A Study of Ethical Egoism.* Kluwer Academic Publishers.
Plato, 360 BCE
  1999 *The Essential Plato.* Alain de Botton, ed. Benjamin Jowett (1871) and M.J. Knight, trans. New York: Quality Paperback Book Club.
Pufendorf, Samuel
  1991 [1678] *On The Natural State of Men.* The 1678 Latin Edition and English Translation. Michael Seidler, trans. Edwin Mellen Press.
Ramsay, Hayden
  1997 *Beyond Virtue: Integrity and Morality.* Palgrave Macmillan.
Sartre, Jean-Paul
  1993 [1943] *Being and Nothingness.* Washington Square Press.
    Shaftesbury, Lord
  2000 [1711] *Shaftesbury: Characteristics of Men, Manners, Opinions, Times.* Lawrence E. Klein, Karl Ameriks and Desmond M. Clarke, eds. Cambridge: Cambridge University Press.
Shaw, William H.
  2000 *Relativism and Objectivity in Ethics.* Heimir Geirsson and Margaret R.Holmgren, eds. Pp. 12–31. Toronto, Canada: Broadview Press Ltd.
Solomon, Robert C.
  1974 *Existentialism.* McGraw-Hill Modern Library College Editions.

Spencer, Herbert
  1999 [1851]   *The Social Statics (Works by and About Herbert Spencer).*
        Michael Taylor, ed. Thoemmes Press.

CHAPTER 8
Chiappini, Rudy
  2008   *Francis Bacon: Anthology.* Milan; New York: Skira.
Curley, Edwin
  1994   *The Ethics and Other Works: Benedict de Spinoza.* Princeton, NJ:
        Princeton University Press.
Fakhry, Majid
  2001   *Averroes: His Life, Works and Influences (Great Islamic Writings).*
        Oxford, England: Oneworld Publications.
Gleick, James
  1993   *Genius: The Life and Science of Richard Feynman.* New York: Vintage
        (Random House).
Gordon, Dane R., and David B. Suits
  2003   *Epicurus: His Continuing Influence and Contemporary Relevance.*
        Rochester, NY: RIT Cary Graphic Arts Press.
Kilcullen, John
  1988   *Sincerity and Truth: Essays on Arnauld, Bayle, and Toleration.* New
        York, NY; Oxford, UK: Oxford University Press.
LoLordo, Antonio
  2006   *Pierre Gassendi and the Birth of Early Modern Philosophy.* Cambridge,
        MA: Cambridge University Press.
Moses, Matthew, Mark, Luke, and John et al.
  2007   *The Holy Bible.* Nashville: Thomas Nelson Bibles.
Pyle, Andrew
  2003   *Malebranch (Arguments of the Philosophers).* New York, NY; Milton
        Park, UK: Routledge.
Stewart, Matthew
  2006   *The Courtier and the Heretic: Leibniz, Spinoza, and the Fate of God.*
        New York, NY: W.W. Norton & Company, Inc.
Weinberg, Steven
  2008   *Cosmology.* New York: Oxford University Press.

BY AUTHOR
Allen, Colin, and Edward N. Zalta (ed.)
  2003   *Animal Consciousness.* Electronic document. The Stanford Ency-
        clopedia of Philosophy.
        http://plato.stanford.edu/archives/sum2003/entries/consciousness-
        animal/.Aristotle, 350 B.C.E.
  1998   *The Nicomachean Ethics (Oxford World's Classics).* Preprint edition.
        J.L. Ackrill and J.O. Urmson, eds. W.D. Ross, trans. Oxford Uni-
        versity Press.
Bacon, Francis
  2000 [1597] *Sir Francis Bacon: The Essayes or Counsels, Civill and Morall
        (The Oxford Francis Bacon).* Michael Kiernan, ed. Oxford University
        Press.
Beauchamp, Tom L. (ed.), David Hume
  1998   *An Equiry Concerning the Principles of Morals.* Oxford: Oxford Uni-
        versity Press.

Beck, B.B.
  1980 *Animal Tool Behavior*. New York: Garland STPM Press.
Becker, Lawrence C., and Charlotte B. Becker (eds.)
  1992 *A History of Western Ethics*. New York: Garland Publishing.
Black, Max
  1964 "The Gap Between 'Is' and 'Should'" *The Philosophical Review*
         73:165–181.
Broderick, James
  1961 *Robert Bellarmine, Saint and Scholar*. Westminster, MD: Newman Press.
Bugnyar, T., and K. Kotrschal
  2002 "Observational Learning and the Raiding of Food Caches in Ravens,
         Corvus Corax: Is It "Tactical" Deception?" *Animal Behavior*
         64:185–195.
Catholic Church
  2003 *Catechism of the Catholic Church*. New York: Doubleday.
Cech, T.R.
  1990 "Self-Splicing and Enzymatic Activity of an Intervening Sequence
         RNA from Tetrahymenia." *Bioscience Reports* 10:239–260.
  1993 "Structure and Mechansims of the Large Catalytic RNAs: Group I
         and Group II Introns and Ribonuclease P." In *The RNA World*. R.F.
         Gesteland and J.F. Atkins, eds. Pp. 239–269. Cold Springs Harbor,
         New York: Cold Springs Harbor Laboratory Press.
Chiappini, Rudy
  2008 *Francis Bacon: Anthology*. Milan; New York: Skira.
Clack, Jennifer A.
  2005 "Getting A Leg Up on Land." *Scientific American*, December:100–107.
Clark, R.W.
  1984 *JBS: The Life and Work of JBS Haldane*. Oxford: Oxford Paperbacks.
Cross, F.L., E.A. Livingstone
  1977 *Oxford Dictionary of the Christian Church*. Oxford: Oxford Univer
         sity Press.
Curley, Edwin
  1994 *The Ethics and Other Works: Benedict de Spinoza*. Princeton, NJ:
         Princeton University Press.
Dally, Joanna M., Nathan J. Emery
  2006 "*Food-Catching Western Scrub-Jays Keep Track of Who Was Watch-
         ing When.*" Science 312(June):1662–1665.
Darwin, Charles
  1995 [1859] *On the Origin of Species*. Gramercy.
Darwin, Charles
  1997 [1871] *The Descent of Man*. P. 698. Amherst, New York: Prometheus
         Books.
Davies, Paul
  1999 *The 5th Miracle: The Search for the Origin and Meaning of Life*. New
         York: Touchstone.
  2000 *The 5th Miracle: The Search for the Origin and Meaning of Life*. New
         York: Touchstone.
Dawkins, Richard
  1986 *The Blind Watchmaker*. New York: W.W. Norton.
  1996 *The Blind Watchmaker: Why the Evidence of Evolution Reveals a
         Universe Without Design*. W.W. Norton & Company.
  2000 *Unweaving the Rainbow: Science, Delusion and the Appetite for
         Wonder*. Houghton Mifflin Co.

de Ramsay, Andrew Michael
  2001 [1728] *The Travels of Cyrus, to Which is Annexed a Discourse Upon the Theology and Mythology of Pagans: Volume 2*. P. 475. Adament Media Corporation.
de Waal, F.B.M.
  1996 "Conflict as Negotiation." In *Great Ape Societies*. William C. McGrew, Linda Marchant and Toshisada Nishida, eds. Cambridge: Cambridge University Press.
  1996 *Good Natured: The Origins of Right and Wrong in Humans and Other Animals*. Cambridge: Harvard University Press.
  1997 *Bonobo: The Forgotten Ape*. Berkeley: University of California Press.
Dobzhansky, Theodosius
  1973 "Nothing in Biology Makes Sense Except in Light of Evolution." *American Biology Teacher* 35.
Emery, Nathan J., Nicola S. Clayton
  2004 "The Mentality of Crows: Convergent Evolution of Intelligence in Corvids and Apes." *Science* 306 (December):1903–1907.
Fakhry, Majid
  2001 *Averroes: His Life, Works and Influences (Great Islamic Writings)*. Oxford, England: Oneworld Publications.
Feuer, Lewis S.
  1959 *Marx & Engels: Basic Writings on Politics & Philosophy*. New York: Doubleday.
Feuerbach, Ludwig
  1957 *The Essence of Christianity*. New York: Harper Torchbook.
Finocchiaro, Maurice A.
  1989 *The Galileo Affair: A Documentary History*. University of California Press.
Franz, Frederick
  1966 *Life Everlasting in Freedom of the Sons of God*. New York: Watch tower Bible and Tract Society.
Galanter, Marc
  1989 *Cults: Faith, Healing and Coercion*. New York: Oxford University Press.
Galileo, Galilei
  2001 *Dialogue Concerning the Two Chief World Systems*. Stillman Drake, trans. Modern Library.
Gallup, G.G. Jr.
  1970 "Chimpanzees: Self-Recognition." *Science* 167:86–87.
Gauguin, Paul, Painter
  1897 *From Where Do We Come? What Are We? Where Are We Going?* Oil on canvas. Museum of Fine Arts, Boston. 54 3/4 x 147 1/2 in.
Geirsson, Heimir, and Margaret R. Holmgren
  2000 "Divine Command Theory." Heimir Geirsson and Margaret R. Holm gren, eds. Pp. 33–37. Ontario, Canada: Broadview Press, Ltd.
George, Robert P.
  2001 *In Defense of Natural Law*. Oxford University Press.
Giese, K.P., N.B. Fedorov, R.K. Filipkowski, and A.J. Silva
  1998 "Autophosphorylation at Thr286 of the Calcium-Calmodulin Kinase II in LTP and Learning." *Science* 279:870–73.
Gilbert, Walter
  1986 "The RNA World." *Nature* 319:618.
Gillan, D.J., D. Premack, and G Woodruff
  1981 "Reasoning in the Chimpanzee: I. Analogical Reasoning." *Journal of*

Experimental Psychology: Animal Behavior Processes 7:1–17.

Gleick, James
  1993 *Genius: The Life and Science of Richard Feynman*. New York: Vintage (Random House).

Gordon, Dane R., and David B. Suits
  2003 *Epicurus: His Continuing Influence and Contemporary Relevance*. Rochester, NY: RIT Cary Graphic Arts Press.

Gould, Stephen J.
  1996 *Full House*. New York: Harmony Books.

Gould, Stephen Jay
  1997 "Foreword: The Positive Power of Skepticism." In *Why People Believe Weird Things*. Michael Shermer, ed. p. ix. New York: W.H. Freeman.

Gray, Patricia M., Bernie Krause, Jelle Atema, Roger Payne, Carol Krumhansi, and Luis Baptista
  2001 "The Music of Nature and the Nature of Music." *Science* 291: 52–54.

Grayling, A.C.
  2008 "Our Mirror on Morality." *New Scientist* 2657 (May):21.

Gribbin, John
  1993 *In the Beginning: The Birth of the Living Universe*. New York: Little, Brown & Company.

Griffin, Donald R.
  2001 *Animal Minds: Beyond Cognition to Consciousness*. Chicago: University of Chicago Press.

Guthrie, W.K.C.
  1962–1969 *A History of Greek Philosophy. Vols 1–3*. Cambridge: Cambridge University Press.

Haidt, Jonathan
  2007 "The New Synthesis in Moral Psychology." *Science* 316(May):998–1002.

Hare, Brian, Michael Tomasello
  2005 "Human-Like Social Skills in Dogs?" *TRENDS in Cognitive Science* 9(9):439–444.

Hauser, Marc
  2006 *Moral Minds: How Nature Designed Our Universal Sense of Right and Wrong*. New York: Ecco Press.

Hermann, Esther, J. Call, M. V. Hernandez-Lloreda, B. Hare, and M. Tomasello
  2007 "Humans Have Evolved Specialized Skills of Social Cognition: The Cultural Intelligence Hypothesis." *Science* 317:1360–1362.

Hofstadter, Douglas
  2007 *I Am a Strange Loop*. New York: Basic Books.

Holdrege, Craig
  2001 *Elephantine Intelligence. Electronic document. The Nature Institute Spring*. http://natureinstitute.org/pub/ic/ic5/elephant.htm.

Horowitz, N.H.
  1955 "On Defining Life." In *The Origin of Life on Earth*. A.I. Oparin, ed. New York: Pergamon.

Hout, Mike, and Claude Fischer
  2002 "Why More Americans Have No Religious Preference: Politics and Generations." *American Sociological Review* 67:165–190.

Hume, David
  1888 [1739] *A Treatise of Human Nature*. L.A. Selby-Bigge, ed. Oxford: Clarendon Press.

Hume, David
  1957 [1757] *The Natural History of Religion*. H.E. Root, ed. P. 76. Stan-

ford: Stanford University Press.

Hume, David
  1998 [1751] *An Enquiry Concerning the Principles of Morals.* Tom L.
    Beauchamp, ed. Oxford: Oxford University Press.

Imanishi, Kinji
  1963 "Social Behavior in Japanese Monkeys." Charles A. Southwick, ed.
    Primate Social Behavior. Toronto: Van Nostrand.

Izard, C., J. Kagan, and R. Zajonc
  1984 *Emotions, Cognition, and Behavior.* Cambridge: Cambridge Univer
    sity Press.

Jaakkola, Kelly
  2005 "Understanding of the Concept of Numerically "Less" by Bottlenose
    Dolphins (Tursiops Truncatus)." *Journal of Comparative Psychology*
    119(3):296–303.

Jensen, Gary
  2003 "Religious Cosmologies and Homicide Rates Among Nations: A
    Closer Look." *Journal of Religion and Society* 8:1.

Jensen, Henning
  1971 *Motivation and Moral Sense in Francis Hutchinson's Ethical Theory.*
    Kluwer Print on Demand.

Kant, Immanual
  1989 [1785] *The Foundations of the Metaphysics of Morals.* Lewis White
    Beck, ed. Prentice Hall.

Keosian, John
  1964 *The Origin of Life.* New York: Reinhold.

Kilcullen, John
  1988 *Sincerity and Truth: Essays on Arnauld, Bayle, and Toleration.* New
    York, NY; Oxford, UK: Oxford University Press.

La Barre, Weston
  1970 *The Ghost Dance: The Origins of Religion.* New York: Dell Publish
    ing Co., Inc.

LaFollette, Hugh
  2000 *The Blackwell Guide to Ethical Theory.* Hugh LaFollette, ed. Ox
    ford, UK: Blackwell Publishers Inc.

LaFree, Scott
  2000 "Meet Me at the Goo." *New Scientist* November:44–47.

Latourette, Kenneth Scott
  1975 *A History of Christianity, Volume 1: Beginnings to 1500 (Revised).*
    San Francisco: Harper.
  1975 *A History of Christianity, Volume 2: Reformation to the Present.* San
    Francisco: Harper.

Lawrence, Bruce B.
  1998 *Shattering the Myth: Islam Beyond Violence.* Princeton: Princeton
    University Press.

Leakey, Richard
  1994 *The Origin of Humankind.* New York: Basic.

Leibniz, Gottfried Wilhelm
  1998 [1686] *Philosophical Texts.* Richard Franks and R.S. Woolhouse, eds.
    Oxford Press

Linden, Eugene
  2002 *Octopus and the Orangutan: More True Tales of Animal Intrigue,
    Intelligence, and Ingenuity.* New York: Dutton Books.

Lock, Andrew, and Charles R. Peters

1996 *Handbook of Human Symbolic Evolution*. Oxford: Clarendon Press.
LoLordo, Antonio
2006 *Pierre Gassendi and the Birth of Early Modern Philosophy*. Cambridge, MA: Cambridge University Press.
Lorenz, Konrad
1997 *King Solomon's Ring: New Light on Animals' Ways*. New York: Plume (Penguin Group USA).
Luther, Martin
1957 [1517] *Luther's Ninety-Five Theses*. Minneapolis: Augsburg Fortress Publishers.
Machamer, Peter
1998 *The Cambridge Companion to Galileo*. Cambridge University Press.
Marquand, Josephine
1968 *Life: Its Nature, Origins and Disribution*. Edinburgh: Oliver & Boyd.
Marx, Karl., Frederick Engels
1957 *On Religion*. Moscow: Foreign Languages Publishing House.
Masserman, J., S. Wechkin, and W. Terris
1964 "'Altruistic' Behavior in Rhesus Monkeys." *American Journal of Psychiatry* 121:584–585.
Mill, John Stuart
2002 [1863] *The Basic Writings of John Stuart Mill: On Liberty, the Subjection of Women and Utilitarianism*. J.B. Schneewind (Introduction), ed. Modern Library.
Miller, S.L, and C. Chyba
1992 "Whence Came Life?" *Sky and Telescope* June:604–605.
Miller, Stanley LLoyd
1953 *"A Production of Amino Acids Under Possible Primitive Earth Conditions."* Science 117:528–529.
Millikan, G.C., and R.I. Bowman
1967 "Observations on Galapagos Tool-Using Finches in Captivity." *Living Bird* 6:23–41.
Momen, Moojan
1999 *The Phenomenon of Religion: A Thematic Approach*. Oxford, England: Oneworld Publications.
Moses, Matthew, Mark, Luke, and John et al.
2007 *The Holy Bible*. Nashville: Thomas Nelson Bibles.
Nielsen, P.E.
1993 "Peptide Nucleic Acid (PNA): A Model Structure for the Primordial Genetic Material?" *Origins of Life and Evolution of the Biosphere* 23:323–327.
Orgel, Leslie E., Stanley Miller
1974 *Origins of Life on Earth (Concepts of Modern Biology)*. Upper Saddle River, NJ: Prentice Hall.
Osterberg, Jan
1988 *Self and Others: A Study of Ethical Egoism*. Kluwer Academic Publishers.
O'Hear, Anthony
1997 *Beyond Evolution: Human Nature and the Limits of Evolutionary Explanation*. New York: Oxford University Press.
Panksepp, Jaak
2000 "The Riddle of Laughter: Neural and Psychoevolutionary Underpinnings of Joy." *Current Directions in Psychological Sciences*: 183–186.

Paul, Greg
  2005 "Cross-National Correlations of Quantifiable Societal Health with Popular Religiosity and Secularism in the Prosperous Democracies, A First Look." *Journal of Religion and Society* 7:1.
Pepperberg, Irene M.
  1990 "Cognition in an African Grey Parrot." *Journal of Comparitive Psychology* 104:41–52.
  1995 "Studies to Determine the Intelligence of African Grey Parrots." Proceedings of the International Aviculturists Society January 11–15.
Plato, 380 BCE
  1995 *The Last Days of Socrates: Euthyphro, Apology, Crito, Phaedo.* Harold Tarrant, ed. Hugh Tredennick, trans. Penguin USA.
Plato, 360 BCE
  1999 *The Essential Plato.* Alain de Botton, ed. Benjamin Jowett (1871) and M.J. Knight, trans. New York: Quality Paperback Book Club.
Premack, David, Ann Premack
  2003 *Unlocking the Mystery of Who We Are.* New York: McGraw-Hill.
Premack, David, G. Woodruff
  1978 "Does the Chimpanzee Have a Theory of Mind?" *Behavioral and Brain Sciences* 4:515–526.
Preuschoft, S., J.A. van Hooff
  1995 "Homologizing Primate Facial Displays: A Critical Review of Methods." *Folia Primatol* 65(3):121–137.
Principe, Lawrence
  2000 *The Aspiring Adept: Robert Boyle and His Alchemist Quest.* Princeton: Princeton University Press.
Pufendorf, Samuel
  1991 [1678] *On The Natural State of Men.* The 1678 Latin Edition and English Translation. Michael Seidler, trans. Edwin Mellen Press.
Pyle, Andrew
  2003 *Malebranch (Arguments of the Philosophers).* New York, NY; Milton Park, UK: Routledge.
Ramsay, Hayden
  1997 *Beyond Virtue: Integrity and Morality.* Palgrave Macmillan.
Reiss, D., Marino L.
  2001 "Mirror Self-Recognition in the Bottlenose Dolphin." *Proceedings of the National Academy of Science* 98:5937–5942.
Rice, G.E. Jr., and P. Gainer
  1962 "'Altruism' in the Albino Rat." *Journal of Comparative & Physiological Psychology* 55(1):123–125.
Santillana, Giorgio di
  1955 *The Crime of Galileo.* Chicago: University of Chicago Press.
Sartre, Jean-Paul
  1993 [1943] *Being and Nothingness.* Washington Square Press.
Schrodinger, Erwin
  1944 *What is Life?* Melbourne: Press Syndicate, University of Cambridge.
Semendeferi, Katerina, A. Lu, N. Schenker, and H. Damaiso
  2002 "Humans and Great Apes Share a Large Frontal Cortex." *Nature Neuroscience* 5(3):272–276.
Shaftesbury, Lord
  2000 [1711] *Shaftesbury: Characteristics of Men, Manners, Opinions, Times.* Lawrence E. Klein, Karl Ameriks and Desmond M. Clarke, eds.

Cambridge: Cambridge University Press.
Shaw, William H.
 2000 *"Relativism and Objectivity in Ethics."* Heimir Geirsson and
  Margaret R.Holmgren, eds. Pp. 12–31. Toronto, Canada: Broadview
  Press Ltd.
Shklovskii, I.S., and Carl Sagan
 1998 *Intelligent Life in the Universe.* Boca Raton, Florida: Emerson-
  Adams Press, Inc.
Shweder, R.A., N.C. Much, M. Mahapatra, and L. Park
 1997 *"The "Big Three" of Morality (Autonomy, Community, Divinity),
  and the "Big Three" Explanations of Suffering."* A. Brandt & P. Rozin, ed.
  Pp. 119–169. Morality and Health. New York: Routledge.
Smith, Adam
 2003 [1776] *The Wealth of Nations.* Alan B. Krueger, ed. Bantam.
Solomon, Robert C.
 1974 *Existentialism.* McGraw-Hill Modern Library College Editions.
Spencer, Herbert
 1999 [1851] *The Social Statics (Works by and About Herbert Spencer).*
  Michael Taylor, ed. Thoemmes Press.
Stark, Rodney, and William Sims Bainbridge
 1996 *A Theory of Religion.* New Jersey: Rutgers University Press.
Stewart, Matthew
 2006 *The Courtier and the Heretic: Leibniz, Spinoza, and the Fate of God.*
  New York, NY: W.W. Norton & Company, Inc.
Suttle, Curtis A., Amy A. Chan, and Matthew T. Cottrell
 1990 "Infection of Phytoplankton by Viruses and Reduction of Primary
  Productivity." *Nature* 347:467–469.
Tappert, Theodore G., and Helmut T.Lehmann
 1967 "Table Talk," *Luther's Work, Vol. 54.* Philadelphia: Fortress Press.
Tattersall, Ian, and Jeffrey H. Schwartz
 2001 *Extinct Humans.* Boulder, Colorado: Westview Press.
Tattersall, Ian, and Jeffrey Schwartz
 2000 *Extinct Humans.* New York: Westview Press.
Tucker, Pomeroy
 1867 *Origin, Rise, and Progress of Mormonism: Biography of Its Founders
  and History of Its Church.* New York: Utah Lighthouse Ministry.
Tully, Timothy P.
 1999 "In Brief." *Scientific American,* November.
Varela, F., H. Maturana, and R. Uribe
 1974 "Autopoiesis: The Organization of Living Systems, Its Characteriza-
  tion and a Model." *Biosystems* 5:187–196.
Visser, Wayne, and Clem Sunter
 2002 *Beyond Reasonable Greed: Why Sustainable Business in a Much Better
  Idea!* Tafelberg: Human & Rousseau.
von Neumann, J.
 1966 *"Theory of Self-Reproducing Automata."* A.W. Burks, ed. Illinois:
  University of Illinois Press.
Watanabe, S., and K. Ono
 1986 "An Experimental Analysis of "Emphatic" Response: Effects of Pain
  Reactions of Pigeon Upon Other Pigeon's Operant Behavior." *Behavioral Processes* 13(3):269–277.
Wechkin, S., Masserman

1964 "Shock to a Conspecific as an Aversive Stimulus." *Psychonomic Science* 2(1):47–48.

Weinberg, Steven
2008 *Cosmology*. New York: Oxford University Press.

Weir, A.A.S., J. Chappell, and A. Kacelnik
2002 "Shaping of Hooks in New Caledonian Crows." *Science* 297:981.

Wheatley, Thalia, and Jonathan Haidt
2005 "Hypnotic Disgust Makes Moral Judgments More Severe." *Psychological Science* 16(10):780–784.

White, Lynn, Jr.
1967 "The Historic Roots of Our Ecological Crisis." *Science* 155(March):1203–07.

Wills, Christopher, and Jeffrey Bada
2001 *The Spark of Life*. New York: Perseus Publishing.

Wilson, David Sloan
2002 *Darwin's Cathedral: Evolution, Religion, and the Nature of Society*. Chicago: University of Chicago Press.

Wilson, E.O.
1996 *In Search of Nature*. Washington, D.C.: Island Press.

Woese, Carl
1967 *The Genetic Code*. New York: Harper and Row.

Wohler, Friedrich
1828 "On the Artificial Production of Urea." *Annalen der Physik und Chemie* 88:253–256.

Woodruff, G., D. Premack
1979 "Intentional Communication in the Chimpanzee: The Development of Deception." *Cognition* 7:333–362.

Zajonc, R. B.
1980 "Feeling and Thinking: Preferences Need No Inferences." *American Psychologist* 35:151–175.

LaVergne, TN USA
13 September 2009
157760LV00004B/6/P